A TREATISE

ON

MILITARY LAW

AND THE

JURISDICTION, CONSTITUTION, AND PROCEDURE
OF MILITARY COURTS.

WITH A SUMMARY OF

THE RULES OF EVIDENCE AS APPLICABLE
TO SUCH COURTS.

BY

LIEUTENANT ROLLIN A. IVES,
FIFTH REGIMENT ARTILLERY,
Ass'T Prof. of Law, U. S. M. A.

SECOND EDITION.

THE LAWBOOK EXCHANGE, LTD.
Clark, New Jersey
2008

ISBN-13: 978-1-58477-884-4
ISBN-10: 1-58477-884-9

The quality of this reprint is equivalent to the quality of the original work.

THE LAWBOOK EXCHANGE, LTD.
33 Terminal Avenue
Clark, New Jersey 07066-1321

Please see our website for a selection of our other publications and fine facsimile reprints of classic works of legal history:
www.lawbookexchange.com

Library of Congress Cataloging-in-Publication Data

Ives, Rollin A. (Rollin Augustus), 1849-1881
A treatise on military law and the jurisdiction, constitution, and procedure of military courts, with a summary of the rules of evidence as applicable to such courts / by Rollin A. Ives.
p. cm.
Originally published: 2nd ed. New York, D. Van Nostrand, 1881.
Includes bibliographical references and index.
ISBN-13: 978-1-58477-884-4 (cloth : alk. paper)
ISBN-10: 1-58477-884-9 (cloth : alk. paper)
1. Courts-martial and courts of inquiry--United States. 2. Military law--United States. I. Title.
KF7609.I9 2008
343.73'01--dc22

2008004134

Printed in the United States of America on acid-free paper

A TREATISE

ON

MILITARY LAW

AND THE

JURISDICTION, CONSTITUTION, AND PROCEDURE
OF MILITARY COURTS.

WITH A SUMMARY OF

THE RULES OF EVIDENCE AS APPLICABLE
TO SUCH COURTS.

BY

LIEUTENANT ROLLIN A. IVES,
FIFTH REGIMENT ARTILLERY,
ASS'T PROF. OF LAW, U. S. M. A.

SECOND EDITION.

NEW YORK:
D. VAN NOSTRAND,
23 MURRAY STREET.
1881.

TO

BREVET LIEUTENANT-COLONEL

G. NORMAN LIEBER,

JUDGE-ADVOCATE, U. S. A., AND PROFESSOR OF LAW AT THE U. S. MILITARY ACADEMY,

THIS WORK IS GRATEFULLY DEDICATED

AS A TOKEN OF APPRECIATION OF HIS ENCOURAGEMENT, COUNSEL, AND ASSISTANCE IN ITS PREPARATION,

BY HIS FRIEND,

THE AUTHOR.

PREFACE.

The Law Military has undergone many changes in this country since the year 1860. Some of these changes have been of a radical character, introducing entirely new features into the administration of military jurisprudence. The relation of the military to the civil power has also, during the same time, received much attention. These considerations would of themselves abundantly explain the *raison d'être* of a new work on military law. It supplies a want which has long been felt.

But, besides this, military law has grown in importance, more persons being affected by it, and powers having been vested in military courts which they never held before. The military officer now comes daily in contact with some question of military law. He needs, therefore, a thorough acquaintance with its principles. That this is felt to be the case is shown by the increased facilities for acquiring it which the government affords him. At the U. S. Military Academy a professorship and an assistant professorship have been established for this purpose. The author of this work has for some time filled the latter position.

The book which he has prepared is intended as a text-book in a course on military law, as well as for use throughout the army; and, in my opinion, he has met with marked success in adapting it to these purposes. To have entered more elaborately into discussions and details would have unfitted it for a text-book, and would not have added to its value as a convenient book of reference in a large majority of such cases as arise in the military service.

It is not the object in this preface to dwell upon the special merits of this work. In two particulars, however, it possesses advantages which will, no doubt, be at once recognized, viz: in its arrangement, and in the fact that it embodies all recent statutory provisions, and important judicial, and other authoritative, decisions on the subjects of which it treats.

It is, perhaps, not out of place here to add a word to what the author has said with reference to the duties of the judge-advocate of a court-martial. In our service he occupies a threefold position —prosecutor, clerk to the court, and legal adviser to the court. In England he holds the two latter only. Now it is by no means a settled question within what limits our judge-advocate should discharge his duties as prosecutor. Certain requirements in the interest of the accused are made of him by law, but there is a broad field not touched by law, within which each will act according to his own notions or prejudices. The safest rule is to be guided by the principle that the government has no interest in convicting an innocent man, and that therefore the court should have before it *the truth.*

There is no reason why a judge-advocate should seek to exclude material evidence for the defense, much less to discolor facts. But, further than this, he generally occupies a position of vantage with reference to the accused, and this is particularly true in the case of undefended enlisted men. He often has in possession facts favorable to the defense of which the accused is necessarily ignorant. In all such and similar cases he should act with *good faith;* never seeking to gain an undue advantage by reason of any ignorance either of law or fact on the part of the accused; and remembering that the government never desires, and that it can reflect no credit on him, to secure a conviction in the teeth of facts. "Put yourself in his place," is a maxim which might be suggestive to the judge-advocate of the course he should pursue.

I take advantage, also, of this opportunity to touch upon another point. Our original Articles of War were copied from the English. With them we adopted their English interpretation and construction. But this fact has not always been kept in view, and the result has been that in some cases words have received an entirely different meaning from that which they were intended to convey. Practice, based upon such interpretation, may perhaps have made it part of our military law, but this is no reason why, if new cases of doubt should hereafter arise, we should not go for information to the source from which the language sprang. It thus becomes important to study the development of the military code of England—a study which will take us back to the beginning of the seventeenth century, and, indeed, through the code of Gustavus Adolphus, from which the English was largely taken, to the continental codes of the fifteenth and sixteenth centuries. In a work such as this it would not be possible, even if it were desirable, to enter such a field. I believe I have correctly stated what it professes to accomplish, and that it has accomplished what it professes will, I am convinced, be the the judgment of its readers.

G. Norman Lieber,
Professor of Law.

West Point, N. Y.,
January, 1879.

CONTENTS.

MILITARY LAW.

CHAPTER I.

MILITARY LAW DEFINED.

THE chief object of this treatise is to present to the reader the subject of *Military* Law as accepted at the present time in our Army; but we are met at the very outset with a difficulty arising from the confounding of this subject with another, entirely different,—*Martial* Law. For a long number of years all *military jurisdiction* was generally termed "Martial Law," and it was not until about the commencement of the present century that a distinction between Military and Martial law was recognized. This distinction is now universally conceded, but we still find the British Parliament passing an annual vote for the "administration" not of Military but "of Martial Law," and each succeeding government has appointed, under patent from the Crown, a "judge martial" paid out of this vote, who wholly disclaims having any other knowledge of "Martial Law" than such as every educated gentleman may possess, or anything whatever to do with any other than "Military Law."[1] In our own country, also, we find noted jurists using these terms interchangeably, speaking of Martial when they mean Military law, and

[1] Clode's Military and Martial Law, p. 157.

the reverse. All this has tended and still tends to a confusion from which we must free ourselves before proceeding to the main object of the text.

In the United States especially is the difference between these two subjects marked. The jurisdiction under the two is derived from different constitutional grants; is exercised by different courts; and is applicable, as a rule to a different class of persons. *Military* law relates to the government and discipline of the military forces of a state, while *Martial* law has for its object something entirely different.

To understand Martial Law fully we must distinguish between it as a foreign or international fact, and the same thing as a domestic or municipal fact.[1]

1st. **As a Foreign Fact.** When a belligerent occupies the territory of an enemy, he has a right by international law to govern it. The political law, so far as the nature of the case demands, is suspended, and military authority supersedes it. If any local courts or authority continue to subsist, it is only through the permission of the commander.

The rule, in this country, is that all civil and penal law shall continue to take its usual course in the enemy's places and territories so occupied, unless interrupted or stopped by order of the occupying military power; but all the functions of the hostile government, legislative, executive, or administrative, whether of a general, provincial, or local character, cease, or continue only with the sanction, or if deemed necessary, the participation of the occupier or invader.[2]

When General Scott occupied Mexico he required the magistrates of the country, municipal or judicial, to continue to administer the laws of the country *among their*

[1] VIII. Opinions Att'y Genl. p 369. [2] G. O. 100, 1863, § 6.

countrymen, but in subjection to the military power. Offenses of Mexicans against soldiers, or of soldiers against Mexicans or against each other, not provided for in the articles of war, were to be tried by *military commissions.*[1]

We have said, in cases of this kind, that military authority is substituted. By this is meant the military authority of the commander, with the sanction of his sovereign: and, *in our armies,* his authority under the direction of the President with the express or implied sanction of Congress.[2] This authority must, however, be exercised in accordance with the laws and usages of war.

Such government is without doubt a form of Martial Law, but the term *Military Government* would seem a better one for cases of this kind.[3]

2d. **As a Domestic Fact.** Under this heading two cases present themselves:—

(*a*) Cases of insurrection or rebellion *within* states or districts occupied by rebels, treated as belligerents.

In this event, such states stand, during the war, almost exactly on the same footing as foreign states, and the rules applicable for their government are the same as those just given.

(*b*) Cases of invasion or insurrection within the limits of the United States, or, during rebellion, within the limits of states maintaining adhesion to the national government when the public danger requires its exercise.

This is what the minority of the court in Milligan's case termed *Martial Law Proper*, and, in free governments like the United States, is the most difficult of exact definition. A single case will illustrate. In 1864, Mr. Milligan, a citizen of Indiana, was arrested and tried by a military commission for "inciting insurrection," "viola-

[1] G. O. 20, Feb. 19, 1847. G. O. 287, Sept. 17, 1847.

[2] Ex-parte Milligan, 4 Howard, 142.

[3] This was the term used by the minority Judges in Ex-parte Milligan.

ting the laws of war," and various other acts of disloyalty; found guilty, and sentenced to be hung. At this time the civil courts were open, and Milligan filed a petition in the circuit court of the U. S. for the District of Indiana, to be brought before the court, and either turned over to the proper civil tribunal to be proceeded with according to the law of the land, or discharged from custody altogether. At the hearing of the petition in the Circuit Court, the opinions of the judges were opposed upon a number of questions, and these questions were certified to the Supreme Court of the United States under the provisions of an act of Congress.

The principal question in the case was as to the jurisdiction of the military commission. Upon this question five of the nine judges held, "that there are occasions when martial rule can be properly applied. If, in foreign invasion or civil war, the courts are actually closed, and it is impossible to administer criminal justice according to law, *then*, on the theatre of active military operations, where war really prevails, there is a necessity to furnish a substitute for the civil authority, thus overthrown, to preserve the safety of the army and society; and as no power is left but the military, it is allowed to govern by martial rule until the laws can have their free course. As necessity creates the rule, so it limits its duration; for if this government is continued after the courts are re-instated, it is a gross usurpation of power. Martial rule can never exist where the courts are open, and in the proper and unobstructed exercise of their jurisdiction. It is also confined to the locality of actual war. Because, during the late rebellion it could have been enforced in Virginia, where the national authority was overturned and the courts driven out, it does not follow that it should obtain in Indiana, where that authority was never disputed, and justice was always administered. And so in the case of a foreign invasion, martial rule may become a necessity in one state, when, in another, it would be mere lawless violence." [1]

The minority of the court,[2] while agreeing with the majority that the military commission had no jurisdiction in this particular case, understood the majority opinion to assert that it was not in the power of Congress to have given it jurisdiction. With this latter doctrine they refused to agree. They held that Congress, under its constitutional authority to raise and support armies, and to declare war, if not from its constitutional authority to provide for governing the forces, could call martial rule into action in times of insurrection or invasion, or of civil or foreign war, within districts or localities where ordinary law no longer adequately secures public safety and private rights; and, furthermore, that it might be called into action temporarily, and in case of justifying peril, by the President at such times.[3]

That the minority opinion expresses the true view of martial law in this country we cannot but believe. The decision of the court was given by the bare majority of one, and, therefore, does not carry the weight of most of its decisions.[4]

[1] 4 Howard, p. 127.

[2] Chase C. J. and Wayne, Swayne and Miller J.J. [3] 4 Howard, 142.

[4] Among the manuscripts of the late Dr. Francis Lieber was found, after his death, one on the subject of Martial Law, written in the form of a note to the fifth and sixth articles of "The Instructions for the government of the Armies of the United States in the field" (G. O. 100, 1863). After distinguishing between martial law in hostile countries and domestic martial law, he says,—"As to Martial Law at home, which may become necessary in cases of foreign invasion, as well as in cases of domestic troubles, it has full sway in the immediate neighborhood of actual hostilities. The military power may demolish or seize property, or may arrest persons, if indispensable for the support of the army, or the attaining of the military objects in view. This arises out of the immediate and direct physical necessity, as much so as the law of trespass is inoperative against those who forcibly enter a house in a case of conflagration. This operation of Martial Law is not exclusive or ex-

Congress, too, seems to have adopted the minority view, for in 1867,[1] four months after this decision, it passed "an act to provide for the more efficient government of the rebel states," empowering district commanders to substitute for the trial of *all* criminals military commissions in the place of the local courts.

A similar view has been taken in England. In the case of the *Queen vs.* Nelson and Brand,[2] Lord Chief-Justice Cockburn concluded that the Crown had no authority, by virtue of its prerogative, to enforce martial law in any part of the realm where the laws of England prevail; but admits that Parliament may call it into being and operation.[3]

General Observations. It will be seen that the Supreme Court uses the term martial *rule* instead of *law*. This conveys a better idea. If the civil courts are closed and military courts substituted, no fixed code of law takes

ceptional. Any immediate physical danger, and paramount necessity arising from it, dispenses with the forms of law most salutary in a state of peace.

"The subject of the greatest difficulty connected with Martial Law is its existence in a country distant from the scene of military action, or in districts which are not in a state of insurrection. How far may it extend in point of geographical limits? How far may it extend in intrinsic action? Can it be dispensed with under all circumstances? How can people devoted to liberty limit its action so that it may not become a means of military despotism?

"It cannot be dispensed with under all circumstances, and if there were a law prohibiting it, it would break through the law in cases of direct and absolute necessity. The salvation of a country is like the saving of an individual life. It is paramount to all else. * * * *

"It has been denied that the government has any right to proclaim martial law, or to act according to its principles, in districts distant from the field of action; or to declare it in larger districts than either cities or counties. This is fallacious. The only justification of martial law is the danger to which the country is exposed, and as far as the positive danger extends, so far extends its justification."—(See pamphlet on Martial Law by Col. G. N. Lieber).

[1] March 2d. [2] Charge of Lord Chief-Justice, London, 1867.

[3] This is not the universally accepted doctrine in England, nor has it been carried out in practice. Acts of Parliament, in fact, recognize the right of declaring martial law as an "undoubted prerogative" of the crown.

the place of the civil code, but the "laws and usages of war," which are a part of the law of nations.

Whenever possible, martial law, in the case of individual offenders, should be carried out by military courts.[1] A place, district, or country occupied by an enemy stands, in consequence of the occupation, under martial law of the invading or occupying army, whether any proclamation declaring martial law, or any public warning to the inhabitants has been issued or not. Martial law is the immediate and direct effect and consequence of occupation or conquest. The presence of a hostile army proclaims its martial law.[2]

In the event of martial law with us, one of the chief features will be the suspension of the privilege of the writ of *habeas corpus*. This was exemplified by the act of Congress of March 3, 1863, authorizing its suspension during the rebellion, throughout the United States, by the President.

After martial law has been proclaimed by the proper authority, the officers engaged in the military service of the state may lawfully arrest any one whom they have reasonable grounds to believe is engaged in insurrection or rebellion, and may forcibly enter and search premises where it is reasonable to suppose that such offenders are secreted. Without the power to do this martial law and the military array of the government would be mere parade, and rather encourage attack than repel it. No more force, however, can be used than is necessary to accomplish the object. And if the power is exercised for the purpose of oppression, or any injury willfully done to person or property, the party by whom, or by whose order, it is committed, would undoubtedly be answerable.[3]

[1] G. O. 100, A. G. O., 1863, § 12. [2] Ibid, § I.

[3] Opinion of the Supreme Court in Luther *vs.* Borden, 17 Howard, 46, cited in Scott's Digest, 378.

Martial law may apply to both civilians and soldiers, as was the case in Mexico, but our Articles of War now embrace most of the military and civil offenses, in time of war, when committed by soldiers, and make them cognizable by courts-martial; where an offense comes under a statute, military commissions cannot try soldiers.

Military Jurisdiction is therefore of two kinds; *first*, that which is conferred by statute; *second*, that which is derived from the common law of war. In the United States the jurisdiction conferred by statute is exercised by courts-martial; that derived by the laws of war by military commissions.[1]

Military Law may now be defined as that part of the law of the land relating to the government of the military forces, and having for its object military discipline.

The term "military forces" as here used includes the armies of the United States, Regular and Volunteer, and the Militia when called into the actual service of the United States.[2] All these forces are subject to military law, and Congress has extended this law to some other classes of persons under certain prescribed circumstances.[3]

Sources. Our military law is principally a statutory code, adopted under the constitutional power given Congress "to make rules for the government and regulation of the land and naval forces."[4] It is, however, composed like the municipal law of a written and unwritten law, and derives its existence from the following sources:

1st. **Statutes of Congress.** Congress has passed frequent statutes since the first establishment of the government, for the regulation and government of the land

[1] G. O. 100 A. G. O. 1863, § 13. [2] Rev. Statutes, § 1342.

[3] Ibid, Sections 1094, 1342, (45th, 46th and 63d Articles of War), 1343, 1360, 1361, 1621, 4824, 4835. For list of these persons, see Chapter IV.

[4] Art. 1, § 8.

forces.[1] The principal of these which form the source of military law are :

(*a*) **The Rules and Articles of War.** The rules and articles of war were derived, originally, from the English Mutiny Act and Articles of War, under the following circumstances. In May, 1775, the Continental Congress met at Philadelphia and proceeded immediately to levy and organize an army. A system of rules for its government was, of course, indispensable.

The members of this Congress were naturally familiar with the English military code. The *local* troops, serving with the English forces sent to this country in 1754, had been in that year brought under the Mutiny Act :[2] while the armies of Gage and Burgoyne were governed by the English code at the time the first "continental troops" were raised.[3]

It was but natural, therefore, that this body should turn to it as a model, and on June 30th the Congress promulgated Articles, sixty-nine in number, for the government of the continental troops.[4] These articles were adopted from the English in the same form as our present

[1] A copy of Revised Statutes was published Feb. 18, 1878. This publication is legal evidence of the laws therein contained in all courts of the United States, but does not preclude reference to, nor control, in case of any discrepancy, the effect of any original act as passed by Congress since Dec. 1, 1873. The references of the text are to this volume of Statutes.

[2] Clode's Forces of the Crown, p. 181.

[3] Massachusetts had on April 5, 1775, adopted articles for the government of her troops, and was followed by Connecticut, (May 31, 1775) Rhode Island, (June 12, 1775) and New Hampshire (June 29, 1775). These articles, fifty-three in number, were essentially the same, and formed the governing code for these troops until articles were promulgated by the Continental Congress. In these articles the death penalty was limited to two cases, "abandoning post" and "making known the watchword to the enemy." (American Archives, 4th series, Vol I., p. 1350, Vol 2, pp. 566, 1153 and 1180 respectively.)

The author has also a copy of articles, (32 in number,) promulgated by the Pennsylvania Committee of Safety, (November 6, 1775,) for the government of an artillery company raised by it.

[4] American Archives, 4th series, Vol. I., p. 1356.

articles, modified, however, to meet the milder views which a people objecting to a "standing army" naturally entertained.[1 & 2] Additions were made in November of that year, but were repealed by act of September 30th, 1776, and new articles adopted. These articles (one hundred and two in number) were modeled after the British form, and arranged in eighteen sections. With some few exceptions they remained in force until 1806.

On September 29, 1789, they were formally recognized and adapted to the new Constitution by the first Congress of the United States.

In 1806, the articles (one hundred and one in number) were rearranged and promulgated by Congress; the divisions into sections dropped, and the old model substituted. These, with some five or six modifications, remained in force for nearly seventy years, and were the governing code of the army, until new articles were enacted by Congress on the 22d of June, 1874.[3]

(*b*) **General Regulations**. Congress did not act under its power "to make rules for the *regulation* of the land forces" until 1813. The regulations of Major General Baron de Steuben,[4] were formally approved and issued by the Continental Congress in 1779, and remained in force

[1] These articles authorized the death penalty in only three cases, the cases spoken of in the Mass. articles, and for "compelling a surrender." In seven cases an officer was to be "cashiered," and in two others "discharged."

[2] These articles probably did not reach the besieging army about Boston, (which the Continental Congress had adopted as the *national* army,) until early in August. In an order dated, Headquarters, Cambridge, Aug. 9, 1775, Washington directs that on the next day they be delivered out to be distributed through the several corps of the army. In the meantime these troops were governed by the articles of the respective colonies. In fact, for some time after the *Continental* articles were distributed among the troops cases happened of persons tried under the *Colonial* articles, their sentences being confirmed by the Commander-in-chief.

[3] In the Army Bill submitted to Congress, Dec. 12, 1878, New Articles of War were proposed.

[4] Inspector General of the Army

up to that date. In 1813 the Secretary of War was authorized, and it was declared to be his duty, "to prepare general regulations, which, when sanctioned by the President, shall be respected until altered or revoked by the same authority."[1] Such a set of regulations was prepared and published in May, 1813. In 1816[2] they were recognized by Congress, subject to such alterations as the Secretary of War might adopt with the approbation of the President. In 1821,[3] Congress approved and adopted a system of regulations prepared by General Scott, but in the following year,[4] this act was repealed, thus leaving the power to alter or modify as it stood by the act of 1816. Several revisions of regulations[5] with important additions have been published by the Secretaries of War under this authority, no legislative sanction being given or required. In 1866,[6] the Secretary of War was directed to have prepared, and to report to Congress at its next session a code of regulations for the government of the army, etc., the *existing* regulations to remain in force until Congress shall have acted on said report. The power of alteration was thus taken away by this act,[7] but, in 1875,[8] Congress recommitted the power to make and publish regulations to the President, the same to be subject to existing laws.

The Supreme Court has held that "the power of the executive to establish rules and regulations for the government of the army is undoubted; and that the power to establish implies, necessarily, the power to modify or repeal, or create anew."[9] A mere order of the President or Secretary of War is not a regulation.[10]

[1] Act of Congress of March 3, 1813.
[2] Act of April 24, 1816.
[3] Act of March 2, 1821.
[4] Act of May 7, 1822.
[5] 1825, 1836, 1841, 1847, 1857, 1861, 1863.
[6] Act of July 28, 1866.
[7] XIV. Opinions Atty. Gen'l Jan. 9, 1873.
[8] Act of March 1, 1875.
[9] U. S. vs. Eliason, 16 Peters, 301, Gratiot *vs.* U. S., 4 Howard 105.
[10] Harvey *vs.* U. S. 3 Nott and Huntington, 42.

General regulations have been defined as a system of ordinances for the administration of the affairs of the army, and for better prescribing the respective duties and powers of officers and men in the military service, and embracing all forms of a general character.[1]

Cadet Regulations. By act of 1812,[2] "Cadets, heretofore appointed in the service of the United States, or that may in future be appointed, may be attached at the discretion of the President of the United States, as students to the Military Academy, and shall be subject to the established regulations thereof." Special regulations for the cadets of the Military Academy have been from time to time adopted by the President, and published by the Secretary of War. The present edition was published February 28, 1877.

Effect of Regulations. The Supreme Court has decided that the army regulations, made pursuant to the authority conferred by Congress, have the force of law.[3]

2d. **Orders**. The articles of war[4] provide, that any officer or soldier, who disobeys any lawful command of his superior officer, shall suffer death, or such other punishment as a court-martial may direct. Published orders are therefore a part of the *lex scripta.*

Standing General Orders have been defined to be executive instructions to do or not to do particular acts. Police and local or interior regulations come under this head.[5]

Of general orders from the War Department courts-martial take judicial cognizance when duly promulgated; but *special* orders, and orders from other authority must be regularly proved, as the court is not bound to take judicial notice of them.[6]

[1] Ex. Doc. No. 275, 43d Congress, 1st Session. [2] April 29th.
[3] U. S. *vs.* Freeman, 3 Howard 567, Gratiot *vs.* U. S., 4 Howard 107.
[4] Art. 21. [5] Ex. Doc. 275, 43d Congress, 1st Session.
[6] U. S. vs. Wiltenburger, 19 Wallace 526.

Verbal Orders form part of the *lex non scripta*. They are those lawful commands which a superior officer may *viva voce*, or otherwise, issue to a subordinate. It is most frequently the disobedience of such orders that renders parties amenable to Article 21.

3d. **Custom of War**. This is recognized as a source of military law by the 84th Article of War, but is only applicable when a doubt arises not explained by the articles.

By "custom of war" is meant that part of the unwritten law derived from the usages of armies in time of peace or war. It is the common law of courts-martial as derived from precedents, which should be followed when well established, unless manifestly wrong.[1]

Custom of war finds its applicability, principally, in the sentence imposed. Thus, in the early military history of the United States, death, by "hanging," was imposed for purely military offenses; but now, though the municipal code of the United States prescribes that "the manner of inflicting the punishment of death shall be by hanging the person convicted by the neck until dead, under *the customs of war*, the death penalty is, for purely military offenses, generally inflicted by "shooting to death with musketry."[2]

Aids. As valuable aids for knowing what the military law is in our country, we may mention:

(1) **Decisions of Courts**. The decisions of the civil courts upon military questions, both in this country and England, are valuable exponents of the law, and are entitled to great weight and consideration by military courts. Constant reference will therefore be made to their rulings. As to English statutes adopted into our legislation, the Supreme Court has held, that the known and settled con-

[1] See U. S. vs. MacDaniell, 7 Peters 2.   [2] Scott's Digest, p. 291.

struction of such statutes by the English courts must be held to be incorporated into the acts adopted by us.[1] Our Articles of War being taken, many of them bodily, from the English Articles, this decision of the Supreme Court should not be lost sight of: and decisions of English courts since their adoption, though no part of our law, are excellent aids for determining what that law is.

(2) **The Rulings, within their respective Spheres, of the Heads of different Branches of the Government on Questions affecting the Military Establishment.** Among these may be specially mentioned the decisions of the Judge-Advocate General, and the different Attorneys-General. The opinions of these officers are entitled to great respect, and military courts should, only after the most careful deliberation, refuse to be governed by them.

As to the effect of the opinions of the Attorneys-General, Judge Black, while filling that office, said,—"The duty of the Attorney-General is to advise, not to decide. A thing is not to be considered as done by the head of a department merely because the Attorney-General has advised him to do it. You may disregard his opinion if you are sure it is wrong. He aids you in forming a judgment on questions of law, but still the judgment is yours, not his. You are not bound to see with his eyes, but only to use the light which he furnishes, in order to see the better with your own. But though opinions from this office have technically no binding effect, it is generally safer and better to adopt them."

In 1875 the following question arose,—"Are the opinions of the Judge-Advocate General of the army, when *confirmed, approved, and published to the army for its instruction* by the Secretary of War, to be regarded by courts-martial as authority to be respected, or are they to

[1] 2 Peters 2, 5 Ibid 264, 12 Ibid 527.

be deemed as nothing worth when in conflict with their own conclusions from misunderstood premises? In other words, are courts-martial to consider themselves not only as judges of the facts and of the weight of evidence, but also as irresponsible makers of the *law* which is to be applied to those facts and that evidence?" Being submitted to the Judge-Advocate General, he decided that,—"As the court has finally declined to adopt the views of its power and duty held by this bureau, it cannot be obliged to do so."[1]

This accords with the decision of the Supreme Court in *Decatur vs. Paulding*.[2] The court there held that, "if a suit should come before this court, which involves the construction of any of these laws [laws of Congress], the court certainly would not be bound to adopt the construction given by the head of a department. And if they supposed his decision to be wrong, they would, of course, so pronounce their judgment."

(3) **The Rulings of Officers having Power to convene Courts-martial.** These should be noticed especially by courts sitting within the sphere of these officers' commands. Beyond these limits such rulings are rarely known, and will be of value or not depending on circumstances.

(4) **The Views of Text-writers upon this Subject.**[3] In conclusion it may be said, and this fact should be borne in mind, that courts-martial, being courts of original jurisdiction, are judges of the law and fact in every case that comes before them. As said by the Supreme Court,—"Where a court has jurisdiction, it has a right to decide every question which occurs in the case."[4]

[1] Opinion J. A. G., Nov. 20, 1875, approved by Secretary of War Nov. 29, 1875. Published in G. C. M. O. 55, Hdq'rs Dept. of California, Dec. 13, 1875.

[2] 14 Peters, 515.

[3] For a list of American and English publications on Military Law see Appendix.

[4] Elliot *vs.* Piersoll, 1 Peters, 328.

CHAPTER II.

COMPOSITION AND CONSTITUTION OF COURTS-MARTIAL.

THE established tribunals in the United States for administering military law are Courts-Martial. They are always composed of commissioned officers, and are courts of special and limited jurisdiction.[1]

The various kinds of courts-martial recognized by our articles are the General, Regimental, Garrison, and Field Officer's Court.

General Courts-Martial may consist of any number of officers from five to thirteen inclusive, but they shall not consist of less than thirteen when that number can be convened without manifest injury to the service.[2]

When our articles were first adopted it was prescribed that General Courts-Martial should not consist of less than thirteen commissioned officers. This was changed, however, in 1786, and the present law as to their composition substituted.

The reason for selecting the number thirteen, is given by Clode[3] as follows: "When provision was made, under the military code, for the trial of an offender by a court composed of the president and twelve officers, it may reasonably be presumed that the controlling analogy which suggested that tribunal, was the civil administration of justice by a presiding judge appointed by the Crown, and

[1] Wise vs. Withers, 3 Cranch, 337. Dynes vs. Hoover, 20 Howard, 80.

[2] Art. 75.

[3] Military and Martial Law, p 104.

twelve jurymen summoned by the sheriff to deal with all the questions of law and fact that might be brought before them."

In the English service the President is appointed by name as such, and has certain functions assigned him, giving him more the character of a judge than in our service.

A question early arose as to what would constitute such "manifest injury" as to allow a court of less than thirteen members to be appointed, but was set at rest in 1827 by the decision of the Supreme Court in the case of *Martin vs. Mott.*[1] It was there laid down that this phrase "is merely directory to the officer appointing the court; and his discretion as to the number that can be convened without manifest injury to the service, being in a manner submitted to his discretion, must be conclusive." Attorney-General Wirt[2] doubted somewhat the legality of this decision, but it is the accepted law.

It must, however, appear in the order convening a court composed of less than thirteen members, that "no other officers than those named can be convened without manifest injury to the service;" otherwise, such court would be illegal, and an execution under its sentence would be murder.

When a court of thirteen is convened, there is nothing in the statutes requiring the court to remain at that number; it may be reduced by death, sickness, challenge, or other reason to five, and still remain a lawful court. The same would be true of any court without regard to the original number convened.

When a court is reduced to the minimum, five, and a member challenged, the remaining four may determine as to the validity of the challenge. A court-martial reduced

[1] 12 Wheaton, 19–35. [2] I Opinions Attorney-General, 299 *et seq.*

below the minimum by the absence of members, is still competent to meet and adjourn from day to day till absentees return, or till the court is dissolved by competent authority.[1]

Regimental and Garrison Courts, until 1786, consisted of five members, except in cases where that number could not conveniently be assembled, when three were sufficient. At that time the number was fixed at three, the junior member acting as recorder.

The Regimental court must be composed of officers of the same regiment or corps.

Regimental Court for doing Justice. This court, authorized by the 30th Article of War, is composed in the same manner as any regimental court.

Field Officer's Court. This court is composed of a field officer of a regiment, for trying offenses in that regiment. In the English service a drum head court-martial was sanctioned in 1830, for punishing on the spot mutiny or insubordinate conduct committed on the march.[2]

The necessity of some such court, able to punish without going through all the forms required of regimental and garrison courts, became manifest during the late war, and was established by Act of July 17, 1862. The statute originally authorized such courts in time of peace, but since the promulgation of the new articles they are limited to times of war.[3]

Persons eligible to sit on Courts-Martial. As before stated, only commissioned officers can sit on courts-martial, and two of our military writers[4] have interpreted the word "commissioned" so as to exclude officers of the Medical and Paymaster's Corps. The reasons assigned are those given by Attorney-General Berrien:[5]—He says, "If

[1] Opinions J. A. G., p. 18. [2] Clode, Military and Martial Law, p. 81.
[3] Art. 80. [4] De Hart, p. 38. Benét, p. 22. [5] Nov. 6, 1829.

we look to the origin of courts-martial in England (from whence we borrow them) it would be difficult to believe that a tribunal which has succeeded there to the ancient court of chivalry, could be composed of other than military men. And if we consider the nature of the subjects which are generally submitted to the decision of these tribunals, the knowledge of military discipline and usage, and frequently of tactics (which is indispensable to those who preside there), it would seem that non-combatants, whose duties do not lead them to acquire this species of information, and who have no rank, either real or assimilated, could not be deemed competent to sit on courts-martial."

The Judge-Advocate General, however, in referring to this subject, stated that, "though it is in accordance with the general usage of the service not to detail officers of the medical corps of the army on courts-martial, where it can be avoided, yet such details are not unfrequently and properly made at stations where commissioned officers are few in number.

"Medical officers being, as a class, men of learning and a high order of capacity and intelligence, no instance is known of any injurious result ensuing from their being appointed on military courts. The proceedings of no trial, where an officer of this corps was a member of the court, have, it is believed, been for that reason disapproved, during the war; and a very considerable number of records of military trials have been passed by this Bureau as regular and sufficient, from which it appeared that such officer or officers had been part of the detail."[1]

Paymasters are not so frequently detailed upon courts-martial as medical officers, but there seems no good reason, in our service, why they should not be, as many of them have acquired a knowledge of military law in the line of

[1] Opinions J. A. G., p. 366.

the army. Courts-martial are called upon to act as judges and jurymen. As jurymen it is hardly necessary to compare the ability of these two classes of officers with that of the average juryman in criminal cases before the civil courts; as judges their competency is certainly equal to that of officers when first appointed from civil life, and who are frequently detailed for court-martial service the moment they are appointed.

In the English service no officer is competent to sit as a member of a *general* court-martial until he shall have held a commission for three years.[1] Such a clause would be valuable in our service, thus giving any officer sufficient time to acquaint himself with military law and the customs and usages of the service.

In reply to a communication of a department commander in 1875, the adjutant-general said the Secretary of War most decidedly disapproves the detail of chaplains as members of courts-martial.[2]

Graduated Cadets with Brevet Rank. The question at one time arose as to whether graduated cadets, with the brevet rank of second lieutenants, attached as supernumerary officers to corps of the army, were commissioned officers within the meaning of the articles of war so as to permit them to sit as members of courts-martial. Attorney-General Berrien held in 1829, that they were not commissioned officers,[3] but a contrary view was taken by the War Department some years later,[4] and by Attorney-General Cushing in 1855.[5] The latter held that a brevet second lieutenant is a commissioned officer; that he can be tried as a commissioned officer; and that he is legally capable as a commissioned officer to try.

[1] Clode, p. 115. [2] Letter dated A. G. O. May 13, 1875. [3] Aug. 17, 1829.
[4] G. O. 11, A. G. O., 1845. [5] VII. Opinions Attorney-Gen'l, July 11, 1855.

Professors of the Military Academy are commissioned officers,[1] but not within the meaning of the 75th Article so as to allow them to be detailed on courts-martial.[2]

Mixed Courts. Officers of the Marine Corps, detached for service with the army by order of the President, may be associated with officers of the *Regular* Army on courts-martial for the trial of offenders belonging to the Regular Army, or to the forces of the Marine Corps so detached; and, in such cases, the orders of the senior officer of either corps who may be present and duly authorized, shall be obeyed.[3] This is a material modification of the previous article, which permitted officers of the marines to be associated with officers of the land forces for the purpose of holding courts-martial, and trying offenders belonging to either arm whenever it might be found convenient and necessary.

Militia and Volunteer Courts. Officers and soldiers of any troops, whether militia or others, mustered and in pay of the United States, are subject to be tried by courts-martial.[4]

This article applies to militia and volunteers, both State and United States.

The courts for the trial of these troops cannot be composed of regular officers, either wholly or in part, though militia and volunteer officers may sit on courts for the trial of officers and soldiers of the regular army.[5]

Regular officers, detailed and sitting upon general courts-martial as volunteers of higher grade, may try volunteers, but only when holding commissions in the volunteer service.[6]

[1] Act of July 28, 1866, Revised Statutes, § 1094.
[2] I. Opinions Attorney-General 469, VII. Ibid, July 11, 1855,
[3] Art. 78. [4] Art. 64. [5] Articles 77 and 78. [6] Opinions J. A. G., p. 43.

CONSTITUTION OF COURTS-MARTIAL.

General Courts-Martial. The President of the United States, being by the constitution Commander-in-Chief of the army, may appoint general courts-martial; and by the 72d Article, whenever any officer therein authorized to appoint a general court-martial, is the accuser or prosecutor of any officer under his command, the President is required to appoint the court.

The Secretary of War may appoint general courts-martial. No principle of law is better established than that the Secretary of War, in ordering a court-martial in any case, represents the President, whose executive agent he simply is in the matter.[1] A court-martial, instituted by G. O. 26, A. G. O., Aug. 27, 1850, expressed a doubt as to the regularity of the order by which it was convened, on the ground that the Secretary of War was not competent to render such an order. The President held it legal.[2] The Supreme Court has also decided that the acts of the War Department are, in legal contemplation, the acts of the President.[3]

Any general officer commanding the army of the United States, a separate army, or a separate department, shall be competent to appoint a general court-martial either in time of peace or war.[4]

Where an officer with the brevet of a general officer is assigned by the President to command an army, or separate department, and placed on duty according to his brevet rank, he is entitled to order a court under this article.

The "army" which a general must command under this article must be held to mean a body of men under military

[1] Opinions J. A. G., p. 25. [2] G. O. 35, A. G. O., Oct. 30, 1850.

[3] U. S. *vs.* Eliason, 16 Peters, 291. Wilcox *vs.* Jackson, 13 Peters, 498.

[4] Art. 72.

organization that is complete in itself, and does not exist as an integral part of some other organization.[1]

In time of war the commander of a division, or a separate brigade of troops, is competent to appoint a general court-martial, but when such commander is the accuser or prosecutor of *any* person under his command, the court shall be appointed by the next higher commander.[2]

The Superintendent of the Military Academy has power to convene general courts-martial for the trial of cadets, and to execute the sentences of such courts, except the sentences of suspension and dismission, subject to the same limitations and conditions now existing as to other general courts-martial.[3]

For many years, and up to 1841, it was customary for commanding officers, to whom the right of convening general courts-martial had been given, to delegate such authority to inferior commanders, at least so far as to authorize them to name or appoint the members of the court; but it was decided that he alone to whom the law has given the authority to act in such cases, must appoint the court; and no right to delegate such authority can be exercised without the express sanction of law.[4]

Regimental Courts. Every officer commanding a regiment or corps shall, subject to the provisions of article eighty, be competent to appoint, for his own regiment or corps, courts-martial, consisting of three officers, to try offenses not capital.[5]

In time of war, however, no soldier serving with his regiment shall be tried by a regimental or garrison court-martial when a field officer of his regiment may be so detailed.[6]

[1] Opinions J. A. G., p. 23. [2] Art, 73. [3] § 1326, Rev. Statutes.
[4] De Hart, pp. 6, 7. [5] Art. 81. [6] Art. 80.

The commander of the Engineer battalion, established by the Act of July 28, 1866, is a commander of a "corps" in the sense of the above article, and is authorized to convene regimental courts.[1]

A regimental commander cannot assemble such courts, except from officers under his immediate command. He cannot go to other posts than his own for officers of his regiment, except by express authority of the department or superior commander.

Garrison Courts. Every officer commanding a garrison, fort, or other place, where the troops consist of different corps, shall, subject to the provisions of article eighty, be competent to appoint, for such garrison or other place, courts-martial consisting of three officers to try offenses not capital.[2]

The presence on duty with the garrison, etc., and as a substantive part thereof, of a single representative of a corps, or a branch of the service other than that of which the bulk of the command is composed, is sufficient to fix upon the body the character of "*one consisting of different corps*," and to empower the commanding officer to assemble a court-martial. Thus the presence of an ordnance sergeant or hospital steward would bring the body within the meaning of this article; not so, however, the presence of a civil physician acting as surgeon, or a hospital matron, or any civil employé of the government.[3]

The words "*or other place*," used in this article, would include any place where the troops consist of "different corps;" viz., arsenals, barracks, draft rendezvous, etc.

The question was submitted to the Judge-Advocate General in 1875—whether a garrison commander could detail for garrison court-martial duty a staff officer of

[1] Opinions J. A. G., p. 26. [2] Art. 82.
[3] Opinions J. A. G., pp. 26–27; also G. O. 5, A. G. O., Jan. 18, 1843.

superior rank to himself. In reply he stated "that the question has not been decided by this Bureau, and as it is not known to have actually arisen in the military administration, it would be premature to discuss it at present. A decided impression, however, is entertained, that a garrison commander, in the exercise of the general authority given him by the 82d Article of War, would be competent to detail for garrison court-martial duty, a medical or other staff officer stationed at the post, though of superior rank to himself." [1]

Field Officer's Court. In time of war a field officer may be detailed in every regiment to try soldiers thereof, for offenses not capital. The colonel, or commanding officer of the regiment, should detail the field officer as a court. If there be but one field officer he cannot detail himself, but may be detailed by the brigade or next superior commander.

Where the detail of a field officer as a court was made by the brigade commander, in a case where there was present in command of the regiment a field officer superior to the one detailed, who would have been the proper officer to make the detail, it was held that such action did not affect the validity of the proceedings of the field officer's court.[2]

As the field officer's court is applicable to the regimental organization only, the commander of a post, whose command is not a regimental organization, is not competent to convene a field officer's court.[3]

[1] Bureau of Military Justice, Aug. 31, 1875.

[2] Opinions J. A. G., p. 173. [3] Ibid, p. 174.

CHAPTER III.

JURISDICTION OF COURTS-MARTIAL.

Source of Jurisdiction. Courts-Martial derive their jurisdiction, in this country, from statutes of Congress. Under its constitutional power "to make rules for the regulation and government of the land forces," Congress has established a military discipline, defined military offenses, provided courts for their trial and punishment, prescribed the jurisdiction and practice of these courts, and the mode of executing their sentences; in fact, has done everything necessary for a proper administration of justice in the army.

Limited Jurisdiction. It was early settled by the Supreme Court that the circuit and district courts of the United States have no criminal jurisdiction but what is expressly conferred upon them by statute,[1] and the reasoning in those cases is equally applicable to courts-martial. Both derive their jurisdiction from the same source—Congress—but not from the same constitutional grant. Civil courts derive their jurisdiction from those clauses [2] of the constitution referring to the *judicial* power, while courts-martial derive theirs from that clause [3] referring to the *war* power of Congress, and these two powers are entirely independent of each other.[4]

[1] U. S. *vs.* Hudson, 7 Cranch, 32; U. S. *vs.* Wiltberger, 5 Wheaton, 76; U. S. *vs.* Bevans, 3 Wheaton, 376.

[2] Art. III. § 1, Art. I. § 8, Clause 9.

[3] Art. I. § 8, Clause 13.

[4] Dynes *vs.* Hoover, 20 Howard, 79.

Courts-martial are, therefore, courts of limited and special jurisdiction, and it should appear upon the record the facts or circumstances which give jurisdiction, either expressly or by legal intendment.[1]

Though limited in their jurisdiction, in cases within their competency courts-martial, when legally constituted and duly organized, are courts whose decisions are as conclusive and complete as any civil court of original jurisdiction.[2]

Responsibility for Excess of Jurisdiction. Courts-martial must confine themselves strictly to their statutory jurisdiction and prescribed mode of procedure, and any excess will render each member responsible in damages to an aggrieved party.

In 1806, a court-martial fined one Wise, a justice of the peace within the District of Columbia. Wise brought a suit against Withers, a collector of militia fines, for entering his house, *vi et armis*, and taking away his goods to satisfy the judgment of this court. The Supreme Court on *writ of error* decided "that a justice of the peace is exempt from the performance of militia duty;" and further said, "it follows from this opinion that a court-martial has no jurisdiction over a justice of the peace as a militiaman; he could never be legally enrolled; and it is a principle, that a decision of such a tribunal, in a case clearly without its jurisdiction, cannot protect the officer who executes it. *The court and the officers are all trespassers.*"[3]

In *Dynes vs. Hoover*,[4] the same court held that where a court is illegally constituted, or acts in a case where it has no jurisdiction over the *subject matter or charge*, or

[1] Turner *vs.* The Bank of North America, 4 Dallas, 11.

[2] Houston *vs.* Moore, 5 Wheaton, 1; Dynes *vs.* Hoover, 20 Howard, 83; Rawson *vs.* Brown, 6 Shepley (Maine), 216; Brent *vs.* Bogardus, 7 Johns, (N Y.), 157.

[3] Wise *vs.* Withers, 3 Cranch, 330, *et seq.*

[4] 20 Howard, 80–83.

one in which, having jurisdiction over the subject matter, it failed to observe the rules prescribed by the statute for its exercise; in such cases all the parties to such illegal trial are trespassers upon a party aggrieved by it, and he may recover damages from them in a proper suit in a civil court by the verdict of a jury.

The court further said,—"When we speak of *proceedings* in a cause, or for the organization of the court and for trials, we do not mean mere irregularity in practice on the trial, or any mistaken rulings in respect to evidence or law, but of a disregard of the essentials required by the statute under which the court has been convened to try and to punish an offender for an imputed violation of the law."

The English practice conforms to this. In 1743, Lieutenant Frye, serving in the West Indies on a British man-of-war, was ordered by his superior officer to assist in arresting another officer. The lieutenant demanded what he had, according to the customs of the naval service, a right to demand, a written order, before he would obey the command. For this he was put under arrest, tried by a naval court-martial, and sentenced to fifteen years' imprisonment. It appears that the depositions of certain illiterate persons, unknown to the accused, were taken and admitted in evidence; that the accused objected to such evidence, but the objection was overruled. In 1746 he brought an action in the Court of Common Pleas against the president of the court-martial, and damages of £1000 were awarded for his illegal detention and sentence; and the judge informed him that he might also bring his action against any member of the court-martial.[1]

Nature and Classes of Jurisdiction. Jurisdiction is the power of a court to try, the capacity to punish. That

[1] MacArthur, Vol I., pp. 268–271.

of courts-martial may be conveniently arranged for discussion under the following heads: *civil* and *criminal, original* and *appellate, exclusive* and *concurrent.*

Civil and Criminal. Courts-martial are tribunals with the *sole* power of trying *criminal* cases. These cases, as a rule, are named in terms in the articles of war; but, by the 62d Article, their jurisdiction is extended to "all crimes not capital, and all disorders and neglects which officers and soldiers may be guilty of, to the prejudice of good order and military discipline." Notwithstanding the apparent indeterminateness of such a provision, it is not liable to abuse; for what those crimes are, and how they are to be punished, is well known by practical men in the army and navy, and by those who have studied the law of courts-martial, and the offenses of which the different courts-martial have cognizance.[1]

Original and Appellate. In all cases save one the jurisdiction of courts-martial is *original.*

The 30th Article provides for an appeal from the regimental court-martial named therein to a general court-martial, but this is the only case where a military court exercises an appellate jurisdiction—nor is there any appeal from the decisions of a court-martial to any other court. In *Dynes vs. Hoover*[2] the Supreme Court said,—"With the sentences of courts-martial which have been convened regularly, and have proceeded legally, and by which punishments are directed, not forbidden by law, or which are according to the laws and customs of the sea, civil courts have nothing to do, nor are they in any way alterable by them. If it were otherwise, the civil courts would virtually administer the rules and articles of war, irrespective of those to whom that duty and obligation has been confided by the laws of the United States, from whose decis-

[1] Dynes *vs.* Hoover, 20 Howard, 82. [2] 20 Howard, 82.

ions no appeal or jurisdiction of any kind has been given to the civil magistrate or the civil courts."

Exclusive and Concurrent. Jurisdiction is likewise exclusive and concurrent.

Over purely military offenses courts-martial have at all times *exclusive* jurisdiction.[1]

In time of war, insurrection, and rebellion, jurisdiction is also conferred over a class of offenses not purely military. These are larceny, robbery, and all those offenses named in the 58th Article, when committed by persons in the military service of the United States.

This jurisdiction is held by the Judge-Advocate General to be exclusive. Where a person in the military service is held in custody of the civil authorities, charged with one of the crimes mentioned in this article, the governor of the State in which the prisoner is confined should be called upon to deliver him up to the military authorities for trial by a military court, he being entitled to such a disposition under the provisions of the article.[2]

Concurrent Jurisdiction. There are certain cases in which the jurisdiction of courts-martial is, in a certain sense, concurrent with the civil courts.

Soldiers do not cease to be citizens by enlisting in and joining the army, and are just as amenable to the civil tribunal as other persons.[3] In entering the military service they take upon themselves new responsibilities without freeing themselves from the old. A civil offense, therefore, may not only constitute an offense against the civil authority, but also against the military, and, as such, be punishable by both. In this sense the jurisdiction of the military and civil courts is concurrent.

[1] See cases cited in Note 1, p. 1, Chap. III., also U. S. *vs.* Mackenzie, 1 N. Y. Legal Observer, p. 371.

[2] Opinions J. A. G., p. 211.

[3] I. Bishop's Criminal Law, 5th Ed., § 46.

This double accountability, where an offense bears criminal qualifications to two jurisdictions, has been frequently affirmed by the Supreme Court.[1] Trial and punishment by both is not regarded as coming within that clause of the constitution which provides that "no person shall be twice put in jeopardy of life or limb for the same offense."

Many cases in our service have settled this question beyond dispute. In 1839 Captain Howe of the Dragoons was charged with "conduct to the prejudice of good order and military discipline," in cruelly beating, kicking, and maltreating a private soldier belonging to his command, all of which cruelty did cause the death of said private. The court-martial convened in April, 1840. The second special plea in bar of trial, presented by the accused, was to the effect that the charges against him were not proper to be tried by a court-martial, but only by a civil court; and that the offense, if committed at all, was committed within the county of St. John, E. F., and that the superior court of the Eastern District of Florida had jurisdiction in said offense. The court sustained this second plea, and decided that they could not take cognizance of the offense for the trial of which the court was convened. The commanding general disapproved this decision, inasmuch as the unmilitary conduct charged ought to have been tried by the court-martial, leaving the homicide to be tried by the civil tribunal.[2]

Subordination to Civil Authority. It is a conceded fact in this country that the military is ever subordinate to the civil, but the question arises, in this connection, which of these courts would first take cognizance of cases

[1] Fox *vs.* Ohio, V. Howard, 434–435; U. S. *vs.* Marigold, IX. Ibid, 569; Moore *vs.* Illinois, XIX. Ibid, 20.

[2] G. O. 25, A. G. O., May 22, 1840. Vide VI. Opinions Attorney-General, June 5, 1854.

of this kind, and whether, after proceedings have commenced, a military court would be bound to deliver up the prisoner to the civil authority.

In the case of Captain Howe, although the court-martial had commenced proceedings, the commanding general, out of respect to the civil authority, deemed it proper to suspend all proceedings in the case, until the decisions of the civil court should be made known.

If this was a case of absolutely concurrent jurisdiction, the court which first took cognizance of the case would attach to itself *exclusive* jurisdiction.[1] But as the jurisdiction is concurrent as to the person, and not as to the offense, this rule does not obtain.

The rule laid down by Attorney-General Cushing, accords with the civil practice.[2] He says, "Any other court having lawful jurisdiction may proceed against the prisoner at the same time for another offense, or for another criminal qualification of the same act; but the latter court cannot take the custody of his person away from another court where jurisdiction has lawfully attached." * * * "If the jurisdiction of a court-martial has not lawfully attached, the commanding officer should upon application by the civil authorities, in accordance with the 59th Article of War, deliver up the prisoner. But if the party escape from the sheriff, or if he be released on bail, or if he be tried and acquitted, or if he be tried and convicted, in each of these cases, as soon as he leaves the manual custody of the civil magistrate, he reverts to the authority of his military superior."[3] He may then be tried by a military court.

Limitations as to Time. The jurisdiction of courts-

[1] Kent's Commentaries, Vol. I. § 341, Note "*a*," also, Smith *vs.* McIver, 9 Wheaton, 532.

[2] Kent's Commentaries, Vol. II., §§ 122–125.

[3] VI. Opinions Attorney-General, April 7, 1854.

martial depends materially upon the time of committal of the offense. The 103d Article provides that no person shall be liable to be tried and punished by a general court-martial for any offense which appears to have been committed more than two years before the issuing of the order for such trial, unless, by reason of having absented himself, or of some other manifest impediment, he shall not have been amenable to justice within that period.

This limitation was first introduced into our articles in 1806, and applies to all offenses.[1] In estimating the time, however, the order convening the court is not to be considered as the order for the prisoner's trial, but the order of the reviewing authority referring the charges to the court for trial.

Where the offense appears to have been committed more than two years before the order for trial, the *onus probandi* would rest upon the government to prove the "absence or other manifest impediment."

In 1872 the Attorney-General gave as his opinion that,—"the words 'other manifest impediment' must be construed with the words immediately preceding, viz. 'reason of having absented himself,' and, taken together, it is apparent that the impediment intended by this act is an impediment similar in kind to absence; that is, one which renders it impossible for a prosecution to take place. I do not think it could be extended to concealment of the offense. The fact that the offense was not discovered by government will not be sufficient 'manifest impediment' to warrant a trial." [2]

Attorney-General Taft held that the "absence" spoken of, in order to bring the accused within the jurisdiction of a court," must be such as to render him not amenable to

[1] XIV. Opinions Attorney General, June 12, 1872.
[2] Ibid., also June 30, 1873.

justice." "The word 'amenable' as used in this article would seem to mean, within the reach and power of the military authorities to bring to trial before a court-martial. Unquestionably the absence of the accused in a foreign land would place the accused beyond such jurisdiction, and thus make him amenable; so, it has been thought, would absence within the limits of the country if he were where the military authorities by reasonable diligence could not discover him.[1]

"It would be difficult, perhaps impossible, to lay down any general rule whereby to determine in all cases under what facts and circumstances the accused may be deemed to be beyond the reach and power of the military authorities to bring him to trial, or beyond the jurisdiction of a court-martial. This is a matter which must needs be left, in each case, to the judgment of the court itself, upon the particular facts and circumstances appearing therein, subject to revision by the proper authority."[2]

Deserters. In the case of *deserters* much difficulty has arisen in determining when the statute of limitations commence to run. As formerly interpreted it was held, that, taking into consideration the language of the 48th Article, the limitation would commence to run from date of apprehension or surrender. This view is very ably maintained by Adjutant-General Townsend in a pamphlet printed in 1876, and is shown to have been the practice of the government for a long number of years.

Two other interpretations have been advanced as to when the limitation commences:

1st. At the end of two years from the date of desertion.

2d. Two years after the expiration of the term for which the soldier enlisted; this being the latest opinion.[3]

[1] § XIV. Opinions Attorney-General, June 30, 1873.
[2] XV. Opinions Attorney-General, Sept. 1, 1876. [3] Ibid.

As there has been much controversy over this point, the Secretary of War, in his annual report of 1877, recommended that it be set at rest by final legislation.

It is settled in reference to this class of offenders, that the enlisting in another regiment, or branch of the service, will not constitute such "absence" or "manifest impediment" as will entitle the government to try after the expiration of two years.[1]

Jurisdiction after Expiration of Service. Much question has arisen among writers on military law as to whether a court-martial has jurisdiction over an officer or soldier after they have been dismissed the service, or their term of service has expired.

English writers maintain that an officer can be brought before a court-martial after being dismissed the service. They base their opinion upon the case of Lord George Sackville.[2] This officer was deprived of his military command and commission, without having been brought to trial, for imputed misconduct at the battle of Minden. He demanded a court-martial, and the question of competency was referred to the twelve judges, who unanimously declared that they saw no ground to doubt the legality of the jurisdiction of a court-martial under those circumstances. He was therefore tried by court-martial, pronounced guilty, and sentenced as follows: "that the said Lord George Sackville is, and he is hereby adjudged unfit to serve his Majesty in any military capacity."[3]

The only case in this country in which this question has been the subject of judicial decision, is that of William B. Bird, which came before the United States District Court for the District of Oregon, in 1871. Judge

[1] Harris' Case, XIV. Opinion Attorney-General, June 30, 1873. G. C. M. O. 63, A. G. O., Aug. 10, 1874.

[2] Tytler p. 113, Hough's Precedents, 6 and 16.

[3] Smollett's England, Vol. 13, p. 271.

Deady said,—"As at present advised, I do not see what provisions of the constitution, or statute, or principle of common law can be invoked to prevent the *arrest and trial* of a person by court-martial for a military offense, committed while such person was an officer or soldier of the army of the United States, *after* the expiration of the term of service, so that the order for trial is issued within the time limited by the article of war."[1]

This, however, does not correspond to the general practice of our government. In 1871 the President announced that the enactments to be found in Articles 48 and 60 are held to show legislative recognition of the general rule, to which the military department of the government also has uniformly adhered in practice, to wit, that officers or soldiers, after they have been regularly discharged from the military service, or after their term of service has expired, unless proceedings against them have been commenced before such expiration, are not (except when otherwise provided by statute) within the jurisdiction of a court-martial for offenses committed by them while in service.[2]

In the case of Joseph White, a discharged soldier undergoing sentence of a general court-martial, the question arose as to whether an offender who has never passed from military control, cannot be made amenable to some tribunal for new crimes committed while a prisoner, and upon this question Major G. N. Lieber, Judge-Advocate U. S. A., recommended that White be allowed to serve out his time of confinement, and that he then be turned over to the civil authorities for trial for the assault and battery. The Adjutant-General, in a letter to the commanding general Department of Dakota, said, "I have the

[1] Scott's Digest of Military Laws, 421.

[2] G. C. M. O., 16, A. G. O., Aug, 30, 1871; see also VIII. Opinions Attorney. General, 328, and IX, Ibid, 182.

honor to inform you that the Judge-Advocate General of the army concurs in the opinion of Major Lieber, and remarks that the want of authority in a military court to try him for the offense he is alleged to have committed, results necessarily from his discharge from the army, which has formally and completely separated him from the military service; that he is now only a citizen suffering punishment as a military convict, under a sentence passed upon him; while as a soldier, he was subject to military discipline and control; that it may be inconvenient for his trial for this offense to be postponed until the expiration of his period of confinement, but this inconvenience, however great it may be, cannot give to a military court jurisdiction over an ordinary assault and battery committed by a citizen. The Secretary of War approves the views of the Judge-Advocate General."[1]

Exceptions. There are, however, as recognized in the order above quoted, certain exceptions to this rule.

First. Where an officer has been arrested, or a soldier confined, for a military offense before expiration of service.

A case illustrative of this was that of William Walker, a seaman in the navy. He was put in confinement, and charges were preferred against him to the Secretary of the Navy before the expiration of the term of his enlistment. The Supreme Court of Massachusetts decided in 1830 that this was "clearly a sufficient commencement of the prosecution to authorize a court-martial to proceed to trial and sentence, notwithstanding the term of service had expired before the court-martial had been convened." The court further remarked, to show the fallacy of a different construction, "that if any of the class of offenses not punishable at common law, and of which

[1] Letter dated A. G. O., Sept. 28, 1872.

no other courts excepting courts-martial can take cognizance, should be committed immediately before the expiration of his term of service, he would escape with impunity. He might be guilty of the grossest insults to his officers; of disobedience of orders in the most critical moment to the ship; and in the hour of battle he might refuse to fight, and there would be no power to punish him."[1]

In the case of Bird, before mentioned, it was held that the jurisdiction of courts-martial under these circumstances, was undoubted.[2]

Second. When the term of service has expired, but no muster out has been made, or discharge given.

The Judge-Advocate General decided, during the war, that officers and soldiers of volunteers remain liable to trial and punishment for military offenses, although their terms of service have expired, if they have not been formally mustered out.[3] The same would be true of a regular soldier until he is regularly discharged.[4]

In the case of *Dinsman vs. Wilkes*, the Supreme Court held that "the decision of the question (whether the commander of a squadron had power to detain a marine after the term of his enlistment expired, if in the opinion of the commander public interest required it) by the commander was final and conclusive, and if the marine did not conform to it he was liable to punishment."[5]

Third. When an officer, dismissed by order of the President, makes, in writing, an application for trial, setting forth, under oath, that he had been wrongfully dismissed, the President shall, as soon as the necessities of the service may permit, convene a court-martial to try such officer on the charges on which he shall have been dismissed, and if

1 American Jurist, April No. 1830.

2 Scott's Digest of Military Laws, 421.

3 Opinions J. A. G., 210.

4 See U. S. *vs.* Travers, 2 Wh. Crim. Cas. 490.

5 XII, Howard, 390.

a court-martial is not so convened within six months from the presentation of such application for trial, or if such court, being convened, does not award dismissal or death as the punishment of such officer, the order of dismissal of the President shall be void.[1]

The President cannot dismiss an officer in time of peace.[2]

Fourth. Where an officer procures his resignation or muster out on false representations.

In this case his discharge may be revoked, and he brought to trial for offenses committed before such discharge. It is a principle of law that fraud vitiates any contract, and that no party is bound by an engagement or obligation into which he has been induced to enter through the fraud or false representation of another. The burden of proof would rest upon the government to show that the discharge was procured through fraud. If, however, the discharge was not fraudulently procured, it cannot be revoked against the will of the party. Having once duly left the service he cannot be caused to enter it without his consent.[3]

Fifth. Where any person in the military service commits any of the offenses named in the 60th Article of War.

The statute of limitations applies, however, to offenses under this article.[4]

Sixth. Where a soldier is a deserter.

Every soldier who deserts the service of the United States shall be tried by a court-martial and punished, although the term of his enlistment may have elapsed previous to his being apprehended and tried.[5]

[1] § 1230 Revised Statutes. [2] § 1229 Revised Statutes.
[3] Opinions J. A. G., p. 240.
[4] XIV. Opinions Attorney-General, June 12, 1872. [5] Art. 48.

In the case of an *officer* dropped for desertion, under the provisions of section 1229 Revised Statutes, and afterwards recaptured, he cannot be tried by a court-martial.[1]

[1] G. C. M. O. 16; A. G. O., Aug. 30, 1871.

CHAPTER IV.

SPECIAL JURISDICTION OF COURTS-MARTIAL.

WE come now to the special jurisdiction of the different courts-martial, and the limitations upon their jurisdiction.

The decision as to which of these courts will have jurisdiction in any case will depend upon the rank of the accused, the nature of the offense, and the punishment that may be inflicted; and, as between regimental, garrison and field officer's courts, whether the offense was committed in time of peace or war.

The only court capable of trying all classes of military offenders and offenses is the general court-martial; and it may try the greatest or the smallest offenses.

Offenses exclusively Cognizable by a General Court. There are certain offenses exclusively cognizable by a *general* court-martial, and these are:—

First. Those which officers may commit under the rules and articles of war.

Article 79 provides that officers shall be tried only by general court-martial; and no officer shall, when it can be avoided, be tried by officers inferior to him in rank. Whether the trial of an officer by officers of an inferior rank can be avoided or not is a question, not for the accused or court, but for the officer convening the court, and his decision upon this point, as upon that of the number of members that can be detailed, is conclusive.[1] From

[1] Wooley *vs.* U. S. 20 Law Reports, 621.

the analogy of the two cases it would seem necessary to state, in an order convening a court composed of officers inferior in rank to the accused, that such detail could not be avoided.[1]

Second. Those which may be punished *capitally*, depending upon the nature and degree of the offense.

The 83d Article provides that regimental and garrison courts-martial, and field officers detailed to try offenders, shall not have power to try capital cases.

General courts-martial, also, can only try such capital cases as are enumerated in the articles of war.[2]

Third. Those against which penalties are denounced greater than a minor court can inflict.

The question of jurisdiction of the minor courts depends upon the punishment, and not upon the offense. If they have jurisdiction of the person, and can award a proper punishment, they have jurisdiction of the offense. The minor courts are forbidden to inflict a fine over one month's pay, or to imprison or put to hard labor any non-commissioned officer or soldier for a longer time than one month.[3]

It often happens that an offense is triable by a general court, or one of the minor courts. "Absence without leave," for instance, if for a short period, would properly be tried by one of the minor courts; if aggravated, by a general court. No definite rule can be laid down to determine before which court such cases should be brought. A discretion must be exercised by the convening authority, and whenever an adequate punishment could not be awarded the accused, if he is found guilty, by one of the minor courts, it should be sent before a general court-martial. The nature of the offense and the circumstances of each particular case must determine.

If one of the minor courts deems that it has no juris-

[1] Opinions, J. A G., p. 22. [2] Art. 96. [3] Art. 83.

diction, on account of inability to award sufficient punishment, it should suspend its proceedings and report the fact to the convening authority.

If this officer, however, differs with them and remands the case for trial, the court cannot refuse to try it. The opinion of a court of inquiry upon this point in 1868, approved and published by the Secretary of War,[1] is here given: "In the opinion of the court, the only ground upon which a garrison court-martial could refuse to try a case, presented to it for trial by the commanding officer of a post, would be the illegality of the order convening the court. By the articles of war it would not have been illegal for the court to have tried the accused under the charges presented by General K. It is simply a matter of discipline, and the responsibility of the commanding officer for this discipline is certainly greater than that of his subordinates. The court are of the opinion that the conduct of Brevet Major B., and Brevet Captain P., in persisting in their refusal to try the case presented to them by the commanding officer, General K., was very reprehensible."

Jurisdiction of Regimental Courts. This court is limited in its jurisdiction to offenses committed by soldiers in a regiment or corps. In one case this court has *exclusive* jurisdiction.

Article 30 provides that any soldier who thinks himself wronged by any officer may complain to the commanding officer of his regiment, who shall summon a *regimental* court-martial *for the doing of justice to the complainant.* This article was adopted from the British, and was intended to afford to enlisted men a quick mode of redress. Though a court for doing justice, it partakes largely of the character of a "court of inquiry," for it is limited to determining

[1] G. O. 81, A. G O., Oct. 9, 1868.

whether a wrong has been committed and to suggesting the proper redress. It cannot inflict a punishment, on account of the limitation in Article 38. The regimental court-martial assembled under this article differs, says O'Brien, from a court of inquiry, in that its primary and essential object is to *remedy* the wrong, and *not* to decide whether or not the wrong done should or should not be punished.

This article has been the subject of much discussion, and has undergone frequent modifications. As first adopted it read: "If any inferior officer or soldier shall think himself wronged by his *captain or other officer commanding* the troop or company to which he belongs, he is to complain, etc." It was interpreted in England, says Simmons, "to refer only to complaints which relate to what is commonly called the interior economy of the company, and have reference to pay or allowances, clothing, messing, the repair of arms or accoutrements, or some similar claim." He further says: "It would not be competent to a regimental court-martial, thus convened, to enter upon an inquiry as to a charge of tyranny or oppression brought forward against the captain or officer commanding a company, and arising out of the ordinary connection of an officer and a soldier, as from duty in the field, or under arms. Such complaints must be made in the usual course to superior officers, and if heard by a military tribunal, it must be by a court for the trial of the accused, and competent to award punishment on conviction."[1]

The Judge-Advocate General, in an opinion delivered since the publication of the "Digest," says: It (the article) does not contemplate a criminal *trial* or *punishment* of the officer, as for a military offense, but only an investigation and adjustment of some matter in dispute arising in the interior economy of the company.[2]

[1] P. 73 (2d Edition.)

[2] Bureau of Military Justice, May 14, 1872. See Macomb's Courts-Martial, p. 193.

When, in 1806, new articles of war were adopted in our service, the words "commanding the troop or company" were left out of this article, leaving the interpretation somewhat in doubt.

A court of inquiry in 1843, entered at length into its meaning, and stated that:—"The American law, on this whole subject, is believed to be the same as the British law, with the single exception that the complaint, under the British law, can only be made against the complainant's captain or other officer commanding his troop or company." They further held that the change made in the articles in 1806 extended the jurisdiction of the court to complaints against *company* officers, whether commanding or not, but no farther; and this on account of the nature of the acts which alone could be complained of.[1] De Hart, agreeing with this court that the only complaints which this article contemplated were such as grow out of the administrative part of the company command, maintained that only the commanding officer of the company could stand in such relation to the soldier, and, therefore, complaints against him could alone be investigated by this regimental court.[2]

The present Code again changed the wording of this article, so as to allow a soldier who thinks himself wronged by "any officer" to complain. The evident intent of this change is to extend the jurisdiction of this court. The wrongs that may be complained of, however, remain the same as they were when the article was first adopted from the British; no modification having been made in that respect. May not complaints of this nature, though, arise against an officer not commanding a company, as for instance the complaint of an ordnance or

[1] G. O. 13, A. G. O., Feb. 20, 1873.
[2] De Hart on Courts-Martial, p. 259, *et seq.*

commissary sergeant against a post quartermaster or commissary?

One requisite would still have to be fulfilled; the complaint must be against an officer of a regiment or corps under the command of the convening authority; for a regimental court could have nothing to do with investigating offenses against officers not under his command.

The following opinion of Col. Lieber, Judge-Advocate's Corps, expresses the accepted view of the jurisdiction of this court.[1] "The object of this court is, in the language of the article, 'the doing justice to the complainant.' It is therefore necessary, in considering the legality of such a court, to look to the end with a view of determining whether the wrong complained of is of such a character that the doing of justice would fall within the province of a regimental court. It is evident that such a court cannot try a commissioned officer or impose on him any punishment for the wrong complained of—for this would be a violation of the 67th (present 83d) Article of War. The powers vested by this article are not punitive, but relate only to such wrongs as are susceptible of redress by the doing of justice to the complainant. Punishing the wrong doer is not to be regarded as, in the sense of this article, doing justice to the complainant. The object can only be attained under this article by putting a stop to the wrongful condition of things which the action of the officer has caused to exist. It is thus with reference to excessive work, irregular details, wrongful stoppages of pay, etc. In such cases the court may recommend a reversal of the orders of the officer, and when such action is by the regimental commander directed to be taken, justice will have been done to the complainant. When the

[1] Approved by J. A. G. in letter dated May 14, 1872, and by Secretary of War, May 16, 1872.

wrong is of such a character as, if committed, to be only met by the punishment of the officer, a general court-martial is the only proper tribunal for its consideration with reference to that punishment."

In the case in which this opinion was given, the court found that the injury complained of had been committed, but failed to designate the manner in which justice should be done. The kind of redress, or whether it should be accorded at all, was left to the discretion of the officer committing the wrong. Colonel Lieber says, "the 33d (present 30th) Article evidently contemplated nothing so indefinite, under that article. The court is assembled for the doing of justice, and must itself determine the nature of the redress required."[1]

Garrison Court. This court possesses a wider jurisdiction than either of the other minor courts. It may try any offenders, not commissioned officers, under the command of the convening authority.

Field Officer's Court. The jurisdiction of this court is expressly confined to times of war, and to offenses committed in the regiment of the field officer. If the regiment is divided into companies at different places, but under the command of the officer appointing the court, jurisdiction still obtains; otherwise, however, if the companies are under another command.

As to offenses and punishments, the same restrictions apply to the three minor courts.

The minor courts are deemed to have jurisdiction, equally with a general court-martial, of offenses not capital committed by "a retainer to camp." An offense of the graver kind, when committed by a retainer, should, like such an offense when committed by a soldier, be referred for trial to a general court.

[1] See O'Brien, pp. 120–130.

These courts have also power to reduce non-commissioned officers to the ranks. Ordnance sergeants and hospital stewards, though liable to discharge, may not be reduced; nor are they to be tried by regimental or garrison courts-martial, unless by special permission of the department commander.[1] The same rule would apply to commissary sergeants.

Jurisdiction of Courts-Martial as to Persons. In general every officer and soldier of the armies of the United States, regular and volunteer,[2] is subject to the rules and articles of war,[3] and amenable to trial by courts-martial. Some of them are made, by statute or by accepted decisions, specially amenable, and Congress has extended these articles to certain other classes of persons.

Retired Officers. By the Act of August 3, 1861, establishing a retired list, it is provided that such officers shall continue to be borne upon the Army Register, and shall be subject to the rules and articles of war, and to be tried by general court-martial for any breach of the said articles. The punishment must be such as would apply to their status. Cases have arisen where retired officers have been tried and dismissed the service.

Officers or Soldiers on Parol are liable to trial by courts-martial, being regarded, so far as pay and allowances are concerned, as in actual service. A violation, on the part of an officer in the United States service, of the *parol of honor*, would properly be chargeable under the 61st Article; and, on the part of an enlisted man, under the 62d Article.[4]

Officers or Soldiers on leave of Absence. Whether an officer on leave, or a soldier on furlough, is liable to trial by court-martial for offenses committed on leave is a

[1] Regulations, par. 895.
[2] See Article 64.
[3] § 1342. Revised Statutes,
[4] Opinions J. A. G., p. 263.

point upon which I find no decision in our service. Some doubt exists upon this point in the English service, though in the case of Lieutenant Poe, tried for misconduct as a passenger on board the "Cæsar" while returning from leave, no objection that the sentence was illegal, on that ground, was taken before the court of Kings Bench. In 1831 the question appears to have been discussed by the Board of Admiralty, and a doubt entertained whether an officer on leave could be tried by a court-martial for a military offense.[1]

In our service, where "retired officers" and "officers on parol" are amenable to trial, the right to try officers or soldiers "on leave" would seem to follow, and this is strengthened by the fact, that by drunkenness or disorder the service may be brought into greater disrepute than if the offense was committed at a military post.

Professors of the Military Academy have always been amenable to trial by court-martial. They are commissioned officers of the army,[2] being in terms, recognized as part of the military peace establishment by the Act of July 28, 1866.

Cadets of the Military Academy are likewise subject to trial by courts-martial, although this was at one time questioned. In 1818 a general court-martial decided that it had no jurisdiction to try cadets. The matter was referred to Attorney-General Wirt, who proved conclusively that they were so amenable.[3] By the Act of 1866 the Corps of Cadets was likewise recognized by Congress as part of the military peace establishment.

Chaplains were, by the Act of April 19th, 1864, subjected to the same rules and regulations as other officers of the army.

[1]Clode's "Military and Martial Law," p. 89.

[2] I. Opinions Attorney-General, p. 469. § 1094, Revised Statutes.

[3] Ibid, Aug. 21, 1819.

Militia Troops. The Constitution authorizes Congress "to provide for calling forth the militia to execute the laws of the Union, suppress insurrections and repel invasions," and also "to provide for governing such part of them as may be employed in the service of the United States."[1] Congress has acted under both of these grants. Under the *first* it has authorized the President to call forth the militia in the cases prescribed in the Constitution,[2] and the Supreme Court has decided that the power is exclusively vested in him to determine when these circumstances exist.[3] Under the *second* it has prescribed that "the militia, when called into the actual service of the United States for the suppression of rebellion against and resistance to the laws of the United States, shall be subjected to the same rules and articles of war as the regular troops of the United States."[4]

The militia may be called out either by requisition upon, or orders to, the State executive, or by orders direct to any subordinate officer of militia;[5] and, as the law now reads, they are subject to the jurisdiction of military law as soon as they are *called into the service* of the United States.

Marine Corps. The Marine Corps, when detached for service with the army by order of the President, are subject to the rules and articles of war prescribed for the government of the army.[6]

Signal Detachment. Observer sergeants and privates of this service, though often separated from the army, are amenable to trial by military courts. The word "soldier," as used in the Articles, includes non-commissioned officers, etc., and other enlisted men.[7]

[1] Art I. § VIII. Clauses 15, 16.

[2] Act of Feb. 28, 1795, and July 19, 1861. § 1642 R. S.

[3] Martin vs. Mott, 12 Wheaton, 19.

[4] § 1644 Revised Statutes.

[5] Houston vs. Moore, 5 Wheaton, 16.

[6] § 1621 Rev. Statutes.

[7] § 1342 Rev. Statutes.

The same rule applies to ordnance and commissary sergeants and hospital stewards.

Soldiers' Home. By the act of March 3, 1859, all persons that may hereafter be admitted into this institution, shall be, and are hereby made subject to the rules and articles of war, and will be governed thereby in the same manner as soldiers in the army.[1]

All inmates of the National Home for disabled volunteer soldiers are subject to the rules and articles of war, and in the same manner as if they were in the army.[2]

Military Prison. The act establishing the military prison[3] provides that all prisoners under confinement in said military prison, undergoing sentence of courts-martial, shall be liable to trial and punishment by courts-martial, under the rules and articles of war, for offenses committed during the said confinement.

The regulations of the prison prescribe that any act of a prisoner, which, if committed by a soldier, would constitute an offense under the articles of war, is to be tried by a general or garrison court-martial according to the nature and degree of the offense, by direction of the general commanding the department.[4]

Retainers to Camps, etc. All retainers to the camp, and all persons serving with the armies of the United States *in the field*, though not enlisted soldiers, are to be subject to orders according to the rules and discipline of war.[5]

By "retainers to the camp" are meant all who voluntarily engage in the service of the United States, such as laborers on military works, or in the hire of the quartermaster or subsistence departments; and also all who, in

[1] § 4824, Rev. Statutes. [2] Ibid, Sec. 4835.
[3] March 3, 1873, amended by Act of May 21, 1874.
[4] G. O. 12, A. G. O., Feb. 19, 1877. [5] Art. 63.

the private service of commissioned officers, voluntarily perform service at a military post or encampment.

"All persons serving with the armies in the field," refers to every description of person, voluntarily found within actual military lines in time of war, accompanying the army for business or pleasure, such as scouts, newspaper reporters, army contractors and the like.

The words "*in the field*," according to the Attorney-General,[1] "imply military operations with a view to an enemy. To decide exactly where the boundary line runs between civil and military jurisdiction as to the civilians attached to an army is difficult, but it is quite evident that they are within military jurisdiction as provided for in Art. 63, when their treachery, defection, or insubordination might endanger or embarrass the army to which they belong, in its operations against what is known in military phrase as 'an enemy.' Persons who attach themselves to an army, going upon an expedition against hostile Indians, may be understood as agreeing that they will submit themselves for the time being to military control. When an army is engaged in offensive or defensive operations, I think it safe to say that it is an army in the field."

For minor offenses against military order and discipline, committed by civilians employed with troops, as retainers or camp followers, it has been customary to expel them from the post or camp where they are employed or stationed. When guilty of crimes or grave offenses they are generally to be turned over to the civil authorities of the locality for trial and punishment. But where employed with troops on the march, or at remote posts and in regions where there is no civil jurisdiction, they may for serious offenses be brought to trial by general

[1] XIV. Opinions Attorney General, April 1, 1872.

court-martial, or for minor offenses by a regimental or garrison court, under the general authority of the 63d Article of War, provided such offenses are of a military character.[1]

Contract Surgeons A doubt has seemed to exist as to whether acting assistant surgeons, hired under contract, were amenable to trial by court-martial, and it was held by the Judge-Advocate General that they were not, except when serving with the armies of the United States in the field, in the sense of the 63d Article of War.[2]

Such persons are, however, obliged to take the oath of office required of every person elected or appointed to any office of honor or profit either in the civil, military, or naval service; [3] they are entitled to pensions the same as officers of the army; [4] to be saluted and to give orders the same as any surgeon; in fact they are placed by the United States Government in the position of commissioned officers so far as relates to their duties as surgeons.[5]

In 1876 a contract surgeon, an alien, who had been honorably discharged from the service of the United States, applied for naturalization papers, claiming the advantages of section 2166,[6] Revised Statutes. Judge Blatchford[7] decided that he was entitled to the provisions of this section, having been in the service of the United States.

Such being their status, it would seem that they should be considered as amenable to military law, at least for offenses committed by them in the execution of their office.

Civil Functionaries Employed in the Service. In

[1] Opinions J. A. G., p. 84. [2] Opinions J. A. G., p. 121.

[3] § 1756 Revised Statutes. [4] § 4693 Revised Statutes.

[5] G. O. 100, A. G. O., Dec. 2, 1875.

[6] This provides that alien soldiers, honorably discharged, are required to reside in the country only one year to become naturalized.

[7] U. S. District Court, Southern District New York, May 13, 1876.

the several staff departments, in the cavalry regiments, and in the national cemeteries the law authorizes the employment of certain civil functionaries who are paid out of army appropriations at fixed salaries.

Much question has arisen as to their amenability to trial by court-martial. In 1869 a paymaster's clerk in the navy, charged with embezzlement,[1] was held by Judge Benedict to be subject to naval jurisdiction and liable to be tried by a court-martial; and again, Judge Hill on a writ of *habeas corpus* decided that a paymaster's clerk in the army, charged with forging vouchers, was liable to be tried by court-martial and not entitled to discharge on such a writ.[2]

The ground of these opinions was that these parties were so amenable because their status was fixed by law, and they were paid out of regular appropriations made for the army and navy.

In 1876 the question arose as to the liability of a quartermaster's clerk to be tried by court-martial under the 60th Article of War. The Judge-Advocate General held that such a clerk *is not* amenable to military trial for any offense whatever *in time of peace.* Such a clerk, he held, might possibly become so amenable if serving with an army in the field, engaged in a warfare with hostile Indians, but under no other circumstances at this period.[3]

The question being referred to Attorney-General Taft, he held that the clerk of a quartermaster *is* so employed in the military service of the United States, as to be amenable to the jurisdiction of a court-martial for any violation of the sixtieth article of the articles of war.[4]

In 1878 the question came before Attorney-General

[1] U. S. *vs.* Bogart. U. S. District Court, Eastern District, N. Y.

[2] In re John Thomas U. S. Dist. Court, Mississippi, 1 Chicago Legal News, p. 245.

[3] Bureau of Military Justice, March 31, 1876.

[4] Opinions Attorney-General, June 2d, 1876.

Devens as to whether civilian clerks employed by quartermasters, and also superintendents of national cemeteries were amenable to the jurisdiction of a court-martial.

In his opinion upon this point he stated, that Attorney-General Taft subsequently contemplated a reconsideration of his opinion (quoted above) and the question was understood to be under re-examination at the time his incumbency at the head of the Attorney-General's Department terminated. He (Devens) held that the question of the amenability of an individual to court-martial jurisdiction under the 60th Article of War is not to be determined according to the nature of his employment, that is to say, whether it is military or not, but solely according to the circumstances of his belonging or not belonging to the military establishment as defined in section 1094 Revised Statutes.

Persons who do not belong to that establishment—who are not a part of the army, as thus fixed and defined—are not subject to such jurisdiction, excepting, of course, where they come within the 63d Article, or within the sections referred to above.[1&2]

Post Traders are subject in all respects to the rules and regulations for the government of the army.[3]

Citizens. In time of *war* citizens are amenable to trial by courts-martial for any of the offenses named in the 45th and 46th Articles of War, and for acting as spies.[4]

In time of war or peace, citizens employed in the military prison who shall suffer a convict to escape, or shall in any way consent to his escape, or shall aid him to escape, or in an attempt to escape, are liable to trial by courts-martial.[5]

[1] G. O. 25, A. G. O., May 21, 1878.

[2] Revised Statutes, Secs. 1343, 1361, 4824, 4835.

[3] G. O., 70, July 26, 1876. [4] Revised Statutes, Sec. 1343. [5] Ibid, Sec. 1360.

CHAPTER V.

ARRESTS AND CONFINEMENTS.

Arrests. The Articles of War direct that officers charged with crime shall be arrested and be confined in their barracks, quarters, or tents, and deprived of their swords by their commanding officer.[1]

An arrest of an officer, as ordinarily understood, does not contemplate bodily restrictions. The officer is simply on his parol not to break the arrest. No bail is required as in the case of civil offenders; but the value of an officer's commission answers the same purpose.

Limits. The requirements of this article, by custom of the service, are not literally enforced. An officer in arrest may, at the discretion of his commanding officer, have larger limits assigned him than his tent or quarters.[2]

Ordinarily the limits of the post where an officer is stationed are allowed, but unless other limits are assigned to him, he must observe a close arrest.

It is customary to fix the limits at the time of arrest, but an officer at any time may apply for an extension of those limits.[3]

Sword. The depriving an officer of his sword is generally omitted, but the same result is obtained, inasmuch as, by Regulations,[4] he cannot wear his sword during that time.

[1] Article 65. [2] Regulations, par. 223.
[3] Regulations, par. 223. [4] Ibid, par. 229.

While under arrest an officer is disqualified from giving any orders, or exercising any military authority; he cannot make a visit of etiquette, or visit officially his commanding or other superior officer unless sent for. In case of business with them he is to make known his object in writing.[1]

Physical restrictions may be imposed upon an officer, when, from the nature of the offense, there would be danger of his escaping. A sentry may be placed over him, and, in extreme cases, he might be confined.

In the case of Lieut. F., an officer who in 1877 embezzled, then deserted, and was afterwards captured, the commanding officer of the post to which he was taken, confined him in an iron grated cell of the guard house, with a guard over him.

Such extreme measures will, however, only be justified in extreme cases, and where there is almost conclusive proof of guilt.

Where an officer intentionally breaks his arrest, the commanding officer would be justified in placing him under guard.

Breach of Arrest is considered one of the most heinous of military offenses, as is shown by the 65th Article, which directs that any officer who leaves his confinement before he is set at liberty by his commanding officer shall be dismissed the service.

The Judge-Advocate General holds that on account of the nature of the punishment, breach of arrest should only be charged under this article upon some determined and decided violation of the order of arrest, in the nature of deliberate contempt of the authority issuing it; and that there can be no technical breach of arrest and violation of the 65th Article, except in case of close arrest and confinement in "barracks, quarters or tent."[2]

[1] Regulations, par. 229. [2] Opinions J. A. G., p. 34.

If a commanding officer, however, out of favor extends the limits prescribed in this article, and an officer willfully and intentionally goes beyond those limits, it is difficult to see why this is not such a "leaving of confinement" as is contemplated by the article.

The Judge-Advocate General holds that in this case and other infractions, not of the severe nature spoken of above, the accused should be tried under the 62d Article.[1]

In all cases of technical breach of arrest—such as exercising military authority, wearing sword, etc.,—the accused cannot be charged under the 65th Article, as the punishment is mandatory and authorizes the sentence of dismissal only in case of "leaving his confinement."

Termination of Arrest. The 65th Article is qualified by the 71st, which declares that, "When an officer is put in arrest for the purpose of trial, except at remote military posts or stations, the officer by whose order he is arrested shall see that a copy of the charges on which he is to be tried be served upon him within *eight* days after his arrest, and that he is brought to trial within *ten* days thereafter,[2] unless the necessities of the service prevent such trial; and then he shall be brought to trial within thirty days after the expiration of the said ten days. If a copy of the charges be not served, or the arrested officer be not brought to trial, as herein required, the arrest *shall* cease. But officers, released from arrest under the provisions of this article, may be tried whenever the exigencies of the service shall permit, within twelve months after such release from arrest.

This article is somewhat incongruous. How can a commanding officer who orders an officer in arrest see that a copy of charges, "on which he is to be tried," be

[1] Opinions J. A. G., p. 46.

[2] Ten days after his arrest. Opinions J. A. G., p. 58.

served upon him within eight days? A copy of the charges preferred might be furnished, but these may be materially altered, or the convening authority may refuse to bring the officer to trial. Again, how can he see that the officer "be brought to trial within ten days?" This rests entirely in the discretion of the convening officer. The commanding officer can, however, unless the provisions of the article are complied with, release the officer from arrest and he is required to do so.

While the article is mandatory and says that under certain conditions the arrest *shall* cease, an officer would not be justified in considering himself released, if these conditions take place. If he so acted, he would do so at his peril. Article 71 says his arrest shall cease when put in arrest "for the purpose of trial." How can he know the intentions of his commanding officer? It is not essential that the officer or soldier should know why he is arrested.[1] An exception is again made "at remote military posts or stations." Who is to judge of the remoteness which will bring a post under this exception? Certainly not the officer arrested. Again, the arrest shall cease "unless the necessities of the service prevent such trial." An officer in arrest is assuredly not the judge of that.

The 71st Article did not contemplate, it is believed, a release by an officer's own will. In the latter part it says, "but officers *released* from arrest under the provisions of this article may, etc.," not officers whose arrest *terminates;* the article should be construed in conjunction with Article 65, which prescribes the gravest punishment for terminating an arrest until released *by the commanding officer.*

If not released from arrest, or restored to duty at the time designated by law, an officer should apply for the

[1] Opinions J. A. G., p. 57.

appropriate relief to the officer who ordered his arrest or his successor. If his application is not granted, it is open for him to apply for redress to the officer superior to the latter, in the manner set forth in the 29th Article of War.[1]

When all other means of justice fail, which must be an extremely rare case, an appeal should be made to the Secretary of War.[2]

Unlawful Arrests. Is there no protection to an officer against illegal arrests by his commanding officer, or being held in arrest contrary to law? In addition to the mode just pointed out, two legal remedies are open to any one placed under military arrest which he deems to be unlawful:—

First. An application for a writ of *habeas corpus* to one of the United States courts or judges.

While no case is known where this has been resorted to in this country, several cases have come before the Court of Queen's Bench in England, in some of which the applicant has been remanded to the military authorities; in others discharged.[3] The United States courts have ever exercised the right of determining, on a writ of *habeas corpus*, whether the custody of a person held by the military authorities is lawful or not. The English courts have refused to interfere by ordering the prisoner's release under *habeas corpus* because his confinement exceeded eight days.[4]

Second. A civil suit against the party illegally arresting.

In the case of an English officer (Captain Wall), where he was kept in prison for nine months before a court-martial was summoned, he recovered £1000 damages

[1] This article in its spirit if not in its language applies to all cases of this character.

[2] Opinions J. A. G., p. 58. [3] Clode's Military and Martial Law, p. 98.

[4] Ibid, p. 102.

against the committing officer. Lord Mansfield stigmatized the conduct of the latter as "malignant." He said: "The principal inquiry to be made by a court of justice in such cases is how the heart stood. If there be nothing wrong there, great latitude will be allowed for misapprehension or mistake." [1]

A similar doctrine has been laid down by the Supreme Court in this country:—In the case of *Wilkes vs. Dinsman*, an action of trespass was brought by the defendant, a marine, against his commanding officer for holding him after his term of service, as claimed by him, had expired. The court held, that a public officer, invested with certain discretionary powers, never has been, and never should be, made answerable for any injury, when acting within the scope of his authority, and not influenced by malice, corruption, or cruelty. Hence, while an officer acts within the limits of that discretion, the same law which gives it to him will protect him in the exercise of it. But for acts beyond his jurisdiction, or attended by circumstances of excessive severity, arising from ill will, a depraved disposition, or vindictive feeling, he can claim no exemption, and should be allowed none under color of his office, however elevated or however humble the victim. [2]

Who may place an Officer in Arrest. None but commanding officers have power to place officers under arrest, except for offenses expressly designated in the 24th Article of War. This article ordains that, All officers of what condition soever, have power to part and quell all quarrels, frays, and disorders, whether among persons belonging to his own or to another corps, regiment, troop, battery, or company, and to order officers into arrest and non-commissioned officers and soldiers into confinement, who take part in the same,

[1] Clode's Military and Martial Law, p. 101. [2] 7 Howard, 89.

until their proper superior officer is acquainted therewith. And whosoever, being so ordered, refuses to obey such officer or non-commissioned officer, or draws a weapon upon him, shall be punished as a court-martial may direct.

This is the only article where the word "officer" includes non-commissioned officer. In the first part of the articles of war it is expressly stated to designate commissioned officers when used therein.

Benét says,[1] "The authority of this article can and should be extended to any glaring impropriety, such as drunkenness on parade, that properly comes under the head of disorders. It was decided by high authority in the British service, that circumstances may occur even upon parade, to justify a junior officer to take upon himself the strong responsibility of placing his commander in arrest; such a measure must alone rest upon the responsibility of the officer who adopts it, and there are cases wherein the discipline and welfare of the service require that it should be assumed."

When a non-commissioned or junior officer orders a superior in arrest, under the provisions of this article, the fact should be immediately reported to the commanding officer.

A court-martial, under the authority of Article 86, has the power of ordering military persons in arrest, who use any menacing words, signs, or gestures, in its presence, or who disturb the proceedings by any riot or disorder.

A court-martial could not arrest an officer for disobedience of its lawful commands, or contempts committed, when absent from its sessions. It should in such cases apply for redress to the convening officer, or to the Secretary of War.[2]

[1] Military Law and Courts-Martial, p. 58. [2] Opinions J. A. G., p. 34.

Courts-martial have no power to order one of its members or the judge-advocate in arrest; the same course must be pursued as just indicated. In 1849 a court-martial ordered its president in arrest, but its action was disapproved by the President of the United States, on the ground that the 86th Article did not authorize a court-martial to punish its own members.[1]

Courts-martial may order in arrest, for the contempts spoken of in the 86th Article, officers superior in rank to every member of the court.[2]

Manner of Arrest. When above the rank of a captain, sealed instructions, in case of arrest, should be sent to the officer in ordinary cases. Under the rank of major it is ordinarily done by one of the commanding officer's staff, who formally reads to the accused the order. It may likewise be done by the mere verbal order of competent authority.

Release from Arrest. The officer who orders the arrest, or his superior, is alone competent to release from arrest. When a junior or non-commissioned officer exercises the authority conferred in Article 24, they could not exercise the power of release. Article 65 requires that the release be by the commanding officer.

General Observations. Regulations direct that officers are not to be put in arrest for light offenses. For these the censure of the commanding officer will, in most cases, answer the purposes of discipline.[3]

In ordinary cases, and where inconvenience to the service would result from it, a medical officer will not be put in arrest until the court-martial for his trial convenes.[4]

It is not necessary that any officer should be placed

[1] G. O. 14, A. G. O., April 12, 1850.

[2] Case of Major John Browne, Samuel's Military Law, p. 635. De Hart, p. 104.

[3] Regulations, par. 222. [4] Ibid., par. 224.

in arrest before being brought to trial; nor can an officer demand an arrest, or persist in considering himself in arrest, after he has been properly released. He may be tried without being in arrest.

It is not necessary to bring an individual to trial because he has been placed in arrest, nor could he demand a trial.

An officer is not prevented from preferring charges while under arrest.

An officer is not necessarily privileged from arrest by virtue of being at the time a member of a general court-martial. But the arrest of an officer while doing court-martial duty should be avoided in any but extreme cases.[1]

Non-Commissioned Officers and Soldiers. Non-commissioned officers are not to be sent to the guard room and mixed with privates during confinement, but to be considered as placed in arrest, except in aggravated cases, where escape may be apprehended.[2]

Any commissioned officer may place a non-commissioned officer in arrest, or a soldier in confinement; but the fact must, as soon as practicable, be notified to his immediate commander.[3]

Soldiers charged with crimes should be confined until tried by court-martial, or released by proper authority;[4] and Article 70 provides that no officer or soldier put in arrest shall be continued in confinement more than eight days, or until such time as a court-martial can be assembled.

Receiving Prisoners by Officer of the Guard. No provost martial, or officer commanding a guard, shall refuse to receive or keep any prisoner committed to his charge by an officer belonging to the forces of the United

[1] Opinions J. A. G., p. 59.
[2] Regulations, par. 68.
[3] Ibid., par. 225.
[4] Art. 66.

States; *provided*, the officer committing shall, at the same time, deliver an account in writing, signed by himself, of the crime charged against the prisoner.[1]

Nothing prevents the receiving of prisoners without such account in writing, but an officer does so at his peril. For the ordinary post offenses, however, it is not customary to furnish a written statement of the crime; and commanding officers of guards frequently receive prisoners brought by non-commissioned officers and soldiers, and confined by order of commissioned officers. Where any doubt exists, in such confinements, the prisoner should be held until the officer by whose order he is confined can be consulted.

Where the officer committing is unknown to the commander of the guard; or, where there is any doubt as to the party being amenable to military law; or where the offense charged is one as to which there may be a question of jurisdiction, the commander of the guard should demand, for his own protection, a "written account signed by the officer, of the crime charged." Without such he renders himself liable in damages in an action before the civil courts for false imprisonment.

While the 67th Article requires the officer commanding a guard to receive and keep *any* prisoner committed to his charge, it must be taken with some limitations. Generally speaking, the word "any" applies to persons amenable to military law, and a commanding officer should satisfy himself that the parties committed are so amenable. It is not always possible, though, to determine whether a prisoner presented is amenable. A deserter, for instance, may be presented in citizen's clothes. Is an officer commanding a guard bound to receive such a person, simply on the written statement of the committing

[1] Article 67.

officer? No case has arisen in our service exactly illustrative of this point, but a decision in the English service in 1850, bears directly upon it. A person who was *prima facie* a soldier was presented by a non-commissioned officer to the commanding officer, and the account in writing required by the article furnished at the time. It proved afterwards that the person was not a soldier, and, on release, he brought an action for assault and false imprisonment. One judge (Earle) held that the article applied "only to those who are soldiers *de facto*, and not to those whose qualifications as soldiers are disputed." It was ruled by the remainder of the judges, "that a commanding officer receiving a soldier charged with desertion by a non-commissioned officer, who delivered a written signed charge of the same, is justified under this article in detaining such soldier. He is bound to receive the prisoner under the article of war, and he is not liable to an action for so doing. It makes no difference whether the crime be civil or military. The fact that a man is *prima facie* a soldier, and enlisted, is sufficient to bring him under the article of war. The duty of receiving arises *eo instanti* as soon as he is presented."[1]

If such imprisonment proves illegal, the *committing* officer becomes responsible, and this was so decided by the United States Circuit Court in California in the case of *McCall vs. McDowell*, in 1867.[2]

Civil Offenders. Commanding officers are sometimes called upon to receive civilians for confinement. Where, for example, a civilian commits a crime upon a military post, the commanding officer would be justified in holding him in confinement until he could be turned over to the authority having jurisdiction of his offense. If a crime is

[1] Wolton *vs.* Gavin, 16 Q. B. Rep., p. 70. Referred to in Clode, p. 100.
[2] 1 Abbott, 212; also cited in Scott's Digest, p. 428.

committed away from a post by a civilian, he would not be justified in holding such prisoner. It may be proper to state that, under these latter circumstances, there would be no objection in allowing a marshal, or sheriff, holding a prisoner under proper warrant, to make use of the guard house where no jail is conveniently near, provided he remains to take charge of the prisoner.

In this connection it should be borne in mind that in forts, arsenals, etc., which have been acquired by the United States, and over which jurisdiction has been ceded by the State in which it is situated, the United States courts have exclusive jurisdiction of all offenses committed therein.[1]

If the jurisdiction has not been ceded by the State, no matter how long the place may have been occupied by the United States, the State courts still retain jurisdiction.[2]

Release from Confinement. To prevent unjust confinement, Article 68 requires that every officer to whose charge a prisoner is committed, shall, within twenty-four hours after such commitment, or as soon as he is relieved from his guard, report in writing, to the commanding officer, the name of such prisoner, the crime charged against him, and the name of the officer committing him, and if he fails to make such report, he shall be punished as a court-martial may direct: Article 69 further provides that any officer who presumes, without proper authority, to release any prisoner committed to his charge, or suffers any prisoner so committed to escape, shall be punished as a court-martial may direct.

The officer of the day is required to release at guard mounting all prisoners under guard, without written charges,

[1] Kent's Commentaries, § 430.

[2] People *vs.* Godfrey, 17 Johns (N. Y.), 225; U. S. *vs.* Ames, 1 Woodbury and Minot (Mass), 76.

unless orders to the contrary be given by the commanding officer.[1]

Control of Courts-Martial over Arrests. A court-martial has no control over the nature of a prisoner's arrest. If brought before them without having been previously placed in arrest or confinement, it could not order him in confinement. It could not extend the limits of his arrest, even to allow him to better make his defense, as it has no control over him except when in its immediate presence. It might suggest greater liberties to the commanding officer, but he alone is responsible, and Simmons cites a case where a commanding officer was justified by his Majesty, in "refusing to accede to the suggestions of a court-martial to grant a prisoner such indulgence as might facilitate the examination of witnesses, and thereby enable him to enter earlier on his defense."[2]

[1] Regulations, par. 226. [2] P. 121 (2d Edition).

CHAPTER VI.

CHARGES AND SPECIFICATIONS.

A Military Charge is a clear, concise statement of an offense, with attendant circumstances. In our service it consists of two parts, viz.: the technical Charge, and the Specification. The former designates the offense in general terms; the latter the specific act, with the circumstances, including time and place, which go to make up the offense.

Taken together they correspond to an indictment by a grand jury in criminal prosecutions; the officer who convenes the court and orders the case for trial, finding the true bill of indictment.

Form for drawing up Charges. The manner of drawing up military charges has been established by custom, the general form of which will be found in the Appendix. There is, however, in the language of Attorney-General Cushing, "no one form of exclusive rigor and necessity in which to state military accusations."[1] The same care is not needed in drawing up military charges as in civil indictments. According to the same authority "the most bald statement of the facts alleged as constituting the offense, provided the legal offense itself be distinctly and accurately described in such terms of precision as the rules of military jurisprudence require, will be tenable in

[1] VII. Opinions Attorney-General, Dec. 1, 1855. I. Opinions Attorney-General, Aug. 29, 1819.

court-martial proceedings; and will be adequate groundwork of conviction and sentence." The two principal essentials in a charge, including the specifications, are :—

1st. That it be laid under the proper article of war.

2d. That it contain averments sufficient substantially to distinguish and constitute the offense.[1] The language of the law should be used when practicable, but the technical expressions used in civil indictments are not necessary.

Charge. Where an offense falls under a specific article it should be so charged, as such was the intent of the framers of the law.

It often happens that an act constitutes an offense against two or more articles. In this event the party preferring the charges must necessarily exercise a discretion; and, as the convening authority generally sees the charges before trial, any error of judgment may be corrected. He may, if he prefer, charge the offense under all the articles. This rule should, however, be borne in mind, that when an offense falls under an article for which a specific punishment is provided, it should be charged under that article. Thus, to charge "Drunkenness on duty" as "Conduct to the prejudice of good order and military discipline," would not be proper. It would give the court a discretion as to punishment where such discretion was not intended by the articles.

The 62d article, known in the English service[2] as the "Devil's article," was added to embrace those crimes not cognizable under the other articles, but which constituted nevertheless offenses to the prejudice of good order and military discipline. It should never be resorted to, therefore, except when an offense is so "prejudicial, etc," and an appropriate article cannot be found under which to

[1] Opinions J. A. G., p. 80. [2] Clode's Military and Martial Law, p. 31.

charge it. Charges are sometimes laid as violation of a specific article; for example, "Violation of the 39th article of war," or the same offense may be more properly charged as "Sleeping on post in violation of the 39th article of war." During the war much fault was found with the former way of laying charges.

In the case of Capt. E——, U. S. Vols., Gen. McClellan said: "The first charge is 'violation of the 42d[1] Article of War.' As often happens, when this slovenly and reprehensible style of framing charges is adopted, the reporting officer or the judge-advocate has mistaken the article under which the act mentioned in the specification is punishable. Again, the office of the greater part of the articles of war is to *ascertain* and *denounce* the appropriate punishment to an offense. There is also this further objection, viz.: many of the Articles of War speak of several *offenses*. It is very seldom intended to impute *all* of these to a prisoner, and the attempt to do this in one charge would be a violation of the rule which requires each charge to be single."[2] "Instead therefore, of charging upon an officer or private, a violation of any Article of War, the reporting officer should name the offense which is punished by the article, and proceed to specify, with the addition of time and place, the circumstances in which the offense consists."[3]

While in civil cases a person can only be tried for one offense at a time, not so with courts-martial; there may be a number of charges, or a number of specifications, each of which constitutes a distinct offense.

Specification. The specification should be explicit and at the same time concise. It is better to follow the terms used in the articles of war where the design is to

[1] Code of 1806.

[2] G. O. 32, Army of the Potomac, Jan. 28, 1862. G. O. 11, A. G. O., Feb. 5, 1862.

[3] G. O. 39, Army of the Potomac, Feb. 4, 1862.

punish a prisoner under a specified article; but, where the word *inebriation* instead of *drunkenness* was used in a charge under the 38th article, the Attorney-General held that it was sufficiently clear to inform him of the military offense for which he was to be tried, and to enable him to prepare his defense, which is all that is necessary in a case of this kind.[1]

The specification should set forth all the facts which go to make up an offense, with time, place, and circumstances.

Averments as to time. Where the time is known it should be set forth exactly, but as it frequently is impossible to give it exactly, a latitude is allowed. To charge an offense as committed "on or about such a time" is considered sufficient.

There is no exact construction to be placed upon the words "on or about," as used in the allegation of time in a specification. The phrase cannot be said to cover any precise or particular number of days, or latitude of time. It is used, in military pleading, for the purpose of indicating to the accused some period, as nearly as can be ascertained and set forth, at or during which the offenses charged were committed, in cases where the exact day cannot be named.[2]

In the case of Colonel D——, U. S. Vols., the first specification to the second charge averred that the accused was intoxicated at some time or times during the seventy days between August 20th and October 29th, 1862. This is not such notice of the time of the offense laid against the accused as enables him to defend himself against the charge. The specification should not therefore have been entertained by the court.[3]

[1] I. Opinions Attorney-General, Aug. 29, 1819. VII. Ibid., Dec. 1, 1855.

[2] Opinions J. A. G., p. 359. I. Opinions Attorney-General, Aug. 29, 1819.

[3] G. O. 193, Army of the Potomac, Dec. 28, 1862. G. O. 4, A. G. O., Jan. 31, 1842.

Averments as to Place. The same rule as to the place applies where it cannot be set forth explicitly. To charge an offense as committed "at or near" such a place is sufficient. The Secretary of War ruled in 1865, that the want of averments as to time and place, if not excepted to by the accused, is not a fatal defect if they can be supplied from the testimony in the record.

Averments as to Circumstances. Every circumstance which constitutes part of the offense should be set forth in the specification, thus showing to the judge-advocate on its face what he is called on to prove. There should be such a correspondence also between the charge and specification, that to have been guilty of one draws with it the necessary consequence that the accused is guilty of the other.[1]

The use of "abusive and indecent language," is regarded a sufficient averment without setting forth the language.[2]

Referring to this point the Commanding General of the Military Division of the Atlantic, in 1874 said: "The records of garrison and regimental courts-martial examined at these headquarters indicate the existence, to a considerable extent, of an impression that when certain language used by enlisted men constitutes the substance of the offense with which they are charged, it is always necessary that such language should be set forth *verbatim* in the specification to the charges. For the sake of certainty this is, as a general rule, desirable, but it is not in all cases indispensably requisite to a military charge. Instances occur of the use of such foul and immoral language, that its repetition in orders to the troops can have none other than a baneful influence. In such cases it is believed to

[1] G. O. 39, Army of the Potomac, Feb. 4, 1862.
[2] G. C. M. O. 3, A. G. O., 1872.

be to the best interests of the service that the specification should simply state the character of the language used, provided always it be done in such terms as will sustain the charge, and distinguish the particular offense. It will then be for the court to determine whether the words proved to have been used, are of the character alleged in the specification. The customs of the service sanction this form of averment.[1]

Rank, Names, etc. The accused should be described by his rank and regiment, and, if a soldier by his battery, troop or company; his Christian and surname should be given, and if enlisted under an *alias* this should be added.

The Judge-Advocate General held a specification fatally defective in which the rank of the accused, an officer, was not set forth, and in which it was not indicated that he had any rank whatever.

Where an error is made as to name, rank, etc., this would not make the specification fatally defective, for the error may be corrected before the arraignment. If a party pleads under a wrong name or title he may be found guilty and punished, for he cannot take advantage of his own wrong.

Dates should be set forth in words and figures, bearing in mind the meaning of the words *instant*, *proximo* and *ultimo*. If the offense is done in the night before midnight, the day before should be the date; if after, the day after.

Intent. As intent often constitutes the gist of the offense, it should be set forth in the specification. Thus, where an act in itself indifferent, if done with a particular intent becomes a crime, the intent should be set forth.

General Observations. Each specification should allege only the circumstances constituting one offense.

[1] G. O. 32, Hdq'rs Mil. Div. Atlantic, Dec. 11, 1873.

Facts of a perfectly distinct nature should not be included in the same specification.

A specification must show that a person belongs to the army, or is amenable to military law; otherwise it would be defective.

A specification must allege some offense, or it is invalid.

Specifications under the charge of "*desertion*" should, in addition to the allegations of desertion and apprehension or surrender, give also the date of enlistment of the accused.

Who may prefer Charges. In our service any officer may prefer charges against another, no matter what the rank of the parties may be, or against a soldier, or person amenable to military law. When preferred they must be sent through the proper channels to the authority competent to convene the court. Where, for instance, a subaltern prefers charges against a soldier, he should send them through the captain of his company. When, acting as adjutant or officer of the day, he confines a soldier and prefers charges, he should send them direct to the commanding officer of the post.

An officer against whom charges have been preferred is under no disability to prefer charges.

A superior may order a junior to prefer charges, and, even though the latter knows them to be false, it would still be an act of insubordination for him to refuse to comply. In subscribing such charges, it would be proper for the subordinate to add that it was done "by order of" his superior officer, since this would be a *fact*, and such fact would belong to the history of the case.[1]

Junior preferring Charges. The following remarks upon juniors preferring charges against superiors are well worthy of notice:

[1] Opinions J. A. G., p. 284.

"Any officer may, undoubtedly, protect himself against a wrong by his superior officer, by an appeal to a common superior. He may even, in conscientious discharge of a public duty, bring to the knowledge of the appropriate authority, any serious violation of duty, on the part of his superior, not affecting himself personally. In the latter case, however, as he voluntarily assumes the office of an accuser, he should be prepared to make good his accusation, or to meet the consequences. In either case he should be peculiarly guarded and circumspect in his language. He should studiously avoid all harshness of expression, everything which would indicate a desire to wound the feelings or injure the character of his superior. If he does this, however grave the charges may be, however calculated they may be *in themselves* to wound the feelings or affect the character of the person against whom they are preferred, they cannot properly be considered as evidence of the design to be disrespectful towards him. If it were otherwise, the more serious the offenses charged, the greater the impunity with which they might be committed. The only questions that can properly arise in such cases are: 1st. Would the facts charged, if true, constitute a military offense? 2d. Are they expressed in proper and becoming language? 3d. Were they preferred to the proper officer and through the proper channels."[1]

Where a subordinate avails himself of this privilege of making complaints, or preferring charges, and, in so doing, uses contemptuous language against his superior, he may be tried and punished for it.[2]

A person may be tried for preferring false charges.[3]

Non-commissioned Officers and soldiers cannot pre-

[1] G. O. 16, A. G. O., March 27, 1851. [2] G. O. 1, A. G. O., January 11, 1856.
[3] G. O. 9, A. G. O., April 1, 1853.

fer charges. They may make complaints, or furnish facts, which shall be the ground for charges, but the charges themselves should be made and signed by a commissioned officer.

Civilians, though not in the military service, can prefer charges. If such person submits formal charges they may be adopted, or new ones may be framed; it is only necessary that they be subscribed by a commissioned officer, and the judge-advocate may always formally authenticate them by his signature.[1]

Courts-Martial may prefer charges against an officer or soldier for using any menacing words, signs, or gestures in its presence, or disturbing its proceedings by any riot or disorder. It might also prefer charges for an act committed away from its presence, as, for example, against an officer, summoned as a witness, who should refuse to appear. The general custom for courts-martial in such cases is to report the fact to the convening authority.

Additional Charges may be preferred at any time against an officer or soldier under charges. If preferred before arraignment, they may be tried along with the original charges; but, if after arraignment, they must be tried separately, or by a new court, as the oath of the members is "to try and determine according to evidence the matter *now* before them." The same remarks apply to amendments to charges.

What Charges may be Tried. While it is certainly most desirable and proper that charges, especially when of a grave character, should be forwarded in the first instance to the authority who has convened, or is to convene the court-martial; yet, if charges are, by the officer preferring them, presented directly to the court, through the judge-advocate, and the court proceed to the trial of

[1] Opinions J. A. G., p. 82.

the same, such action would not affect the validity of its findings and sentence thereon; and, even if not indorsed at all, or in any manner formally referred to the court or judge-advocate for trial, it will be sufficient if the prisoner is actually brought before the court for trial, and the charges appear authenticated by the signature of some responsible officer.[1]

The order convening a court sometimes reads: "A general court-martial is hereby appointed for the trial of such persons as may be brought before it by authority from these headquarters"; when it so reads, only such charges as are referred to the court for trial by the convening authority can be tried by it.

Charges of "Habitual Drunkenness" and "Utter Worthlessness," sustained by specifications of offenses which have already been punished by sentence of court-martial, are deemed unauthorized by law; but at the same time, it is necessary for the efficiency of the army that its ranks should be purged of men characterized by such charges. Cases of that kind may be tried under a charge of "Conduct to the prejudice of good order and military discipline," with separate specifications for each one of the acts of drunkenness which has not already been made the occasion of a trial by court-martial. It will rest with the court to judge from the evidence adduced whether dishonorable discharge would be the proper penalty for the misconduct alleged.[2]

When to be Preferred. Charges should not be preferred unless there is strong reason to believe that an offense has been committed, and that it can be proved. Apropos to this the following General Order of May 7th, 1801, from the Horse Guards, is quoted: "To prefer ac-

[1] Opinions J. A. G., pp. 82 and 129.

[2] G. O. 11, A. G. O., January 24, 1873

cusations which cannot be maintained, at the same time that the practice is highly inconvenient and injurious to the service, reflects much disgrace upon those who bring them forward."[1]

Commanding officers, before forwarding charges, should examine each case carefully as to this point, and also to determine whether the case should not properly be brought before one of the minor courts. To facilitate such examination, and as an aid to the judge-advocate who conducts the case, the names of all witnesses should be appended to the charges.

Alteration of Charges. Charges after having been preferred may be altered by the convening authority by additions, or erasures, or he may draw up entirely new charges upon the facts stated.

Much question has arisen as to the power of a court-martial to amend material averments as to charges, or to reject and throw out altogether a charge or specification. The Judge-Advocate General holds that a court has this power, and founds his opinion upon the belief that the welfare of the service requires that the discretion of a military court should, so far as is consistent with strict law and fixed usage, be placed beyond the control of executive orders, and that its *independence* as a *judicial* body should, thus far, certainly be recognized and acknowledged.[2] In favor of this view he cites Kennedy,[3] and De Hart.[4] It would certainly seem, however, as if there were some cases in which courts could not exercise this power. Such a case happened in 1877. Charges had been technically corrected by the judge-advocate of the department before reference for trial. The judge-advocate of the court, in forwarding the proceedings, stated that he was

[1] Simmons, p. 139 (2d Edition). [2] Bureau of Military Justice, Oct. 3, 1869.
[3] Pages 75 and 76, note, and p. 61. [4] Page 101.

ordered by the court to disregard such correction, and arraign the prisoner on the charges as originally drawn. In this, says the reviewing authority, the court wholly transcended its power, and the judge-advocate of the court should have disregarded such irregular exercise of authority.[1]

Courts-martial should exercise great care in amending material averments. When, however, there has been an error in the name, rank, or regiment, etc., of the accused, or in the date or place, the judge-advocate should make the proper corrections before arraignment, or the court might order such to be made.

The words and terms of the charge and specification cannot be changed after the arraignment of the prisoner.[2]

Delaying or Accumulating Charges. The practice of delaying charges, or allowing them to accumulate, is contrary to the principles of justice.

In Lieut. Gassaway's case, Attorney-General Wirt, quoting from Tytler, says: "Every charge should be preferred at the time when the fact or facts on which it turns are recent; or, if knowingly passed over (as was clearly the case here), ought not either in *candor* or *justice* to be in future brought into question."[3]

By General Orders in 1813, from the Horse Guards, his Majesty declared that an officer has failed in his most essential duty to the service, by *delaying* to bring forward charges, and that permitting charges to lie dormant justifies the impression that the prosecutor is not actuated by public motives alone in their institution.[4]

[1] G. C. M. O. 13, Hdq'rs Dept. of the Missouri, March 24, 1877.
[2] G. C. M. O. 21, A. G. O., Feb. 17, 1877.
[3] I. Opinions Att'y-Gen., Aug. 29, 1819. Tytler's Essay on Mil. Law, p. 165.
[4] Simmons, p. 137 (2d Edition).

CHAPTER VII.

CHALLENGES AND PLEAS.

A Challenge, as understood in military law, is an exception to members of a court who are to pass judgment on a trial.

The right of such challenge is recognized by the 88th Article of War, which says, "Members of a court-martial may be challenged by a prisoner, but only for cause stated to the court. The court shall determine the relevancy and validity thereof, and shall not receive a challenge to more than one member at a time."

Challenges at common law are divided into two general classes: *peremptory*, and those *for cause stated*. Peremptory challenges, *i. e.*, those which assign no cause, are forbidden by the 88th article.

Challenges for Cause are to the *array*, or to the *poll*.

Challenges to the Array are objections to the whole court on account of its illegality.

While the article says that the court "shall not receive a challenge to more than one member at a time," this does not preclude a challenge to the whole array; for this is a challenge which goes to the very organization of the court, denying its legal existence as a court. Even if not made, where the ground of the challenge is true, the proceedings of such a court would be invalid.

Such challenges would not, as a rule, be made if courts-martial examined, before commencing proceedings, the order convening the court and the charges.

Challenges to the array would be proper for the following causes:

1st. That the officer convening the court had no authority to convene such a court.

2d. That the order does not state, in a court composed of less than thirteen members, that "no other officers than those named can be assembled without manifest injury to the service."

3d. That the officer convening the court for the trial of a commissioned officer, or of an enlisted man in certain cases,[1] is the accuser or prosecutor.

4th. That the court is illegally constituted from having an incompetent member or members on it: *for example*, where a court for the trial of militia officers was composed in part of regular officers.

If any of these challenges are valid the accused cannot be called upon to plead.

Challenges to the Poll are usually divided into *principal* and challenges *to the favor*.

A Principal Challenge is one where the cause assigned carries with it *prima facia* evidence of suspicion.

The following examples, taken from actual practice, would come under this head, and, when made, should be allowed by the court.

1st. That a member of a court-martial preferred the charges and was a material witness.

2d. That a member was an inferior officer to the accused in the same regular regiment, in the line of promotion, and thus interested in his conviction.

3d. That a member or members of the court were members of a court of inquiry detailed to investigate the same charges.

4th. That in a new trial, upon the application of the

[1] See 73d Article of War.

accused, a member of the court appointed for the rehearing of the case sat as a member on a former trial.

While the fact, in each of these cases, would not invalidate the proceedings of a court, if no objection was made by the accused, yet, when objection was made on these grounds and overruled, it was held good ground for the disapproval of the proceedings and sentence.[1]

Challenges to the Favor are those where an allegation of bias, prejudice, or malice is made. The dividing line between *principal* challenges and challenges *to the favor* is not very clearly marked, but this is of little importance in court-martial cases.

The following causes are cited as coming under this head:

1st. Previous expression of opinion.

2d. That the member had expressed hostile feelings and was prejudiced against the accused.

It sometimes happens that soldiers challenge their company commanders. This alone would not be sufficient cause for challenge, but, if on the ground of prejudice, and the prejudice could be proved, it would follow the same rule as to any other prejudiced member.

3d. That a member is a witness for the government.

Whether the court will excuse a member on such a challenge or not, must depend upon the circumstances of each case. Where a material witness, he should be excused.

In each of these cases the challenge should be substantiated by evidence, unless the ground of objection is admitted by the member.

The member challenged is allowed to make a statement to the court, and this, together with the cause of challenge, is matter of record. Courts-martial sometimes

[1] Opinions J. A. G., p. 31. G. O. 118, A. G. O., March 24, 1864.

receive the statement of a challenged member without putting him on oath, and, if no objection is made by the accused, this is permissible; but the accused has the right to examine the member as to his competency upon the *voire dire.* He may also call witnesses to prove his incompetency, which the judge-advocate has the right to re-establish by cross-examination or by new witnesses.

At a general court-martial held at Fort Leavenworth in 1853, the accused challenged a member for "bias, prejudice, and malice." The member then stated that "he had no prejudice or bias against the accused which could in the remotest degree interfere with his doing justice in the case, but, being challenged, he requested to be relieved from sitting on the court." This the court refused and overruled the challenge. The accused then requested that the member might be "put on his *voire dire,* in order that he might examine him as to the extent of any prejudice he might entertain;" which application the court refused. The ground of the decision is not expressed; whether it was that the court considered that the member ought not to be examined, and that the cause of challenge must be shown by other proof; or whether they thought the explanation already made by him sufficient. In commenting upon the case the Secretary of War said: "It was never doubted that a juror may be examined as to his bias or prejudice, or his opinions on the matter for trial, except that it was at one time held that opinions formed and expressed, as they may be proved by extrinsic evidence ought to be so proved. But that distinction is not now maintained in the courts of this country; and an accused is now allowed in all cases, for the better security of an impartial trial, to show the mind of the juror by examining him before the court; and the only exception is where the cause of challenge goes to the disgrace or discredit of the juror. In regard to the sufficiency of the explanation made by the member, the court ought to have considered that it was not a denial, but in some degree an admission of bias and prejudice, qualified by the member's opinion that it could not influence his judgment in the trial. This, however, was the matter of which the court was to judge, after inquiring into the nature and grounds of his feelings towards the accused. And as to the proof in this regard the law allows the accused the testimony of the member in the mode he demanded. The refusal of the court to allow the benefit of the necessary legal evidence to prove his cause of challenge would have set aside the trial, had the verdict been of conviction."[1]

A question has arisen as to whether a challenged member should retire during the deliberation on the challenge. Some difference of opinion has existed upon this point, but, while it will not invalidate the proceedings for him to remain, the better opinion is that he should retire, the better to allow full freedom of discussion.[2]

Where an accused has more than one cause of challenge to a particular member, he should state all at the time of making the challenge.

Excusing a Member. No exact rule can be laid down for determining when a court-martial should excuse a challenged member. It should not be too severe, and on the other hand it must avoid too great leniency. In the case of Captain L——, a member was challenged on the ground that he was a material witness for the prosecution. No evidence was offered that he was such, yet, without inquiring of him whether he was at all biased from any

[1] G. O. 21, A. G. O., July 27, 1863.

[2] He is required to retire until the decision is made, in the Articles recently proposed.

previous knowledge of the facts at issue, the court decided in favor of the challenge. The Secretary of War, referring to their action, said, "Courts should, of course, incline to liberality in accepting every reasonable cause of challenge; but the admission of an objection without any reason shown beyond a mere supposition or prejudice of the prisoner, tends in effect to introduce into courts-martial the allowance of peremptory challenges—a practice wholly unknown to our military code." [1]

Time for Challenging. The proper time for making challenges is after the reading of the order convening the court, at which time the judge-advocate should afford the opportunity. A challenge to the *array* should be the first made, but though properly made at this time, it would have to be entertained at any time, even after the sentence, as it calls in question the very legality of the court.

If there are no challenges to the *array*, or such challenges are overruled, then follow the challenges to the *poll*. Courts-martial are not as strict in reference to challenges as the civil courts; and where, during the course of a trial, reasons for challenge should become known to the accused, not known when the opportunity for challenge was offered, courts-martial would ordinarily allow the challenge to be made, and, if valid, excuse the member.

General Observations. A member excused by reason of challenge in one case, is not excused from sitting in other cases.

New members, or supernumerary members, are challengeable whenever they take their seats.

The record must always show that opportunity for challenge was offered.

The judge-advocate is not challengeable.

[1] G. C. M. O. 66, A. G. O., Sept. 21, 1866.

While the Article of War only authorizes the prisoner to challenge, by custom of the service, the judge-advocate may exercise the right, but the cases are rare when the privilege is taken advantage of.

While less than five members cannot perform any judicial function as a general court-martial, yet they may perform such acts as are preparatory and necessary to the organization of the court; and, if five are present, and one of them is challenged, the right of the four remaining to determine upon the challenge would seem necessarily to result; but where the court allows the challenge, being reduced below the minimum, it cannot proceed with the trial.[1]

When a member is challenged on the minor courts-martial, the two remaining members may determine as to the validity of the challenge.

It is not deemed essential to the validity of a field officer's court that the accused should appear from the record to have had an opportunity of challenge. It is advisable, however, if any valid objection to being tried by the field officer, detailed as the court, is presented by the accused, that such objection should be set forth in the record as a fact for the information of the reviewing authority.[2]

PLEAS.

Every prisoner upon arraignment before a court-martial is called upon to plead.

A *plea* is the answer by matter of *fact* to the charges preferred.[3]

Pleas are of various kinds, and may be divided for discussion into the following general classes:

1st. Pleas in bar of trial. 2d. Pleas in bar of judgment. 3d. Pleas to the matter of the charge.

[1] Opinions J. A. G., p. 21. [2] Opinions J. A. G., p. 176.
[3] Bouvier's Law Dictionary, Vol. II., p. 340.

They are given in this order as this is the natural order of pleading, each subsequent plea being an admission that there is no foundation for the former.

Pleas in Bar of Trial are divided into *pleas to the jurisdiction*, and *special pleas*.

Pleas to the Jurisdiction. A plea to the jurisdiction sets forth a reason why the court cannot legally proceed with the trial.

The decisions of the Supreme Court, cited in Chapter III., upon the liability of members of courts-martial for excess of jurisdiction, should be carefully borne in mind, in deciding upon pleas to the jurisdiction.

The accused may plead under this head:

1st. Where arraigned before a minor court, that the offense is alone cognizable by a general court-martial.[1]

2d. While an officer or soldier, that the crime is one alone cognizable by a civil court of criminal jurisdiction.

The case of Captain Howe illustrates this.[2]

While courts-martial in time of peace have no jurisdiction to try purely civil offenses, such as manslaughter, larceny, burglary, etc., yet, when these crimes are charged as "Larceny to the prejudice of good order and military discipline," or simply as "Larceny, etc.," and the specification shows an offense against good order and military discipline, they can be tried.

3d. That the accused is not amenable to military law, He may deny that he is an officer or a soldier.[3] While certain prescribed formalities are necessary for enlistment, such as signing the enlistment papers, taking the oath, etc., yet, where a volunteer soldier, duly mustered into the service, received pay and performed the duties of a soldier, it was held that he should be treated as duly enlisted, though he may not have signed the enlistment articles:

[1] Vide Chapter IV. as to jurisdiction of the minor courts.

[2] Vide Chapter III., p. 39. [3] Vide Chapter III. p. 43.

also, where a person had rendered service as an enlisted man, and as such been armed and clothed by the government, though he may not have been paid, he is estopped from denying the validity of his contract of enlistment upon the ground of any informality therein.[1] Inasmuch as it is often difficult, especially in the field, to procure the best evidence of the contract of enlistment, the enlistment papers, it has been the practice to accept as sufficient presumptive proof thereof, such facts as show on the part of the accused an acquiescence in the status of a soldier, as the receipt of pay, the doing of military duty, etc.[2] Where, under this plea, the question hinges upon some fault in the enlistment papers, the judge-advocate should produce them, and may afterwards introduce other evidence.

Under this third head a person may plead that he is not a retainer to the camp, etc., within the meaning of the 63d article.

"Pleas to jurisdiction" and "challenges to the array" are sometimes used interchangeably, and what would constitute a good challenge to the array is reserved as a plea to jurisdiction. The following appears to be the chief difference. A "challenge to the array" denies the legality of the court, not only to try the particular case in question, but all cases of a similar kind, and sometimes all cases of whatever nature. A "plea to jurisdiction," while acknowledging that the court is lawfully organized, denies its right to try this particular case.

Special Pleas in bar of trial set forth a reason why the accused should not be called on to answer to the charge.

The following pleas come under this head:—

(First.) Former Acquittal or Conviction. The articles

[1] Opinions J. A. G., p. 156. [2] Opinion J. A. G., p. 167.

of war direct,[1] that no person shall be tried a second time for the same offense, but a question arises as to what constitutes such trial, as will make this plea valid.

We will first discuss the cases which would not render this a valid plea. They are :—

(*a*) Where a court of inquiry had examined the charges and expressed an opinion.

(*b*) Where the accused was tried by an illegally constituted court, or one which had no jurisdiction of his offense.

For example, where a person was tried by a court convened by an officer having no authority to convene such court; or, where a person was tried by a minor court for an offense of which a general court alone had jurisdiction.

(*c*) Where proceedings were commenced against an accused, but abandoned without formal acquittal or conviction: or, where the trial had proceeded to a certain stage, and a *nolle prosequi* was entered.

(*d*) Where the accused was arraigned upon one set of charges, and these charges were withdrawn, and others, somewhat different, were substituted, and the accused was then rearraigned upon the second set.

(*e*) Where a court-martial was finally dissolved by the reviewing officer because unable to agree upon a finding.

The case is regarded as analogous to that of a jury dissolved on account of hopeless disagreement.[2]

(*f*) Where the court was reduced below the minimum by the death, resignation, etc., of one of the officers, and the accused brought before a new court.

(*g*) Where the accused pleaded a former acquittal or conviction, and it was not for the same *identical* offense.

Captain Howe, having been acquitted by the civil

[1] Art 102. [2] U. S. vs. Perez, 9 Wheaton, 579.

courts, was rearraigned before the court-martial, which had suspended its proceedings, for the military part of his offense. He pleaded this acquittal by the civil courts, but it was held invalid, and he was tried, found guilty, and punished.[1&2]

The United States courts have decided that under the constitutional provision which declares that "no person shall be subject for the same offense to be twice put in jeopardy of life or limb," the jeopardy spoken of "can be interpreted to mean nothing short of the acquittal or conviction of the prisoner, and the judgment of the court thereon."[3]

Applying this to courts-martial it may be said, that where a competent court-martial has formally come to a finding and sentence, and the proceedings are forwarded to the reviewing authority, this constitutes such a trial as was contemplated in Art. 102, and will be a valid plea of *autrefois acquit* or *convict*. That the reviewing authority deems the sentence inadequate, or disapproves the proceedings for any cause, except want of jurisdiction, will not render the trial a nullity.

The plea of *autrefois acquit*, or *convict*, is the privilege of the accused which he may waive. If he does not choose to use it, courts will not take notice of it so as to bar a trial.

It would be a good plea of former acquittal where a person tried for an offense, which included another, and acquitted, was arraigned for the lesser offense. *Example.* Having been found not guilty of "desertion," and afterwards arraigned for "absence without leave."[4]

[1] Vide Chapter III. p. 39. [2] G. O. 25. A. G. O. May 22, 1840.

[3] U. S. *vs.* Haskill, 4 Wash. C.C. R. 409. U. S. *vs.* Shoemaker, 2 McLean, 114. U. S. *vs.* Perez, 9 Wheaton, 579. Opinions J. A. G., p. 37, *et seq.* I. Opinion Attorney-General, Aug. 29, 1819.

[4] Opinions J. A. G., p. 282.

(Second.) Pardon. This constitutes a good plea in bar of trial. In the case of a general pardon the court would have to take notice of it without its being formally plead; but a special pardon should be brought to its notice in the pleading.

In the case of a deserter returned to duty, by the authority competent to order his trial,[1] this would be a good ground for plea of pardon. Where such return to duty was not by this authority, this would not constitute a valid plea.[2]

A release from arrest cannot be regarded as a pardon. In 1819 Lieut. Gassaway plead a former arrest on the same charges and a discharge without trial, but the Attorney-General held that this was not a valid plea.[3]

A pardon to an officer by a post commander, for offenses which he has no power to pardon, is not a good plea.[4]

The Supreme Court has decided that the power to pardon may be exercised at any time after the commission of the offense, even while legal proceedings are pending.[5] A court-martial would be forced, therefore, to accept such plea, if valid, at any time during the trial.

(Third.) Statute of Limitations. No person shall be liable to be tried and punished by a general court-martial for any offense which appears to have been committed more than two years before the issuing of the order for such trial, unless, by reason of having absented himself, or some other manifest impediment, he shall not have been amenable to justice within that period.[6]

It is difficult, sometimes, to determine when a party is

[1] Under par. 159, Regulations. [2] Opinions J. A. G., p. 139.

[3] I. Opinions Attorney-General, Aug. 29, 1819.

[4] G. C. M. O. 13, A. G. O., Aug. 3, 1871.

[5] Ex parte Garland, 4 Wallace, 334 *et seq.* [6] Art. 103.

so amenable, after the expiration of two years.[1] Captain Howe,[2] among other pleas, plead the "statute of limitations." "The record of his case showed that the general court-martial to try the charges was ordered on the 10th of April, 1840, within seven months after the offense had been committed; that when arraigned before the court the accused pleaded the pending proceedings against him, in the indictment in the civil tribunal; and that, therefore, he himself showed to the court-martial the impediment to the progress of that court. The record also exhibits the suspension of the proceedings in the military court, because of that impediment, and that the impediment was removed on the 20th of October, 1841; and that, by general orders of March 2d, 1842, the trial of Captain Howe was ordered to be proceeded in by the re-assembling of the court-martial on the 10th of May next, which was done accordingly. Thus the record shows that the prosecution was ordered in four months and four days after the offense was committed, and that it was actually proceeded in within less than six months after the impediment was removed, making less than eleven months of delay to prosecute the offense, when the time of the existing impediment, and cause of suspension of the proceedings instituted in the court-martial, is deducted from the time intervening between the commission of the offense on the 6th of of December, 1839, to the continuation of the proceedings of the court-martial assembled on May 10, 1842, according to the order of March 2, 1842."[3] The court-martial decided that this plea was not valid, and its opinion was approved by the Attorney-General.[4]

Though an accused might be willing to waive the privilege conceded in Art. 103, the court could not try

[1] See discussion in Chapter III., p. 40, *et seq.*

[2] Vide Chapter III.

[3] VI. Opinions Attorney-General, p. 513.

[4] Ibid.

the case. The article is a restriction upon the court, as well as a benefit to the accused.[1]

(**Fourth.**) **Total or Partial want of Specification.** This would be a valid plea in bar, where the specification is vague as to time, place, or circumstances.

In the case of Lieut. F—, of the Militia, the accused declined to plead to the specification to the first charge, and to the first charge, on the ground that the specification was defective, in not alleging the commission of any particular act but merely repeated the words of the charge, stating a conclusion rather than a fact. The court overruled the objection, but the reviewing authority decided that it was well taken.[2]

(**Fifth.**) **Pleas in Abatement.** A plea in abatement is a temporary plea in bar. In practice, it has merely the effect, if granted, of delaying the trial. It might be resorted to in the following cases :—

(*a*) Where the accused had not been furnished with a copy of the charges preferred against him.

(*b*) Where the copy furnished is materially different from the one upon which he is arraigned.

(*c*) Where there is a misnomer or false addition. In such case, the accused is bound to state his proper name, and point out the correct changes, otherwise he may be tried on the charges as they stand.

If the accused makes no objection to the name or designation under which he is charged, he may be tried and punished, even though they be erroneous.[3]

In the first two cases the court should grant sufficient delay to enable the accused properly to defend himself.

Pleas in bar of Judgment. These are pleas in way of

[1] I. Opinions Attorney General July 25, 1820. VI. Ibid. Dec. 30, 1853.
[2] G. C. M. O. 26, Army of the Potomac, July 26, 1864.
[3] III. Opinions Attorney-General, June 24, 1840.

justification or excuse, and may present good cause why the accused should not be called upon to answer.

The following cases would come under this head :—

First. Where the accused at the time of commission of the crime was *non compos mentis*.

This is a generic term, and includes all the species of madness, whether it arise from 1, idiocy; 2, lunacy; 3, drunkenness; or 4, sickness.[1]

Idiots are persons born without understanding. In law they are held incapable of committing crimes.

Lunatics. Lunacy is the state of one who has had understanding, but by disease, grief, or other accident has lost the use of reason.[2]

For crimes committed during actual lunacy a person is not responsible. Lunacy, however, is a thing of degrees, of great varieties, and it is exceeding difficult in many cases to obtain positive proof of its presence.

Sir Mathew Hale says:[3] "It is very difficult to define the indivisible line that divides perfect and partial insanity, but it must rest in circumstances duly to be weighed and considered both by the judge and jury, lest on one side there be a kind of inhumanity towards the defects of human nature, or on the other side too great indulgence given to great crimes." The *onus probandi* rests upon the party making this plea.

Lucid Intervals. Lunatics frequently have *lucid intervals*, when there is a return, more or less complete, to a sane state. For a crime committed during such time, when the party is sufficiently sane to know right from wrong, he is responsible. It is the duty of a party who contends for a lucid interval to prove it; for a person

[1] Bouvier's Law Dictionary, p. 234.

[2] Blackstone Com., § 304.

[3] I. Hale's P. C., p. 30.

once insane is presumed so, until it is shown that he has had a lucid interval or has recovered.[1]

Intoxication. It is a rule of the common law that intoxication cannot be set up as an excuse for a criminal offense. In some cases it has been held that it aggravates rather than mitigates. But that this is true in all cases, is opposed to our sense of reason, and does not accord, it is believed, with the practice of courts-martial in this country. If an officer, for example, should drink, without any intention of becoming intoxicated, and, while under this influence, should refuse to obey a lawful command of his superior officer, while this would not excuse him, it would in many cases mitigate.

Wharton says, although now drunkenness cannot be said to aggravate a crime in a judicial sense, yet it is well settled that it forms no defense to the fact of guilt.[2]

Upon this point there has been much discussion, and it would be impossible in a work of this kind to present the different views that have been maintained. One thing seems settled, that evidence of intoxication may be given in the prisoner's behalf, but why should such evidence be allowed if it is to have no effect? The effect must depend upon the circumstances of each case, and courts-martial must judge for themselves what value to give to it. When the question of premeditation or intent forms part of the charge, evidence of intoxication would be of value in determining the degree.

Continental jurists divide drunkenness into three kinds, 1st, Intentional; 2d, Culpable; and 3d, Inculpable. In the first case, it is no excuse; in the second, it reduces the degree of criminality and mitigates the punishment; in the third, the liability to punishment ceases.[3]

[1] Bouvier's Law Dictionary p. 89, and cases there cited.

[2] Wharton's Am. Crim. Law, § 39. [3] Greenleaf on Evi, Note I, § 374.

Sickness. A person from sickness may be *non compos*, so as to excuse him for the commission of a crime.

In 1851, Captain K was charged with "mutinous conduct," "breach of arrest," etc. He pleaded guilty, but averred that he was in a state of temporary derangement produced by opium, administered to him by the physician of the post. The court found him "guilty" and sentenced him "to be cashiered;" but the President arrived at the conclusion, from the evidence, that he was laboring under temporary insanity, and refused to approve the sentence.[1]

Second. Where there is understanding and sufficient will, but not exerted at the time of the act. *Example*, An accidental injury while doing a lawful act.

The act itself must be lawful and the injury resulting arise from ignorance, misfortune, or chance. If the act itself is unlawful, and a consequence ensue which the party did not foresee or intend, as the death of a man or the like, his want of foresight is no excuse. A difference here is also made between an act which is merely a *malum prohibitum*, and one in its original nature wrong and mischievous.[2]

Ignorance of Law. Ignorance as to law is no excuse for a criminal offense.

Military men are presumed to be conversant with military law, general regulations, general and special orders which it is their duty to know, and ignorance will be no excuse for their non-observance.

Mistake as to Law would often be a good plea in bar of judgment. In the case of *Jenkins vs. Waldron*,[3] the court said,—"It would, in our opinion, be opposed to all the principles of law, justice, and sound policy to hold that officers, called upon to exercise their deliberate judg-

[1] G. O. 28, A. G. O., June 9, 1851. [2] Blacks. Com. § 27 and note 8.
[3] 11 Johns. (N. Y.) 121.

ments, are answerable for a mistake in law, either civilly or criminally, when their motives are pure and untainted with fraud or malice." [1]

Third. Where there is compulsion or evident necessity. Compulsion may be lawful or unlawful. When a person is compelled by lawful authority to do that which he ought to do the compulsion does not affect the validity of the act. Thus, in the case of an officer or soldier obeying the lawful command of his superior officer, he would be excused for any harm that might result. But the question as to lawful or unlawful compulsion in case of an order issued, brings up the extremely delicate question of the right to disobey the order of a superior officer.

The Articles of War [2] declare that any officer or soldier [3] who disobeys any *lawful* command of his superior officer shall suffer death, or such other punishment as a court-martial may direct.

The introduction of the word "lawful" shows that there may be some commands, issued by lawful authority, which an officer or soldier is not required to obey. In civil life it is a settled rule that a person committing an illegal act cannot justify his conduct upon the ground of a command from another. Is the same thing true in the army?

In the case of *McCall vs. McDowell* the judge said,—"The circumstances of the two cases (in civil life and in the army) are entirely different. In the former case the party giving the command and the one obeying it are equal in the eye of the law. The latter does not act upon compulsion; he is a free agent, and at liberty to exercise his judgment in the premises. Personal respon-

[1] See also Wilkes *vs.* Dinsman, 7 Howard, 131.

[2] Art. 21.

[3] The term "camp follower" is here introduced in the Articles recently proposed.

sibility should be commensurate with freedom of action to do or to refrain from doing. For acts done under what is deemed compulsion or duress, the law holds no one liable. In contemplation of law the wife is under the power and authority of the husband. Therefore for even criminal acts, when done in the presence of the latter, she is not held responsible. The law presumes she acted under coercion of her husband, and excuses her. If the law excuses the wife on the presumption of coercion, for what reason should it refuse a like protection to the subordinate and soldier when acting in obedience to the command of his lawful superior? The latter may be said to act, particularly in time of war, under actual coercion. As a matter of abstract law it may be admitted that ultimately the law will justify a refusal to obey an illegal order. But this involves litigation and controversy, alike injurious to the best interests of the inferior and the efficiency of the service. The certain vexation and annoyance, together with the risk of professional disgrace and punishment which usually attends the disobedience of orders by an inferior, may safely be deemed sufficient to constrain his judgment and actions, and to excuse him for yielding obedience to those upon whom the law has devolved both the duty and responsibility of controlling his conduct in the premises. True, cases can be imagined, where the order is so palpably atrocious, as well as illegal, that one must instinctively feel that it ought not to be obeyed by whomsoever given. But there is no rule without its exception. This one is practical and just, and the possibility of extreme cases ought not to prevent its recognition and application by the courts.

"Between an order plainly legal and palpably otherwise—particularly in time of war—there is a wide middle ground, where the ultimate legality and propriety of orders depends, or may depend, upon circumstances and conditions of which it cannot be expected that the inferior is informed or advised. In such cases, justice to the subordinate demands, and the necessities and efficiency of the public service require, that the order of the superior should protect the inferior; leaving the responsibility to rest where it properly belongs."

The judge further said,—"Except in a plain case of excess of authority, where at first blush it is apparent and palpable to the commonest understanding that the order is illegal, I cannot but think the law should excuse the military subordinate when acting in obedience to the order of his superior."[1]

In General Orders of 1852,[2] it is said,—"It is possible a commanding officer may transcend his authority; but in all cases the inferior should act upon the reasonable presumption [of law] that his superior was authorized to issue an order which he might be authorized to issue. If the subordinate act otherwise, he does so at his peril, and subjects himself to the risk of being punished for disobedience. This rule applies equally whether the legality of the order depends upon a question of fact or a question of law."

Compulsion from Fear. Another species of compulsion arises when a person is by physical force, or by threats which induce a fear of death, compelled to do an act contrary to his will. This might be pleaded in cases of mutiny or rebellion. The only force that will excuse is a force upon the person, and present fear of death; and this force and fear must continue all the time the party remains with the rebels.[3]

(Fourth.) Necessity. The plea of necessity is often a

[1] See also Martin *vs.* Mott, 12 Wheaton, 19.
[2] G. O. 34, A. G. O.
[3] 4 Blacks. Com., p. 30, note 13.

good plea in bar of judgment. In case of a mutiny, or in quelling a riot, it may be necessary to wound or even kill persons to accomplish the purpose, or in making an arrest, or preventing an escape, an officer or soldier may have to make use of extreme measures. If brought to trial for such action the plea of necessity will be proper as before stated.

Where an officer or soldier, acting under lawful orders, has certain discretionary powers given him, or where by statute a discretion is conferred upon him, he is to judge of the measures to be used, and he never should be made answerable for any injury when acting within the scope of his authority, and not influenced by malice, corruption, or cruelty.[1] His position, in such case, in many respects becomes *quasi* judicial, and is not ministerial, as in several other cases of liability by mere ministerial officers.[2] In *Martin vs. Mott*, the Supreme Court laid down that whenever a statute gives discretionary power to any person, to be exercised by him upon his own opinion of certain facts, it is a sound rule of construction that the Statutes constitute him the sole and exclusive judge of the existence of these facts.[3]

(Fifth.) Former Punishment. A plea of former punishment, if proved, would appropriately be a bar in judgment. What will constitute such punishment as will make this an appropriate plea, must depend upon the circumstances of each particular case.

When a punishment has been illegally inflicted without trial, it cannot be set up in bar of trial,[4] although it may be a good plea in bar of judgment.

These causes, which constitute good pleas in bar of

[1] Wilkes *vs.* Dinsman, 7 Howard, 131.

[2] 11 Johns. 108. Kendall *vs.* U. S. 12 Peters, 511. Decatur *vs.* Paulding, 14 Peters, 516.

[3] 12 Wheaton, 31.

[4] G. O. 27, Army of the Potomac, Oct. 16, 1861.

judgment, are generally not pleaded, as such, before courts-martial, but embodied in the defense.

Pleas to Matter of the Charge. Where the accused has none of the before mentioned pleas to make, he should then plead to the matter of the charge "guilty," or "not guilty."

Guilty. He may plead "guilty" to certain portions of the charge, but "not guilty" to others; or "guilty excepting certain words."

The following General Order, publishing the remarks of Gen. Hancock upon the trial of an officer, may be profitably read in this connection.

"In the second specification the accused was charged with being, while on an important duty, 'grossly intoxicated' and 'totally incapable to perform the duty assigned him.' He pleaded guilty to this specification with the exception of the words 'grossly' and 'totally,' and was convicted on his plea, no evidence being introduced to establish the allegations as laid. In my opinion this was a great mistake, shutting off, as it did, all proof of the degree of the offense with which the accused stood charged. If this was to be resorted to as a precedent, similar pleas might frequently be resorted to for the very purpose of withholding the facts in cases of flagrant violation of military law, and thereby increasing the chances of a favorable recommendation or action on review."[1]

A court might properly refuse to admit a plea of guilty to a specification to which the accused added the words "but alleging no criminality thereto." It is a plea of a *conclusion* which it is for the *court*, if the facts warrant it, to arrive at upon the evidence.[2] Such a plea, however, has been allowed and not objected to by the War Department.[3]

[1] G. C. M. O. 69, A. G. O., 1877.
[2] Opinions J. A. G., p. 281.
[3] G. C. M. O. 75, A. G. O. 1875.

It often happens that the accused pleads "guilty," and then makes a statement not in accord with his plea. In the case of desertion, for example, a soldier often pleads "guilty," and then states that he intended to return; now intent to remain away is the gist of desertion, so that the plea and the statement do not correspond. The court should in these cases regard the statements as neutralizing each other, and should have the accused instructed as to his legal rights, and advised to change his plea with a view to the hearing of testimony.[1]

Standing Mute. When a prisoner, arraigned before a general court-martial, from obstinacy and deliberate design stands mute, or answers foreign to the purpose, the court may proceed to trial and judgment as if the prisoner had pleaded not guilty.

A prisoner may, however, stand mute from other causes:—

1st, He may be mute by the visitation of God.

2d, He may not have sufficient intellect, or may not sufficiently understand the course of proceedings to enable him to make a proper plea.

The article in these cases evidently contemplates a different course; and the practice is for the court to suspend its proceedings until the prisoner is able to plead, or is of sufficient intellect, or is able to understand the proceedings, evidence, etc., so as properly to defend himself.

Controlling Pleas. It is not competent for a commanding general, by a general order, to control parties in their pleas when arraigned before a general court-martial. If they insist upon pleading "guilty" they cannot be pre-

[1] G. C. M. O. 2, A. G. O. 1872. G. C. M. O. 63, A. G. O. 1874. G. C. M. O. 205, A. G. O. 1876.

vented from so doing. He may however require the judge-advocate of general courts to introduce all the testimony in their power whether the party plead "guilty" or "not guilty."[1]

[1] Opinion of the J. A. G., published in Gen. Orders of the Army of the Potomac.

CHAPTER VIII.

OATHS.

Definition. The definition of an oath has differed with different writers. As defined by Tyler,[1] "an oath is an outward pledge given by a juror (or person taking it) that his attestation or promise is made under an immediate sense of his responsibility to God." Greenleaf says, that a security to this extent, for the truth of testimony, is all that the law seems to have deemed necessary; and with less security than this, it is believed that the purposes of justice cannot be accomplished.[2]

The various oaths which have to be used in military jurisprudence will now be discussed.

Oath of Members. The members of a court-martial, whether general, regimental, or garrison, are required, before they proceed to the trial of any case, to take the following oath: [3]

"*You, A. B., do swear that you will well and truly try and determine, according to evidence, the matter now before you, between the United States of America and the prisoner to be tried, and that you will duly administer justice, without partiality, favor, or affection, according to the provisions of the rules and articles for the government of the armies of the United States; and if any doubt should arise, not explained by said articles, then according to your conscience, the best of your understanding, and the custom of war in like cases;*

[1] Tyler on Oaths, p. 15.

[2] Greenleaf on Evidence, Vol. 1, par. 328. [3] Art 84.

and you do further swear that you will not divulge the sentence of the court until it shall be published by the proper authority; neither will you disclose or discover the vote or opinion of any particular member of the court-martial, unless required to give evidence thereof as a witness, by a court of justice in a due course of law. So help you God."

This oath defines the duty of members of courts-martial. It has been changed only in form since adopted into our articles, and, in substance, has remained the same for the last two hundred years.[1] As will be seen, on examination, it contains several distinct asseverations. Each member of the court promises :—

1st. "To well and truly *try* and determine *according to evidence*."

"Courts-martial are governed by the common law rules of evidence in criminal cases, except where Congress has enacted otherwise, so that the evidence upon which they decide must be *legal* evidence.

"It sometimes happens that there is a difficulty in properly proving a material point in issue, and that a departure from the rule might seem to be desirable," but this is not permissible. "Though we may not discover its real use, yet we may not dispense with what the law requires."[2]

An erroneous view has sometimes been held by members of courts-martial, that where a competent witness has testified to a fact, and his testimony has not been contradicted by other evidence, they are bound by this part of their oath to find guilty. Wharton says, "such evidence as is permitted to be detailed to a judge or jury is said to be competent; its effect upon the mind of the triers depends upon its credibility." A verdict of

[1] Clode's Military and Martial Law, p. 112.

[2] Porter *vs.* Haskell, 11 Maine Reports 177. Cited from a pamphlet on "Evidence" by Major Gardner, J. A. Corps, p. 30–31.

"guilty" should, therefore, only be given when the members are satisfied of the guilt of the party.[1]

2d. To try the matter *now* before it.

As before stated, no alteration of the charges can be made, nor new charges be tried under this oath after arraignment.[2]

3d. To administer justice according to the rules and articles of war etc., and, if any doubt arises not explained by those articles, then according to their conscience, the best of their understanding, and the custom of war in like cases.

4th. Not to disclose or discover the vote or opinion of any particular member of the court unless required to give evidence thereof, as a witness, by a court of justice, in due course of law.

In the year 1748 the last two clauses were added to the oath of members of courts-martial in the British service, and gave rise to much subsequent controversy; the latter part of their oath reading, "he would not upon any account at any time whatever, disclose the vote of any member unless thereto required by Parliament." This oath being brought to the notice of the Commons in the year 1750, the Secretary of War assigned the following reasons for it: 1st. "Though it would be impossible to have the members of the court-martial independent of the commander-in-chief, yet as the best method of preventing his influence being used, this oath was adopted;" and 2d. "That from the personal intimacy between the accused and the members, great bitterness of feeling might arise if such a disclosure were made as would make the votes of the judges notorious."

"These reasons were then accepted and ever since

[1] As to what constitutes satisfactory evidence, see Chap. XXV., p. 346.

[2] G. C. M. O., 39, A. G. O. June 10, 1867.

have been considered sufficient, for the oath stands in the mutiny act of 1868, with the qualification that disclosure may be made if the member be required to give evidence thereof by a court of justice, or a court-martial, in due course of law."[1]

Our oath does not contain the words "or a court-martial," nevertheless, a court-martial is considered a court of justice within the meaning of the oath.

In 1868 Lieut. P— was tried for violating his oath as a member of a court-martial, "by disclosing the vote of one or more members of the said general court-martial," and, "by disclosing a part and portion of the proceedings of the said general court-martial during secret session." In commenting on the case the convening officer said,— "The officer ordering the case for trial presumed that the accused had divulged the vote and opinion of one or more members of the court, given in a case then on trial, or which had been completed. Disclosing the vote and opinion of a member given in closed court, is evidently one of the irregularities contemplated in the 99th (present 62d) article of war; but the gist of each of the specifications on which the accused was arraigned and tried, is the violation of a duly administered oath. From the evidence contained in the record, it appears that the accused divulged the vote and opinion of one or more of the members, given while the court was considering, with closed doors, a subject in no way connected with the case then properly before it for trial. The oath, administered in compliance with the 69th (present 84th) article, is binding only in matters pertaining to the case which is actually being tried. This is evident from the language of the oath itself."[2]

[1] Clode's Forces of the Crown, p. 168.

[2] G. C. M. O. 113, Hd.'qr's. Dept. of Missouri, June 6, 1868.

How Administered. The oath is administered to the court by the judge-advocate after the challenges have been fully decided upon; or, if the accused does not desire to challenge, immediately after his statement to that effect. The early custom was for each member to hold up his right hand and repeat the oath after the judge-advocate.[1] The present custom is for the members, standing, to raise their right hands, while the judge-advocate, standing, says, "You (calling the name of each member of the court) do swear," etc.

Immediately after the court is sworn, the President of the court administers the following oath to the judge-advocate,

"*You A. B. do swear that you will not disclose or discover the vote or opinion of any particular member of the court-martial, unless required to give evidence thereof, as a witness, by a court of justice, in due course of law; nor divulge the sentence of the court to any but the proper authority, until it shall be duly disclosed by the same. So help you God.*"

The members and the judge-advocate may be affirmed if they object to taking the oath. The judicial form of affirmation is as follows:

"*You A. B. do solemnly, sincerely, and truly declare and affirm, etc.*"[2]

The articles of war are mandatory as to who shall administer the oaths before a court-martial, and the order in which they shall be administered. On a naval court-martial, however, where the order of swearing the members and judge-advocate was reversed, the Attorney-General held that it was not a fatal defect.[3]

Oaths for Minor Courts. Our articles of war did

[1] Macomb's Martial Law, p. 76. [2] See Chap. XXV, p. 327.
[3] XIII Opinions Att'y Gen'l, Jan. 20, 1871.

not prescribe the taking of any oath by the minor courts until 1806, nor the English articles until 1805.[1]

As the junior member ordinarily has performed the duties of judge-advocate on these courts, some question has arisen as to the proper manner of administering the oaths. The following is the proper mode prescribed in 1871:[2]

The junior member of the court being its recorder, administers to the other two members the oath prescribed in the article for members, after which the presiding officer administers to the recorder the following oath, which combines with the oath of a member the additional obligation required of a judge-advocate, or person officiating as such:

"*You, A. B., do swear that you will well and truly try and determine according to evidence, the matter now before you, between the United States of America and the prisoner to be tried, and that you will duly administer justice, according to the provisions of 'an Act establishing rules and articles for the government of the armies of the United States,' without partiality, favor or affection, and, if any doubt should arise, not explained by said articles, according to your conscience, the best of your understanding, and the custom of war in like cases; and you do further swear that you will not divulge the sentence of the court to any but the proper authority, until it shall be duly disclosed by the same; neither will you disclose or discover the vote or opinion of any particular member of the court-martial, unless required to give evidence thereof, as a witness, by a court of justice, in a due course of law. So help you God.*"

These oaths having been duly taken, the fact will be sufficiently stated as follows:—

[1] Clode's Military and Martial Law, p. 126.

[2] G. O. 49, A. G. O., May 18, 1871.

"The court, including the recorder, was then duly sworn according to law in the presence of the prisoner."

A Field Officer, sitting as a field officer's court, is not required to take an oath. The law imposes this duty upon him as an officer of the army, and he discharges it under the sanction of his military oath.[1]

Whenever the same court-martial tries more prisoners than one, and they are arraigned on separate and distinct charges, the court is to be sworn at the commencement of each trial.[2] It is not considered a compliance with this regulation to call several prisoners into court at the same time, and swear the members of the court once before them all.[3]

Witnesses. Art. 92 prescribes that all persons who give evidence before a court-martial shall be examined on oath or affirmation in the following form:

"*You swear (or affirm) that the evidence you shall give in the case now in hearing shall be the truth, the whole truth, and nothing but the truth. So help you God.*"

The law does not prescribe who shall administer the oath to witnesses, but the custom is for the judge-advocate to administer it in general courts, and in the minor courts the junior member, in the absence of a judge-advocate. In a field officer's court, the officer himself is authorized to administer it.

The general custom is for the witness to be sworn by holding up his bare right hand, while the judge-advocate repeats the oath.

Voir Dire. It sometimes becomes necessary to examine a *member* touching his competency to serve on a court-martial, or a *witness* as to his competency to give evidence. This is called an examination on the *voire dire*, and the oath to be administered is as follows:

[1] Opinions J. A. G., p. 175. [2] Regulations, par. 892.

[3] G. O. 60, A. G. O. April 16, 1873.

You do swear that you will true answer make to such questions as may be put to you, touching your competency to serve as a witness (or a member) in this case: So help you God.

In 1867, a court refused to allow a member to be sworn on the *voire dire* as to competency, on the ground of its incompetency to administer the oath before being sworn as a court. The Secretary of War held that the judge-advocate had power to administer the oath.[1]

Reporters. By act of March 3, 1863, the judge-advocate of a military court shall have power to appoint a reporter, who shall record the proceedings of, and testimony taken before, such court, and may set down the same in the first instance in short hand. The reporter shall, before entering upon his duty, be sworn, or affirmed faithfully to perform the same.[2]

No reporter can be employed except in cases of importance, and when the other duties of the judge-advocate will not allow him to take down the testimony in the ordinary way.[3]

The following oath should be administered to reporters or clerks to a court-martial,

You do swear (or affirm) that you will faithfully perform the duties of a reporter to this court, and duly record the proceedings of and testimony to be taken before said court. So help you God.

Interpreters. It may become necessary to employ an interpreter to a court-martial. In such case he should be sworn to perform his duties faithfully. The following oath would be proper:

You A. B. do swear (or affirm) that you will faithfully interpret to the best of your ability, for the use of this court,

[1] G. C. M. O. 35, A. G. O. June 3, 1867.

[2] Rev. Statutes §. 1203. [3] G. O. 208, A. G. O., 1863.

whatever may be submitted to you by order of the court for that purpose. So help you God.

Courts of Inquiry. The Articles of War[1] provide that the recorder of a court of inquiry shall administer to the members the following oath :

"*You shall well and truly examine and inquire, according to the evidence, into the matter now before you, without partiality, favor, affection, prejudice, or hope of reward. So help you God.*"

After which the president of the court shall administer the following oath to the recorder:

"*You A. B. do swear that you will, according to your best abilities, accurately and impartially record the proceedings of the court and the evidence to be given in the case in hearing. So help you God.*"

The witnesses before a court of inquiry are required to take the same oath as is taken by witnesses before courts-martial.[2]

Retiring Boards. The law requires that the members of a retiring board shall be sworn in every case to discharge their duties honestly and impartially.[3] The following oath should be administered by the recorder:

You A. B. do swear (or affirm) that you will honestly and impartially discharge your duties as a member of this board in the matter now before you. So help you God.

The recorder takes the same oath as the recorder of a court of inquiry.

DEPOSITIONS.

In cases not capital, the depositions of witnesses residing beyond the limits of the State, Territory or district in which any military court may be ordered to sit, if taken on reasonable notice to the opposite party and duly

[1] Article 117. [2] Article 118. [3] Revised Statutes, § 1247.

authenticated, may be read in evidence before such court in cases not capital.[1]

Three things are necessary that a deposition may be read in evidence before a court-martial:

1st. The party must reside beyond the State, Territory or district where the court may be sitting.

If, however, the opposite party will consent, the depositions of witnesses residing within the State, Territory or district may be taken.[2] This might be necessary where a person is unable from sickness to attend the court, or where a party intends leaving the country.

2d. Reasonable notice must be given to the opposite party.

What will constitute such notice is a matter for the court to determine. In civil cases before the United States courts the notice must be sufficient to allow the opposite party to be present at the taking of the deposition; allowing time after the service of the notification, not less than at the rate of one day (Sundays exclusive), for every twenty miles of travel.[3] The notice to the opposite party must state the name of the witness, and the time and place of the taking of his deposition.[4]

3d. The deposition must be duly authenticated.

The old Article[5] indicated justices of the peace as the proper officers before whom depositions were to be taken; and an Act of 1863[6] directed that *any* officer authorized to take depositions by the laws of the State, district or Territory in which the witness is examined, may take a deposition to be used in evidence before a military court. The present article, though framed from the act of 1863, fails to state by whom a deposition must be authenticated.

[1] Article 91. [2] See I. Opinions Attorney General, March 15, 1825.
[3] Greenleaf on Evidence, Vol. I. § 322. [4] Revised Statutes, § 863.
[5] 74th. [6] March 3d, chapter 75.

We find, however, that the Revised Statutes provide for the taking of depositions *de bene esse* in civil cases, and authorize the depositions to be taken before any judge of any court of the United States, or any commissioner of a circuit, or any clerk of a district or circuit court, or any chancellor, justice, or judge of a supreme or superior court, mayor or chief magistrate of a city, judge of a county court or court of common pleas of any of the United States, or any notary public, not being of counsel or attorney to either of the parties, nor interested in the event of the cause.

A deposition authenticated by any of these persons would doubtless be accepted by any military court.

In general, the examination of a witness is made by interrogatories and cross-interrogatories previously prepared, and sent by the judge-advocate to the magistrate who is to take the deposition.

Every party deposing in civil cases is required to be cautioned, and sworn to testify the whole truth, and carefully examined. His testimony must be reduced to writing by the magistrate taking the deposition, or by himself in the magistrate's presence, and by no other person, and must, after it has been reduced to writing, be subscribed by the deponent.[1]

[1] Rev. Stat. § 864.

CHAPTER IX.

TRIAL.

The hour having arrived at which the court is ordered to convene, the members take their seats in the order of their rank: the president sitting at the head of the table, and the other officers on his right and left alternately according to rank. The decision of the proper authority in regard to the rank of the members cannot be reversed by the court.[1] The judge-advocate sits at the foot of the table. A table and chairs are provided for the accused and his counsel to the right of the judge-advocate, and a chair for the witnesses at the judge-advocate's left.

When ready to proceed the president calls the court to order; the judge-advocate then calls the names of the members, noting the absentees. (The cause of absence of any member should be ascertained by the judge-advocate; and where reasons are submitted in writing, they should be appended to the record properly referenced.)

If there are more than five members present the court generally proceeds with the trial. It may, however, delay or adjourn to await the attendance of absent members.

It would be well at this time for courts-martial to read over the charges, and the order convening the court, to see if they are legally convened, and whether they have jurisdiction of the offender and the offense. This is not generally done, however, but if any doubt exists in the

[1] Regulations, par. 884.

minds of members, or the judge-advocate, now is the proper time to decide upon it.

A court-martial, except when cleared for deliberation, is always open to the public during a trial.

Reading Order. The accused then comes before the court, and, standing, is cautioned by the judge-advocate to listen to the order convening the court, which the latter then reads to him, and asks him if he has any objection to being tried by any member present named in the order.

The rules laid down in Chapter VII. should be followed in deciding upon challenges.

Counsel. When the challenges, if any, are decided upon, the judge-advocate should ask the accused if he desires to introduce counsel. He may make such application at any stage of the trial, and sometimes this will be necessary to enable him to conduct the examination of a member on the *voire dire.*

The accused is entitled to counsel upon his trial as a *right,* and this right the court cannot properly refuse to admit. Wherever it is refused and it appears that the accused could have procured counsel within a reasonable time, if proper facilities had been afforded him, the proceedings should be disapproved.[1]

This privilege being acknowledged, the court should not refuse an application for postponement, to secure counsel, unless it appears that the continuance will result in an unreasonable delay, prejudicial to the interests of the service.[2] Any person of good standing, civil or military, may be admitted to act as counsel, but a court-martial has the same right as a civil court to refuse to admit an improper person. A court must be governed by the particular circumstances of each case, and where it refuses to allow a particular person to act as counsel, or to post-

[1] Opinions J. A. G., p. 127. [2] Ibid, p. 284.

pone its proceedings to afford opportunity for securing counsel, the reviewing authority will have to judge as to whether such action was sufficiently injurious to the accused to require disapproval of the proceedings.

A court has no right to relieve a member to act as counsel, it belonging exclusively to the appointing power to fix the number of members of the court.[1]

Persons having an interest in the trial cannot insist upon being admitted to act as counsel, or have others do this in their behalf. This was exemplified in the trial of Commander Mackenzie, U. S. N., in 1843, who was charged with "*murder on board a U. S. vessel on the high seas.*" On the third day of the trial the judge-advocate presented a paper signed by two eminent legal gentlemen, stating that "they had been employed by the relatives of Midshipman Philip Spencer, one of the persons for the murder of whom Commander Mackenzie was then upon trial, to attend the trial and take part therein, by examining and cross-examining the witnesses who might be produced, and propounding such questions, and offering such suggestions in relation to the proceedings, and presenting such comments on the testimony, when the same shall be concluded (under the approbation of the court) as they might deem necessary." The court, after mature consideration, decided that the application could not be granted.[2]

Counsel to assist Judge-Advocate. Counsel may be assigned to assist the judge-advocate. Should a judge-advocate, in an important and complicated case, feel the need of such assistance, the course spoken of in Chapter XXII. should be pursued.

Privileges of Counsel. The counsel for the accused

[1] G. C. M. O. 62, A. G. O. Aug. 10, 1874.

[2] Trial by J. F. Cooper, pp. 8, 9, De Hart, p. 318.

simply assists him in examining witnesses, raising objections, and in making his statement.

The questions to witnesses are written out by him, or by the accused, and handed to the judge-advocate, who asks them.

If the counsel desires to make an argument on any point it is submitted in writing, and may be read by him to the court, or by the accused, or judge-advocate. When a reporter is appointed, it is customary to allow the counsel to propound questions directly to the witnesses, and to make arguments as in civil trials.

Delays. The question of counsel having been settled, application for delay, if desired, should now properly be made. Applications for delay or postponement of trial must, when practicable, be made to the authority convening the court. When made to the court, it must be before plea, and will then, if in the opinion of the court well founded, be referred to the authority convening the court, to decide whether the court should be adjourned or dissolved, and the charges reserved for another court.[1]

Courts-martial are authorized, for reasonable cause, to grant continuances to either party, for such time and as often, as may appear to be just: *provided*, That if the prisoner be in close confinement, the trial shall not be delayed for a period longer than sixty days.[2] Where the accused desires a delay to secure the attendance of absent witnesses, it is necessary that it distinctly appear on oath,[3] 1st, that the witness is material, and how; 2d, that the accused has used due diligence to procure his attendance; and 3d, that he has reasonable ground to believe, and does believe, that he will be able to procure such attendance within a reasonable time stated.[4]

[1] Regulations, par. 886. [2] Article 93. [3] Regulations, par. 887

[4] The judge-advocate is also required to take the same oath in the Articles recently proposed.

Court Sworn. If the trial is to proceed, the members and the judge-advocate of the court are then sworn.[1]

Should it appear from the charges that the statute of limitation[2] is applicable to the offense, the judge-advocate should establish, if possible, before calling upon the accused to plead, the fact that he was not amenable to trial during that time.

Arraignment of Accused. The court being sworn, the judge-advocate reads the charges and specifications in their order to the accused (the accused standing) and then addresses him as follows:

You have heard the charge and specification preferred against you, how say you to the specification, guilty or not guilty?

How say you to the charge?

If there be more than one charge or specification, the arraignment is in the following order,—to the specifications to the first charge,—then to the first charge, and so on through all the charges and specifications.

The accused may make any of the pleas spoken of in Chapter VII.

The general plea is "guilty," or "not guilty."

Guilty. If the plea is "guilty" it is a general rule of law that no testimony on the merits is to be introduced. In the case of Cadet C., the court refused to receive testimony after plea of "guilty." The Attorney-General held "that it is the duty of the court in all cases where the punishment of the offense charged is discretionary, and especially where the discretion includes a wide range and great variety of punishment, and the specifications do not show all the circumstances attending the offense, to receive such testimony as the judge-advocate may offer, for the purpose of illustrating the actual character of the

[1] Vide Chapter VIII, on Oaths, p. 113–117. [2] See Article 103.

offense, notwithstanding the party accused may have pleaded 'guilty.' If there be any exception to this remark, it is when the specification is so full and precise as to disclose all the circumstances of mitigation or aggravation which accompanied the offense; where that is the case, or where the punishment is fixed and no discretion is allowed, explanatory testimony cannot be needed."[1]

Upon this point the suggestion of the Judge-Advocate General, published in orders, is given:[2] "As instances of bald and unsatisfactory records of trials not rarely occur in practice, a *general* order, it is suggested, might well be published, advising officers detailed upon courts-martial, that in all cases, whether of desertion, drunkenness on duty, or other offense committed either by officers or soldiers, where the plea is guilty and the specifications do not set forth in full detail the facts and circumstances of the offense charged, it is properly their duty, as well as their right, to require and receive evidence sufficient to inform the reviewing authority as to the degree of the criminality of the acts found to have been committed."[3]

Not Guilty. If the plea is "not guilty," the trial proceeds. The judge-advocate may open the prosecution by a statement of the facts he intends proving, but this is not customary, and would rarely be done, except in very complicated cases where he specially desires the court to follow the evidence in its sequence.

He now calls his first witness for the prosecution, and, if there are persons present whom he has summoned as witnesses on either side, he requests them to retire.

Objection to Witness. The accused, if he objects to the witness on the ground of his incompetency, should

[1] Opinion of the Atty-Gen., published in O. 32, A. G. O. April 22, 1834.
[2] G. C. M. O. 69, A. G. O. Oct. 29, 1877.
[3] See also Chapter VII. p. 110.

now make his objection known, and, if he desires, may call witnesses to prove his incompetency.

In 1873 an officer asked to have summoned certain additional witnesses to impeach the credibility of three important witnesses for the prosecution, and was refused by the court. The Secretary of War disapproved their action and said: The case is deemed to present a fit occasion for reminding courts-martial that the least denial to an accused person of any proper facility or opportunity for defense, can serve only to defeat the ends of justice and may often lend impunity to guilt.[1]

He may also ask to have the witness put on the *voire dire*, that he may examine him as to his competency.[2] The same right is accorded the judge-advocate as to witnesses for the defense.

If the evidence subsequently given upon the matter in issue should prove the incompetency of the witness, on motion of the adverse party his testimony may be stricken out.

Oath. If no objection be made to the witness, or, being made, if his competency is established, the oath is then administered.[3]

The party producing now commences the direct examination.

All questions are recorded, and the answers in the words of the witness.

Objection to any question may be made by the court, or the adverse party. If of a minor nature, the court may determine upon it without being cleared. If a question is objected to, the reasons should be stated, and, together with the reply of the opposite party, should be recorded. The court is then cleared and the point decided by it.

[1] G. C. M. O. 21, A. G. O. July 24, 1872.

[2] G. C. M. O. 35, A. G. O. 1867.

[3] Vide Chapter VIII. on Oaths, p. 119.

The court is then opened, the accused and counsel resume their seats, and the decision is announced by the judge-advocate. If the question is rejected, it follows the rule as to all proceedings of a court; it should not be stricken from the record, except with the assent of both parties and permission of the court. The decision of the court should likewise appear on the record. "It is not usual nor would it be right, to detail the grounds which might have led the court to the result finally adopted. The decision only of the court, both as to interlocutory and final judgments, is made known, but in no case the details of any discussion or the judgment of particular members."[1]

When the majority of the members of a court-martial have come to a decision upon any question, raised in the course of the proceedings, no individual of the minority, whether the president or other member, is entitled to have his *protest* against the decision entered upon the record.[2]

The judge-advocate should first prove the connection of the prisoner with the offense, and be careful to prove the fact that the person is amenable to military law; also the times and places set forth in the specification.

Cross-Examination. After the direct examination follows the cross-examination, followed by the re-examination, and, if desired, the re-cross-examination.[3]

Examination by Court. While the court, or any member with permission of the court, may ask questions of the witnesses at any time, it is deemed better to refrain from so doing until the judge-advocate and accused have finished. The court asks questions to clear up doubts or explain discrepancies.

A question put by a member, if objected to, but allowed to be asked by the court, should be recorded as

[1] Simmons § 469, (6 Ed). [2] Opinions J. A. G. p. 302.
[3] Vide Chapter XXV. p. 340–344.

"question by the court;" if rejected, as "question by member."

The decision of the court is final as to what questions may be put, and no one, whether member, judge-advocate, or accused, can insist upon a question being asked.

It often happens that the judge-advocate or the accused has omitted to ask a question which they desire to be put. Such question should be submitted to the court, and is, as a rule, permitted, being entered on the record as a question "by the court."

Reading over Testimony. When the witness has given his testimony in full, before dismissal from the stand, the judge-advocate should read it over to him, and notify him, that if he wishes to make any corrections in it, he will be allowed to do so. It should not be read to him, wholly or in part, before he is cross-examined.

Witnesses may be recalled by the court at any stage of the proceedings, for such examination as it may deem necessary, or they may return of their own accord, and, with permission of the court, (which should be granted) correct any portions of their testimony. If the correction is material to the issue, it would be proper to leave the testimony on the record as it originally was given, and note the correction; this for the benefit of the reviewing authority. When a witness comes the second time on the same trial before a court to testify, he need not be resworn, although he should be cautioned that in testifying he is still on oath.

The judge-advocate calls all the witnesses desired for the prosecution, and their testimony being finished, announces that he here rests the prosecution.

The witnesses for the defense are then called and examined in the same manner as has been described, the accused commencing the direct examination; the questions of the accused being put through the judge-advocate and the answers recorded by him.

The accused has a right to call all necessary witnesses whose testimony will assist his defense, and the court should allow him considerable latitude in questioning witnesses; but as it frequently happens, especially with soldiers, that the accused desires to call unnecessary witnesses, the court will exercise its discretion in allowing such action, being careful, however, to do nothing which will prejudice his case. The accused has a right to call witnesses as to character, and it is often for his advantage to do so.[1]

After the examination of the witnesses for the defense the judge-advocate may, if he see fit, summon new witnesses, or recall any of the previous witnesses to rebut the testimony elicited in the defense, and the accused may in such event establish the fact in issue by new witnesses.

Originating Evidence. Some question has arisen as to the power of a court-martial to originate evidence; that is, to call witnesses not called by either party. While this places a court-martial somewhat in the light of a prosecutor, yet there may be points which the court desires to have cleared up, and the Judge-Advocate General says that it is authorized to call before it to give testimony, witnesses whom neither the prosecution nor the defense have summoned, and this even after both have closed their case.[2]

Simmons says,—"The custom of service would justify the calling as a witness any individual alluded to in the evidence before the court, who may be at hand, and whose examination might afford a probability of elucidating a special point which may be dubious, but it is apprehended that this is the utmost extent to which a court would be

[1] Chapter XXIV., p. 314. [2] Opinions J. A. G., p. 128.

authorized to go. A court-martial might involve itself in an inextricable labyrinth, were it to stay proceedings and adjourn in order to obtain testimony."[1] De Hart[2] and Benét[3] cite the views of Simmons, and maintain that a court can originate evidence only to the extent stated by him.[4]

Sick or Absent. If the court desires to hear the testimony of a sick or absent witness, it may adjourn to such time as his presence may be secured, subject, in case of unreasonable adjournment, to being reconvened by the reviewing authority. Where the witness is sick at the post where the court is sitting, it may adjourn to his quarters, and take the testimony. In such case, the accused and his counsel should be allowed to be present to cross-examine, and exercise the rights accorded them by law. The established rule of law is that a court-martial cannot receive testimony against an accused except in his presence. This, however, is a personal privilege which he may waive.[5]

Courts-martial will necessarily often be called upon to decide points affecting the rights and privileges of the accused in his defense, and in this connection may well be read the remarks of the Secretary of War in a recent order,—"Courts-martial had much better err on the side of liberality towards a prisoner than by endeavoring to solve nice and technical refinements of the laws of evidence, assume the risk of injuriously denying him proper latitude for defense."[6]

[1] Simmons, p. 413 (2d Ed.) § 948 (6th Ed.) [2] P. 85.

[3] P. 357. Kennedy (p. 141) same view.

[4] A court-martial is authorized of its own motion, and at any stage of the proceedings, to summon any witness whose testimony appears material to the case on trial, in the Articles recently proposed.

[5] I. Opinions Attorney-General, March 15, 1825.

[6] G. C. M. O. 32, A. G. O. Oct. 31, 1872.

Statement. After the examination of the witnesses for the defense, the accused has a right to make a statement; and for this purpose the court should allow him sufficient delay for preparing it.

The following remarks from the War Department in reference to the *statement* of an accused, should be borne in mind by the members of courts-martial, and by parties being tried :—"Great latitude is undoubtedly always allowed to an accused in offering his defense. Any argument fairly deducible from the evidence tending to show malice in the prosecution, or to impeach the credit of witnesses may be advanced; but this privilege ought not to be abused, so as to make an argument the vehicle of satire and personal ridicule, and convert a means of defense into a weapon of attack." In this particular case the Secretary said, referring to the defense,—"A document characterized by so many personalities, and such unbecoming levity of style, would barely be tolerated in any civil court, and is still less admissible in a court-martial, and towards a person standing in the relation in which Col. G. stood towards the accused, and the court would have been justified in refusing to receive it." [1]

A party may be tried by a court-martial for language used in a written defense before another court.[2]

"It is competent for a court-martial to caution the prisoner as he proceeds, if they should think proper, and to state to him that, in their opinion, such a line of defense as he may be pursuing, would probably not weigh with them, or operate in his favor; but to decide against hearing him state arguments which, notwithstanding such caution, he might persist in putting forward as grounds of justification or extenuation, such arguments not being

[1] G. O. 16, A. G. O. March 27, 1851.

[2] G. O. 2, A. G. O. Jan. 15, 1856. G. O. 25, A. G. O. Dec. 8, 1859.

illegal in themselves, is going beyond what any count would be warranted in doing."[1]

Value of Statement. The exact value of a statement cannot be defined in law, but must depend upon the particular case, and the character of the party making it. Not being stated under the sanction of an oath, great temptation is offered to state facts absolutely false, or at least to give erroneous impressions of, or interpretations to facts. On the other hand proper consideration should be given to a statement.

The judge-advocate may, if he thinks proper, call witnesses to rebut statements made in the defense, with power in the accused of cross-examining, and calling witnesses to prove the truth of his statements.

The defense of the accused is usually read to the court by himself, but may be read by the judge-advocate, and, unless the court objects, by the counsel for the accused. Simmons cites a case where the counsel was not permitted to read the defense as being contrary to precedent.[2] Such rule does not obtain in this country, and, in cases where there is a reporter, courts-martial frequently allow the counsel to make the defense in the form of an address to the court.

Reply of Judge-Advocate. The judge-advocate has the right of reply, or he may submit the case without remark. The latter is the common custom, except in complicated cases. The court should grant time to the judge-advocate for preparing a defense, if he so desires it.

A reply is, or ought to be, a commentary on the evidence introduced by the prisoner, and on remarks made by him in enforcing that evidence, or in arraigning the

[1] Letter from the English Judge-Advocate General to the Deputy Judge-Advocate in Lieut. Dawson's trial, cited by Simmons, p. 196 (2d Ed).

[2] Simmons § 586, (6th Edition).

testimony offered in support of the prosecution. No new matter ought to be introduced at this stage of the trial, without the special leave of the court; and then it should be supported by witnesses, and the prisoner should be allowed to rejoin, and remark upon such new matter. Especially the prosecutor ought not to be permitted, under color of replying to the prisoner's defense, to give additional testimony at this stage of the trial, and, by a statement of facts, made when the prisoner has not the opportunity of cross-interrogating him, and which he has not made when he was sworn as a witness, to attempt to explain or contradict what has previously been given in evidence. Hough denounces such a course as irregular; but if it is pursued, he says, it is but fair, either that the court should *stop* the prosecution from going into such new matter, or, if he be *permitted* to go on, to *hear* the prisoner afterwards in *reply* to such new matter.

In the case of Capt. H., the judge-advocate applied to be heard by the court in an argument that he proposed to present, and this request was denied by the court, on the ground that the accused had interposed no address on his part. The action thus taken was disapproved, it being held that the judge-advocate of a court-martial has an undoubted right at the close of a trial, to address the court for the purpose of commenting on the whole evidence and the law applicable to it; and that this right is in no degree abridged by a waiver on the part of the accused of his like privilege.[1]

Where an accused pleads "guilty," he has still the right of calling witnesses in extenuation of the offense, or witnesses as to character, and also to make a statement to the court.

Adjournment. If an adjournment has taken place

[1] G. C. M. O. 11, A. G. O. May 1, 1872.

during the case until another day, the members resume their seats at the appointed time, and the judge-advocate notes the names of those present and absent as before indicated.

The accused and his counsel are called before the court, and the proceedings of the preceding day verified, corrected and approved. The trial then commences at the point where it had been left off on the preceding day.

Regimental Court for doing Justice—Mode of Procedure. When a court is convened under the 30th Article of War, the mode of procedure differs somewhat from that of the ordinary court-martial.

Both parties furnish the judge-advocate a list of witnesses, who are summoned by him as in any court. Both are allowed the right of challenge. After the court is sworn, the complainant states his grievance, and calls any desired witnesses to support it. The officer complained of may then call his witnesses, and make a statement, if he desires. The court may ask such questions of the witnesses as it desires, and the rules as to cross-examination and re-examination, are the same as in any court. Either party may be sworn. After all the evidence is presented and statements made, the court is then closed and an opinion rendered. In their opinion, if the court finds the injury complained of established, they should point out the mode of redress. The proceedings should then be forwarded to the regimental commander for approval.

Either party may appeal from the decision of this court to a general court-martial. In such cases the mode of procedure is as follows: Both parties furnish a list of witnesses to the judge-advocate. The right of challenge is afforded to both parties (to the appellant first). After the court is sworn the appellant states his grievance, and calls any desired witnesses to substantiate it, after which the other party produces his witnesses, and makes any desired statement. Either party may be sworn. The court is then closed for deliberation.

In giving an opinion, the court should simply state whether appellant has substantiated his grievance or not.

If the court deems the appeal groundless and vexatious, the party appealing shall be punished by the court at its discretion.

CHAPTER X.

FACTS INCIDENT TO THE TRIAL.

Behavior of Members. All members of a court-martial are to behave with decency and calmness.[1]

It is rare that any grounds of complaint arise upon this score; but, during the war, the reviewing officer of a general court-martial reported "that the members of the court were guilty of 'conduct prejudicial to good order and military discipline,' in drinking with the accused at various times and holding private conversations with his counsel, and of other irregularities, going to show that they had no proper sense of their duty, or appreciation of the obligations of their solemn oaths;" and recommended the dismissal of the members, whereupon the President dismissed seven members. In time of peace for any improper behavior, a member would render himself liable to trial.[2]

A court-martial cannot itself punish one of its members for disorderly behavior.

At a general court-martial assembled at Oregon City Nov. 16, 1849, Capt. and Brevet Lieut. Col. Backenstos—senior member and presiding officer of said court-martial—was sentenced "to be expelled from the court, and to be cashiered" for positive, willful, and repeated contempt of court. The specification named that "Captain B. did refuse to put a motion for the adjournment of the court; did violently assert that he only had authority to order the adjournment; did arbitrarily declare the court ad-

[1] Article 87. [2] G. C. M. O. 123, A. G. O. March 8, 1865.

journed; and did boisterously leave the court in defiance of its expressed will; that, being called to return, he did refuse; that, being then ordered into arrest by the court, he did, on the next day of the session, attempt to take his seat as presiding officer, and did remain in the court after it was ordered to be cleared, and did disturb the proceedings till peremptorily ordered to retire."

The President disapproved the proceedings on the ground that the 76th (present 86th) article did not confer on a court-martial power to punish its own members. He further stated that "the presiding officer of a court-martial (besides the duties and privileges of a member) is only its organ. He speaks and acts for it in each case, when the particular rule has been prescribed by law, regulation, or its own resolution. He announces the adjournment when the prescribed hour has arrived. He cannot adopt an hour different from that which has been prescribed, without the approbation of a majority of the court when in session. This right of regulating its own sessions is important and necessary, and the limitation placed on it by the 72d Art. of War (present 95th) was obviously intended to secure full and fair deliberation. In this and all deliberations of the court, the equality of the several members was intended to be preserved. It is not doubted that any disorderly conduct of a member of a court-martial to the prejudice of good order and military discipline would constitute an offense cognizable by another court under the Article of War applicable to the case."[1]

Where an officer, a member of a court-martial, refused to make any explanation in regard to his absence from the court, it was held a contempt of court, though, in this case, not triable by the court to which the contempt was offered.[2]

[1] G. O. 14 R. G. O., April 12, 1850. [2] Army and Navy Jour., Feb. 17, 1877.

Absent Members. The right of an absent member to take or resume his seat, and take part in the proceedings of a court, has been a subject of discussion.

Where a general court-martial has been ordered, and the names of the officers and supernumeraries to compose it are set forth in the warrant, and, by reason of the non-attendance of one of the officers on the first day, a supernumerary takes his place, and the court, thus organized, proceeds to business, the absent member cannot properly thereafter be added to the court upon his arrival, until the case on trial has been disposed of, if at all.[1] Attorney-General Berrien says,—It is irregular for a member of a court-martial who has been absent during a portion of a trial, and who therefore did not hear the witnesses testify, to take part in sentencing the accused.[2] Attorney-General Cushing says,—In practice it is unusual for members, who have not heard the whole trial, to participate in giving judgment; but there is no law to prohibit their doing so, or to compel them if they refuse. Whether the absent members shall act or not upon his return, must depend upon his own views of propriety, and not upon those of the court, which is nowhere clothed with power to expel a member.[3]

Should such an absent member resume his seat, it should appear upon the record, and, if the court thinks, under the circumstances, that the member should be excluded, its only recourse is to suspend its proceedings and report the matter to the reviewing authority.

Judge-advocate's Absence. Where the judge-advocate is absent, the court should suspend its proceedings until his return. He cannot authenticate proceedings which have not taken place in his presence.

[1] I. Opinions Att'y Gen. Nov. 18, 1824.
[2] II. Opinions Att'y Gen., March 2, 1831.
[3] VII. Opinions Att'y General, April 11, 1855.

Excusing Members. The court has no power to excuse one of its members. A member may be relieved by order of the convening authority, but, after a trial has commenced, only the most urgent necessity should prompt the reviewing officer so to act.

Nolle Prosequi. When a court has commenced a trial and arraigned a prisoner, it must proceed to judgment, unless the charges are withdrawn, or a *nolle prosequi* entered.

Some question has arisen as to who may enter a *nolle prosequi.* It is held that the President has power to order a *nolle prosequi* at any stage of a criminal proceeding in the name of the United States;[1] and the Secretary of War, as the constitutional organ of the President, has this power. The convening authority, and even the judge-advocate of his own motion, may move to enter a *nolle prosequi.* The court will decide whether to allow it or not.

Where the convening officer, or higher authority, directs the entering of a *nolle prosequi* through the judge-advocate, the court-martial should allow it to be entered, since the prosecution proceeds by order of the government, and it ought to be allowed to abandon a case if it thinks proper.

Some discussion has arisen as to whether a court itself could direct the entering of a *nolle prosequi,* or a withdrawal of the charge. The following remarks in a late order strike the author as the correct law upon this point: "Where charges and specifications, duly preferred, have undergone proper inquiry at post headquarters, received official scrutiny and revision at these headquarters, and are referred to the judge-advocate of a court-martial for trial, it is the duty of the court to 'well and truly try and

[1] V. Opinions Att'y Gen. p. 729.

determine according to the evidence, etc.,' the charges etc., presented; and they are not authorized and cannot be justified or permitted to negative the order of the Commanding General of the department in relation thereto. The judge-advocate of a general court-martial is the prosecuting officer of the government, and as such, is responsible for the presentation of the evidence concerning the same, and is not subject to the orders of the court when they are in conflict with the orders referring the case for trial. If the judge-advocate failed to present evidence attainable, or if, when presented, it failed to establish the guilt alleged, the court should acquit the accused in whole, or in part, according to the nature and extent of the testimony, but to do more is to assume powers not consistent with the honored and responsible duties of triers of a cause in hearing."[1]

Hours of Session. Proceedings of trials can be carried on only between the hours of eight in the morning and three in the afternoon, excepting in cases which, in the opinion of the officer appointing the court, require immediate example.[2] When the latter case arises, the order convening the court should contain the proviso,—"The court is authorized to sit without regard to hours," or words to that effect. It is a fatal defect where the court sits outside these hours unless specifically authorized.

Control over Court. A military court is not under the control or dictation of the convening authority or any person in conducting its proceedings. Tytler says, "The king can no more interfere with the procedure of courts-martial in the execution of their duty than he can with that of any of the fixed courts of justice."[3] The same is true in this country. Where a court refused to comply with an order from the military district com-

[1] G. C. M. O. 79, D. P. but see Chapter VI. p, 87. [2] Article 94. [3] P. 130.

mander, requiring that in all cases where the accused pleaded "guilty," evidence exhibiting the facts of the offense should be introduced by the prosecution and entertained by the court, the judge-advocate general *advised* that the dissolving of the court, with a reprimand was the only remedy of the convening authority. For him *to bring to trial* the members of the court who had concurred in the refusal, with a view of establishing their offense by the testimony of other members and the judge-advocate, would be without precedent and improper.[1]

Unless the members act willfully, maliciously, and corruptly, they cannot be held responsible for their action in any case so long as they have jurisdiction, and confine themselves to the rules of procedure prescribed by law.

Joinder. No legal objection exists, when two or more persons have joined in concert in the commission of an offense, to joining them in the charges, specifications, and trial, though the practice has been to try but one case at a time.

The practice of trying enlisted men by court-martial on joint instead of separate charges for desertion, theft of public property, and offenses of a similar type, not necessarily involving concert of action, being at variance with approved custom, is regarded as injurious to the service and will be discontinued.[2]

Where persons are joined in trial each should have the opportunity of challenge, of examining and cross-examining witnesses, in fact, the same rights which are accorded a prisoner when tried singly. The proceedings should be made up separately in each case.

Contempts of Court. Courts-martial are authorized in certain cases to punish for contempts. They may punish, at discretion, any person who uses any menacing

[1] Opinions J. A. G. p. 122. [2] G. O. 78, A. G. O. Aug. 7, 1872

words, signs, or gestures, in its presence, or who disturbs its proceedings by any riot or disorder.[1] They cannot punish their members in such cases, but any member is liable to punishment at the discretion of another court-martial, and his improper language or other disorderly conduct should be reported to the authority appointing the court by appropriate charges or otherwise, as the court of which he is a member may direct. Courts-martial must limit themselves strictly to this article. They are not authorized to punish persons for contempts committed out of their presence; although if a military person should be guilty of such conduct, the attention of the reviewing authority might very properly be called to it. In 1873, an officer acting as counsel for the accused was tried for sending a contemptuous message to a court after having been excluded from the court room.[2]

When military persons are guilty of contempts, they may either be punished summarily, or be placed in arrest, and have charges preferred against them.

The contempts rendered punishable summarily by this article are of a public and self-evident kind, not depending on any interpretation of law admitting explanation, or requiring further investigation.

Some doubt has arisen as to the power of courts-martial to punish *civilians* for contempts committed in violation of the 86th Article. Under the old article, in which the authority to punish does not seem quite as strong as in the new, De Hart[3] inclined to the *right* to punish civilians, and Benét maintained that the right existed. Both hold, however, that as courts-martial have no appointed means of enforcing their mandates against civil-

[1] Article 86. [2] G. C. M. O. 37, A. G. O. Oct. 3, 1873.
[3] P. 106–108. [4] P. 37–38.

ians, supposing the existence of a power to make such mandates, a procedure against them would be vain and nugatory; and yet the disturbances of the proceedings of a court-martial should not pass unnoticed. Where the court sits within the limits of a garrison, or territory subject to military jurisdiction, the court can cause the offender to be ejected from its presence and put beyond the military limits, and when the court holds its sessions in towns or at places not known as military posts, such persons may likewise be put out of the presence of the court; and, should further disturbances be made or attempted from the outside of the court room, the civil authorities may be appealed to, to proceed against the offenders for breach of the peace.[1] This mild view of the power of a court-martial to maintain order in its presence does not seem consistent with the dignity of a judicial body. Courts-martial are as competent, in cases within their jurisdiction, as any other court, and it would be an anomalous sight to see a civil court appealing to another court (especially a *federal* appealing to a *state* court) to maintain order in its presence. In the English Code, the corresponding article requires civilians to be taken before a civil magistrate to be punished according to law;[2] but in our article the power is given to the court itself. The United States civil courts are authorized to punish contempts by fine or imprisonment, but could not punish contempts before a court-martial.[3] Punishments by imprisonment would seem appropriate in the case of grave contempts before courts-martial.

The breach of this law by civilians has been and will doubtless be of rare occurrence, and, should it occur in

[1] De Hart, p. 108.

[2] Art. 161, Code of 1872.

[3] Rev. Stat. § 725.

future, courts-martial should exercise a wise discretion as to the punishment they inflict.

Every court is the exclusive judge of its own contempts.[1]

[1] Ex. parte Nugent, 1 American Law Journal, 107.

CHAPTER XI.

FINDING.

THE evidence being finished, and the defense made, the court is then cleared, and closed for deliberation and finding. The entire testimony, or any part of it, is read over by the judge-advocate, at the desire of the court, or a member thereof. In complicated cases it is better to have the whole testimony read over, but every court must be the judge of its necessity in each particular case.

Recalling Witnesses After the case is finished and the court closed, it may, if it deem it necessary, recall any witness for the purpose of explaining discrepancies, or clearing up doubts in the minds of the members. In such cases the accused should always be present. The accused may himself be recalled for explaining points of his statement not clear.

Deliberation For the purpose of arriving at a correct finding, due deliberation should be had before proceeding to a vote; and a full and free discussion with this intent is, therefore, generally entered into. If this discussion can be carried on by the members without disclosing their probable vote upon the general question of guilt, it is much better. From the deference that is paid in the army by juniors to their superiors, the older members should be extremely careful not to take advantage of this discussion to influence the junior members in their findings; while the junior members should remember, especially at this time, that they are acting as jurymen, and that, in maintaining an honest opinion they are doing simply what their oath requires, and in so doing will command the respect of their superiors.

The members should bear in mind the oath which they have taken, "to well and truly try, and determine according to evidence." They must not decide facts on their personal knowledge; but should be in a state of legal ignorance of everything relating to the question in dispute before them until established by legal evidence or legitimate inference from it. No communication of a member or of the judge-advocate of facts within their personal knowledge, should be received at this time. If a member of the court has knowledge of facts connected with the trial, he should ask to be sworn, and depose to these facts at the proper time.

Voting. After due deliberation, and when the court is ready to vote upon the finding, the judge-advocate proceeds to take the sense of the court, commencing with the first "specification" to the first "charge" and so on, in the same order in which the pleading was made. To obviate mistakes, and especially so where there are a number of specifications, it is best for the judge-advocate to read over each one before taking the vote.

The manner of voting, which is the same on all questions before a court-martial, is prescribed by the Article of War.[1] In giving their votes the members are to begin with the officer lowest in rank. The object of this is to prevent the judgment of superiors having too much influence with inferiors.

The judge-advocate keeps the record of the vote, and announces the finding, which in all cases save one, is determined by a majority vote. Art. 96 provides that no

[1] 95th.

person shall be sentenced to suffer death, except by the concurrence of two-thirds of the members of a general court-martial. As there are certain offenses for which the sentence of death is mandatory, it is held that the *finding* of "guilty" in such cases must be by a two-thirds majority; and this must appear on the record.

Where a court consists originally of an even number, or by any circumstances becomes so reduced, and the vote upon a finding is equally divided, the accused has the benefit of such vote and should be declared "not guilty."

The affirmative of any proposition can be adopted in a court-martial only by a majority vote, and all tie votes on the findings inure to the benefit of the accused.[1]

Care should be taken by the judge-advocate in recording the vote not to give any clue to the convening authority of the way in which any member voted. Where the record stated in the finding to a specification, "the vote was a tie and he is consequently not guilty," the Secretary of War held that "a tie vote on that issue was an acquittal and should have been recorded as a finding of 'not guilty.'" The state of the vote should never be expressed in the finding or sentence, except in cases where it is by law required to be stated.[2] To say that the finding was unanimous, while it would not vitiate the proceedings, is irregular and is a violation of the oath, as it discloses the vote of every member.

Manner of Voting. Courts-martial have different forms of voting upon and recording their sentences. The following are some of the forms met with in practice:

The court "confirms the plea of the accused," or "confirms his plea and finds him guilty," or "is of the

[1] G. C. M. O. 17, A. G. O. Sept. 15, 1871.

[2] G. C. M. O. 1, A. G. O., Jan. 16, 1872.

opinion that the accused is guilty." All these are sufficient, but for the sake of uniformity the following form is recommended when the finding is "guilty" or "not guilty."

The court, having maturely considered the evidence adduced, finds the accused —— ——, — Regiment U. S. Infantry:

Of the specification, "Guilty," or "Not Guilty."

Of the charge, "Guilty," or "Not Guilty."

As the findings of courts-martial are frequently anomalous, and do not contain the actual sense of the court, it is recommended to every court to be extremely careful at this stage of their proceedings to see that their findings are consistent. The gist of many charges under a specific article, for example, lies in a single word. A single case will illustrate. A person was tried under the 55th Article for "maliciously destroying the property of an inhabitant of the United States," and the court found him "guilty" except the word "maliciously," and proceeded to sentence him. Such finding was held void as his action did not constitute an offense under this article—if it was not malicious.

To find "not guilty" of a specification, but "guilty" of the charge, where there is a single specification, would be an absurdity.[1]

Where the finding is guilty of the specification, but not guilty of the charge, or of any lesser kindred offense, there is nothing left upon which a sentence can rest. It is equivalent to finding that the state of facts set forth in the specification do not make out the specific offense charged.[2]

Where the evidence does not prove the averments set forth in the specifications, the accused is entitled to a

[1] G. O. 95, Army of Potomac, March 6, 1862. [2] Op. J. A. G. p. 179.

verdict of acquittal; and where there is a doubt in the mind of a member, he should vote for acquittal, as it is considered better that many guilty men should go free rather than that one innocent man should suffer. Members of courts-martial should never forget the standard principle of criminal law, that a man is to be considered innocent until proved guilty.

A court-martial may properly find as follows:—

1st. Guilty or not guilty of all the charges and specifications, or of any particular charge or specification.

In cases of virtual acquittal, the term "guilty" is improperly used. The phrase truly expressive of the judgment of the court would be "proved," or "the facts found as stated," adding in either case the words "but no criminality attached thereto." The term "guilty" should be employed only when the prisoner is convicted of an actual crime, or offense deserving the award of punishment.[1]

While acquitting an accused, the court may nevertheless animadvert on his conduct. Thus in 1827, in the case of Lieut. B., the court remarked as follows: "The court, while it acquits the accused of the technical crime of disobedience of orders, considers his conduct in refusing the summons to attend the commanding officer of his company highly improper and reprehensible."[2]

Where there are a number of specifications to the same charge, the court may find "not guilty" of some of these specifications, but "guilty" of the charge, provided the evidence to the specification of which they find "guilty" is sufficient to constitute an offense under the charge.

2d. Guilty of certain parts of a charge or specification, and not guilty of others.

The form of recording such a finding is "Of the charge

[1] G. O. 11, A. G. O. Feb. 15, 1851. [2] O. 4, A. G. O. Jan. 19, 1827.

(or specification) 'guilty,' except the words ——, and of the excepted words 'not guilty;'" or it may substitute correct words or allegations in the place of excepted words, in which case it would be recorded "'guilty except the words ——, substituting therefor, etc."

3d. The court does honorably acquit the accused. Courts-martial, though finding "not guilty," may by their very silence leave an impression of guilt, and as the reputation and honor of an officer are largely in the hands of the court trying him, where entire innocence is proved, this form of finding would very properly be used. It should, however, be used with care. The Duke of Wellington, speaking on this point, said, "It is difficult and needless at present to define in what cases an 'honorable acquittal' is peculiarly applicable, but it must appear to all persons to be objectionable in a case in which any part of the transaction is disgraceful to the character of the party under trial. A sentence of honorable acquittal should be considered by the officers and soldiers of the army as a subject of exultation, but no man can exult in the termination of any transaction a part of which has been disgraceful to him; and, though such a transaction may be terminated by an *honorable* acquittal by a court-martial, it cannot be mentioned to the party without offense, or without exciting feelings of disgust in others. These are not feelings which ought to be excited by the recollection and mention of a sentence of honorable acquittal."

4th. Where the accused is charged under a specific article, and the evidence does not prove the offense under this article, but does prove a lesser kindred offense, the finding may be "not guilty, but guilty of the lesser offense."

In the case of *Dynes vs. Hoover*, the Supreme Court held that where a seaman was charged with deserting, and the court found him "guilty of attempting to desert," the court had jurisdiction.[1] So in the case of soldiers charged with desertion, a court frequently finds "not guilty, but guilty of absence without leave."

It must be borne in mind, however, that the accused cannot be found guilty of another article setting forth an entirely different offense. Thus, where a soldier was charged under the 39th article with "sleeping on post" and the court found him "not guilty," but "guilty" of the 40th article, (quitting his guard, etc., without leave) the Judge-Advocate General held the finding irregular and void.

In 1864 the Secretary of War decided that an accused brought to trial under any specific article might legally be convicted under the 99th article,[2] where the evidence established the commission of an act contrary to good order and military discipline, but did not sustain the specific charge—but the reverse of this would not be true, *i. e.*, a finding of "not guilty" of "conduct to the prejudice etc.," but "guilty" of some specific article.

A court could never find a person guilty of an offense that entailed a punishment greater than the one upon which he is charged.

Courts cannot resort to the *general* article to evade other articles of war. If the offense is proved under the specific article it must so find. Courts have sometimes done this where the accused is charged under an article for which the punishment is mandatory, and which they believe too severe for the case. Such action is wholly illegal and to be reprobated in the strongest terms. The court is assembled for finding out the facts, and, by their oaths, they agree to find according to the facts proved. If they believe a mandatory punishment too severe, they

[1] 20 Howard, 65. [2] Present 62d.

have a way open to them by recommending the accused to the clemency of the reviewing authority.

Animadversions. The court has a right, and it is often proper that it should animadvert upon the conduct of the accuser, prosecutor, or other persons. The question having been raised of the authority of a general court-martial, by proper animadversions, to bring to the notice of the military commander to whom the proceedings are sent, any conduct of the prosecutor or other military person which may be developed before the court in the due course of trial, the General-in-Chief thought it proper to affirm such right in clear cases, as one well settled by the practice of armies, and that its judicious exercise tends to promote justice and discipline.[1]

In the English service, where the power of summary dismissal resides in the Crown, it has often happened that such animadversions of courts-martial have been followed by summary dismissal. In our service such action of courts-martial might be followed by bringing the party animadverted upon to trial.

Animadversions on Charges. Simmons cites a number of instances, where courts-martial have declared charges "frivolous, vexatious and groundless," "malicious," "not originating in a desire to promote the good of the service," "proceeding from warmth of temper and ignorance, insubordination, animosity, resentment, revenge or conspiracy;" and other cases, where courts have declared, in their opinion, that the prosecutor was actuated "by no illiberal or improper motive," or, "by a sense of duty and regard for the benefit of the service," or that his conduct was "regular and impartial," or "laudable and honorable." Such remarks, he says, have generally been produced by strong assertions or insinuations of the prisoner, not supported by

[1] G. O. 3, A. G. O. Jan. 27, 1873.

evidence, and have occasionally accompanied an acquittal; at other times a conviction.[1]

So in this country. In the case of Bvt. Lieut.-Col. R. the court said that "it is constrained to express the opinion that this prosecution has grown out of personal and private animosities existing among some of the officers at this post, and that these charges would not have been made had these feelings not arisen."[2]

On Witnesses and Parties not before the Court. The court might remark upon and censure insinuations or prevarications of witnesses, and sometimes might deem it proper to call attention to irregularities of persons not before the court. In all such cases the court should be careful not to do injustice to parties, as cases might arise where such action would render every member liable to an action for defamation.

Failure to Agree. If a court cannot agree upon a finding, all that can be done is for the convening authority to dissolve the court and convene a new court for the trial of the accused. If the court refused on insufficient grounds to arrive at a finding, and, being reconvened persists in its refusal, the convening officer on dissolving the court might reprimand the members, but could not bring them to trial.[3]

Reconsidering Finding. A court may reconsider its finding at any time prior to its final adjournment. A motion to reconsider should come from a member who voted with the majority, and the court will determine whether the motion should be granted or not.

Keeping Vote. De Hart,[4] following Tytler,[5] holds that the judge-advocate should keep the record of how the different members vote, to meet the possible contingency

[1] P. 225 (2d Edition). [2] G. O. 36, A. G. O. July 10, 1851.
[3] Opinions J. A. G. p. 122. [4] P. 177. [5] P. 149.

of being required to give evidence of the same before a court of justice. Benét[1] maintains that this memorandum *must* be destroyed, while Simmons holds that the decision upon this point must be left to each judge-advocate. The custom in our service in taking a vote, is simply to note the number of votes for and against, and not to write down the names of the members and their votes. The judge-advocate, therefore, rarely ever has a memorandum in his possession. If he, or any member of the court, should desire to keep such memorandum, there is nothing to prevent their so doing. But, as the cases are rare where a court of justice would call on them to testify on this point, and as such memoranda are liable to become known, the practice is to be discountenanced.

[1] P. 145.

CHAPTER XII.

PUNISHMENTS.

THE court having come to a finding, the next thing in order is the sentence; but, in order to understand more fully the rights and duties of the court at this stage, it is deemed advisable to devote a separate chapter to the subject of punishments before proceeding to the consideration of the sentence.

Object of Punishment. As to the object of punishment and the manner of securing it, the following remarks are deemed worthy of notice.

"The repression of crime by corrective discipline depends mainly on the punishment operating widely *as an example*, and thus exercising a deterring influence on others, and, in a minor degree, by the individual himself being deterred from future offense from fear of the consequences, or by his being so reformed that he ceases to commit crime from a better motive than that of fear.

"The first of these objects will be promoted by carrying into effect a system of discipline known to be of a severe and stringent character, such as will make men prudently resolve to keep clear of it if they can. It should also dwell on the memory of one who has once been subject to it, as a disagreeable and certain consequence of crime, and thus tend to prevent its repetition.

"At the same time, however, that a severe discipline with more extended objects is maintained, there can be no doubt that efforts should be made to prevent the repetition of crime by an endeavor to reform the individual." [1]

Punishments. Courts-martial, upon conviction, are required to name a punishment appropriate to the offense.

The punishments which courts-martial may inflict are derived from the regulations,[2] articles of war, and customs of the service.

In several cases the articles of war prescribe the punishment, in others they limit it, but in the majority of cases it is left to the discretion of the court.

The general court-martial is the only one that can inflict the grave punishments, as the minor courts cannot try capital cases or commissioned officers, or inflict a fine exceeding one month's pay, or imprison, or put to hard labor any non-commissioned officer or soldier for a longer time than one month.[3]

The various punishments which may be inflicted upon *officers* by the sentence of a general court-martial are:

(1) **Death.** The death penalty, however, cannot be inflicted except by concurrence of two-thirds of the members of a general court-martial, and only in the cases mentioned in the articles of war.[4]

By the municipal code of the United States it is provided that "the manner of inflicting death shall be by hanging," [5] and officers or soldiers if found guilty of a criminal offense, the sentence for which should be death, would be punished in that way; the same manner would be adopted in the case of a spy, or mutineer where death resulted.

During the Revolution some cases happened where deserters were punished by hanging, but, by the *custom*

[1] Extract from an article on the Discipline and Management of Military Prisons in the "Aide Memoire to the Military Sciences," Part I, Vol. III. London, 1848. [2] Par. 895. [3] Art. 83. [4] Art. 96. [5] Rev. Stat. § 5325.

of war now, for purely military offenses the death penalty is inflicted by "shooting to death with musketry."

(2) **Any Punishment except Death.** In certain of the articles[1] courts-martial may for the offenses named therein, when committed in time of peace, inflict any punishment except death. The word *any*, as used in this connection, must be limited to those punishments which it is customary to inflict according to the custom of war.

(3) **Cashiering.** In our articles the punishment of cashiering appears in two instances only. Prior to the revision of the articles in 1874, the words, "cashiering" and "dismissal" appeared frequently. It would seem that the two words have ever been perfectly synonymous, although upon this point there is a difference of opinion. For a long number of years, however, both in the English service and in our own, the legal effect of both have been the same; and when new articles were adopted in 1874, the term "cashiering" was dropped and "dismissal" substituted in all but the two instances cited, and in these it is presumed it was overlooked. Singularly enough, in the English Code of 1872 "dismissal" was dropped and "cashiering" substituted.[3]

Though the two terms are retained in our articles they both have the same effect.[4 & 5]

(4) **Dismissal.** When an officer is dismissed from the service for cowardice or fraud, the *sentence* shall further direct that the crime, punishment, name, and place of abode of the delinquent shall be published in the newspapers in and about the camp, and in the State from which

[1] Arts. 47 and 51. [2] Articles 8 and 50.

[3] The term "cashiering," is substituted for "dismissal" in the Articles of War recently proposed.

[4] The Articles spoken of in Note 3, though substituting "cashiering" for "dismissal," speak of an officer's being dismissed in several cases.

[5] See pamphlet upon the subject by Col. Lieber, J. A. Corps.

the offender came, or where he usually resides; and after such publication it shall be scandalous for an officer to associate with him.[1]

Dismissal with disability to hold any office or employment in the service of the United States, is a mandatory punishment for the offences named in certain of the articles.[2]

Dismissal and requirement to refund to the United States a certain amount, is mandatory for the offenses named in Article 15.

Summary Dismissal. The power of summary dismissal of officers up to 1866 rested in the President, as commander-in-chief, at all times; but at present it is provided [3] that no officer shall, in time of peace, be discharged or dismissed from service except upon and in pursuance of, the sentence of a court-martial to that effect, or in mitigation thereof. This power is still retained to the President in time of war, and he is justified by law and authority in summarily dismissing an officer, even after trial by court-martial, and a finding of "not guilty," where the testimony in his opinion sustains an aggravated charge.[4] Frequent cases of such dismissals occurred during the war, upon the recommendation of the reviewing authority.

(5) **Suspension.** This may be from rank, command and pay, or from two of these combined, or from either, at the option of the court.

A sentence of suspension merely by a court-martial does not deprive the party of pay and emoluments.[5]

When a court-martial suspends an officer from com

[1] Art. 100. [2] Articles 5 and 14. [3] Art. 99.
[4] IV. Opinions Atty. Gen'l, pp 1 and 611.
[5] VI Opinions Atty. Gen'l, Oct. 21, 1853.

mand, it may also suspend his pay and emoluments for the same time according to the nature of his offense.[1] There is a similar provision in the Naval Code, in reference to which Attorney General Nelson held, that the power of a court to suspend the pay and emoluments of an officer does not extend beyond the time of his suspension from service. It is incidental to that service.[2]

Where an officer is suspended from rank and pay, the Adjutant General held in 1874 that, during such suspension, he is entitled to quarters in kind or commuted unless deprived by sentence of a general court-martial; [3] but a similar application for quarters and fuel in 1876 was disapproved by the Secretary of War.

This punishment is deemed to be, as a rule, a bad one. The following remarks of the President in the case of Surgeon S. are deemed well worthy the consideration of courts-martial, "In consideration of the inconvenience to the public service which results from the long absence from duty of an officer suspended by sentence of a general court-martial, and from the further consideration in the particular case of Assistant Surgeon L. H. S., that the sentence of the general court-martial, in this case, would operate, if fully executed, to promote above him in his corps, certainly nineteen officers now below him, and perhaps more, the President has been pleased to order that the sentence now in force against Asst. Surgeon S. be mitigated by substituting one year in place of two years, wherever those words occur in that sentence. And the President further directs that by a publication in General Orders from the War Department, general courts-martial in the army before which the question may properly come, be invited to consider whether an effectual and

[1] Art. 101.
[2] IV. Opinions Atty. Gen'l, p. 323.
[3] Letter A. G. O., February 1874.

appropriate penalty may not be inflicted without injury to the service, by adjudging a certain loss of rank instead of suspension from rank for a period of time, the effect of which upon an officer is not certain when the sentence is pronounced, but which must operate to the prejudice of the service in removing an officer from duty."[1]

In 1873 the Secretary of War said, in approving a sentence of reduction in rank of an officer, that he did not deem it advisable that such sentences should be made by courts-martial, as, in some instances they would result in great injury to other officers.[2]

Suspension from rank cuts an officer off from any promotion to which he might have been entitled if not so suspended; but even this works very unequally. The recommendation of the President obviates all this, and has been resorted to frequently by courts-martial. In the case of Asst. Surgeon W., the court sentenced him "To forfeit all rank and claims and privileges arising from services rendered previous to the date of the promulgation of this sentence; to be placed at the bottom of the list of assistant surgeons in the army, and to be reprimanded in General Orders,"[3] which was approved and executed.

The Adjutant General held in 1876 that an officer sentenced to suspension from rank and command cannot be granted leave of absence.[4]

(6) **Confinement.** This may be to certain limits, as to the limits of the post, or closer confinement.

Officers may be confined in the penitentiary, but Art. 97 directs that no person in the military service, shall, under the sentence of a court-martial, be punished by confinement in a penitentiary, unless the offense of which he

[1] G. O. 43, A. G. O. Dec. 22, 1852. [2] War Dept., Dec. 10, 1873.
[3] G. O. 28, A. G. O. June 9, 1851. See also O. 53, A. G. O. Sept. 13, 1828.
[4] Hdq'rs. of the Army, A. G. O. Dec. 18, 1876.

may be convicted would by some statute of the United States, or by some statute of the State, Territory or district, in which such offense may be committed, or by the common law as the same exists in such State, Territory, or district, subject such convict to such punishment.

Confinement in the penitentiary could not be awarded for a purely military offense.

Officers have been sentenced to confinement in the post guard-house, although such punishment is exceedingly rare, and is not to be approved. In the case of Bvt. Major A., tried for "contempt of court," the court sentenced him "to be confined in charge of the officer of the guard in the post guard-house at this post (Fort Leavenworth, Kansas) during his pending trial, or during the pleasure of the court, and denied all communication with any one except his counsel."[1 & 2]

(7) **Reprimand, Public or Private.** Where a public reprimand is the sentence of a court-martial, it generally proceeds from the convening officer, and is read at the head of the regiment, or promulgated in a general order.

Where a court-martial convened from the headquarters of a department, sentenced an officer to be reprimanded in orders from the War Department, it was doubted if any part of the sentence was valid. It would seem not competent for the court to remove the sentence from the decision of the authority which the law has appointed to review and decide it.[3]

The Articles[4] direct that any officer who behaves irreverently at any place of divine worship shall be brought before a general court-martial, there to be publicly and

[1] G. C. M. O. 36, A. G. O., June 7, 1870.

[2] Officers for desertion may be dishonorably discharged from the service and confined at hard labor for not less than two nor more than five years, at the discretion of the court, in the Articles recently proposed.

[3] G. O. 15, A. G. O., April 12, 1852.

[4] Art. 52.

severely reprimanded by the President thereof. In the English service, prior to 1833, this punishment was applicable summarily upon the order of a superior or commanding officer. Now, however, their article declares that it shall follow conviction; hence a trial is necessary and approval. The latter seems much more in accord with the rules of justice, although not with the wording of our article.[1]

(8) **To be put in Arrest.** Any officer or soldier who uses any reproachful or provoking speeches to another officer or soldier, shall be put in arrest.[2]

(9) **Fine.** Fine or imprisonment is made a discretionary punishment for the offenses named in Article 60.

The punishments recognized by law as applicable to non-commissioned officers and soldiers, which courts-martial can inflict are:

(1) **Death.**

(2) **Any Punishment but Death.**[3]

(3) **Dishonorable Discharge** with or without forfeiture of pay and allowances, and with or without confinement.

A sentence of a court-martial adjudging a dishonorable discharge, to take effect at such period in a term of confinement as shall be designated by the reviewing authority, is contrary to law—as being a delegation of a portion of the judicial power to determine the measure of punishment.[4]

A court cannot sentence a soldier "to be honorably discharged;" and where the sentence of a court was simply "to be discharged," the Judge-Advocate General held that this must mean a *dishonorable* discharge.

(4) **Confinement.** Soldiers are sentenced to various kinds of confinement. It may be,

[1] A trial is necessary, and an officer or soldier is to be punished at the discretion of a court-martial only upon conviction, in the Articles of War recently proposed. [2] Art. 25. [3] See Articles 47 and 51.

[4] G. O. 90, A. G. O. Oct. 19, 1872.

1st. **Confinement at hard labor,** with or without ball and chain. This may be in the penitentiary, military prison, post guard-house, or such place as the reviewing authority may direct.

When the offenses of which a prisoner is convicted, or part of them, are punishable with confinement in a penitentiary, but the sentence simply prescribes confinement "at such place as the proper authority may direct," the reviewing authority may designate a penitentiary or a military prison.[1]

When a court-martial, however, has sentenced a prisoner to a "military prison" for any offense, no power is competent to increase the punishment by designating a "penitentiary" as the place of confinement. It is to be hoped that courts will be instructed so that they will not cause men convicted of penal offenses to be sent to the Leavenworth Prison, as it is desired to keep criminals apart from those sentenced for military offenses, not penal.[2]

Confinement of soldiers in the penitentiary is limited by the provisions of Art. 97.

If any State or a military department has made provision by law for confinement in a penitentiary thereof, of prisoners under sentence by courts-martial of the United States, the department commander may designate such penitentiary as a place for the execution of any such sentence to penitentiary confinement; but if no provision has been made by any State in the department, the record will be forwarded to the Secretary of War for designation of a prison. The authority which has designated the place of confinement, or higher authority, can change the place of confinement, or mitigate or remit the sentence.[3]

[1] G. C. M. O. 52, A. G. O. June 11, 1877.
[2] Letter of Adjutant-General, Sept. 12, 1878.
[3] G. O. 90 Hdqrs. of the Army, Oct. 30, 1868.

2d. **Simple Confinement.** A soldier so confined may be required to assist in performing the ordinary police of the garrison.

3d. **Solitary Confinement simply, or on bread and water diet.**

Solitary confinement, or confinement on bread and water diet, shall not exceed fourteen days at a time, with intervals between the period of such confinement not less than such periods; and not exceeding eighty-four days in any one year.

4th. **Confinement and requirement to ask pardon** for the offenses named in Art. 25.

A sentence of confinement for a period extending beyond the period of a soldier's enlistment is not forbidden by law.

A sentence imposing an imprisonment until a fine, imposed by the same sentence, is paid, is sanctioned by the common law and by modern legislation.[1]

In sentences for embezzlement there *should* be a direction that the prisoner should be confined until he should have made restitution to the United States of the amount of public money found to have been embezled. Without this provision in a sentence, there is no means, in the case of an officer not bonded, of enforcing such restitution beyond the extent of his pay.[2]

When a sentence imposes confinement in a *military prison*, the one at Fort Leavenworth, Kansas, is understood, as the Judge Advocate General holds this to be the only legally established military prison.[3]

5th. **Forfeiture of Pay and Allowances.** Any for

[1] In all cases where fines other than forfeitures of pay are imposed by sentence of general courts-martial or military commissions, the prisoner is to be confined until the fine is paid, unless a limit has been fixed by the sentence to the period of such confinement, by the Articles recently proposed.

[2] G. C. M. O. 27, A. G. O. Sept. 12, 1872.

[3] Letter A. G. O. Nov.14, 1878.

feiture of pay by a court-martial reverts to the United States. A court cannot assign or make over the pay of a soldier to any other person, nor can a soldier be required to receipt for money paid without his consent to another person.[1]

A court-martial, except in cases which may arise, under the 32d[2] Article of War, have not authority to find a verdict of debt against a soldier, and to direct, by their sentence, the payment of debts to sutlers or other persons.[3]

Where soldiers are married, forfeiture of pay has frequently the effect of punishing the innocent family of the accused, and, for this reason, the Judge-Advocate General recommends that in such cases the punishment be cautiously employed.[4]

It is sometimes stated in sentences of forfeiture that a soldier shall forfeit so much of his "monthly pay per month." The addition of the words "monthly pay" as employed in such sentences adds nothing to the meaning of the sentence, affects in no manner its legal import, and is in any case wholly superfluous.[5]

6th. **Reprimand Public or Private.**

7th. **To be reduced to the ranks** when non-commissioned officers.

When it is intended to punish a non-commissioned officer by confinement it is proper to reduce him first.

Courts-martial, though they may sentence the non-commissioned staff to discharge, cannot sentence them to be reduced.[6]

By "custom of the service" other punishments are inflicted on soldiers, which are held valid, and often a

[1] G. O. 2, A. G. O. Feb. 28, 1857, G. O. 163, A. G. O. April 15, 1854.
[2] Present 54th. [3] G. O. 21, A. G. O. April 3, 1851.
[4] Opinions J. A. G. p. 309. [5] G. O. 121, A. G. O. Oct 15, 1874.
[6] Regulations, par. 895.

sentence combines two or more of the above named punishments.

Deserters. Every soldier who deserts the service of the United States shall be liable to serve for such period as shall, with the time he may have served previous to his desertion, amount to the full term of his enlistment.[1] This provision not being positive, the Secretary of War held in 1843 that it was necessary to embody in the sentence of the court, in every case of the conviction of a deserter, that he shall make good the time lost by his absence from the service—if such be the intention of the court.[2] Regulations prescribe, however, that a soldier *shall* make good the time lost by desertion, unless discharged by competent authority;[3] and the Judge-Advocate General holds that the deserter is liable, as such, to make good to the service the time lost by his desertion, irrespective of the terms of his sentence, if tried and convicted by a court-martial.[4]

By an order of 1865, it was further provided that non-commissioned officers or soldiers who have absented themselves without authority from their company or regiment, or posts of duty, shall also in fulfillment of their contract, make good the time lost by reason of unauthorized absence, *upon such being found by a court-martial.*[5] It is not necessary therefore to include this requirement in the sentence.

In reckoning the time of service of a deserter, he is to be considered as again in service when delivered up as a deserter to the proper authority.[6]

When deserters enlist in other regiments, their period of service during such enlistment cannot be estimated in

[1] Article 48th. [2] G. O. 45, A. G. O. July 15, 1843.
[3] Par. 158. [4] Opinions J. A. G. p. 139.
[5] G. O. 16, A. G. O. Feb. 8, 1865. [6] Regulations, par. 161.

making good the time lost by desertion under their first enlistment.[1]

Deserters forfeit all pay and allowances due at the time of desertion. No retained pay under the act of May 15, 1872, can accrue to the benefit of a soldier who has deserted at any time during his enlistment.[2]

Forfeiture of pay due at date of desertion, as well as that accruing for the period of unauthorized absence, results *by operation of law* whether or not the soldier is tried or sentenced. But of course, in the great majority of cases, this liability as well as that of making good the time lost by desertion, can properly be enforced, and justice be done, only by bringing the offender to trial, and having the fact of desertion judicially determined.[3]

The reward of thirty dollars authorized to be paid for the apprehension and delivery of a deserter by G. O. 325, A. G. O., 1863, is charged against a deserter whether expressly provided for in the sentence or not.[4]

A soldier who is tried by a general court-martial for "desertion," but only found guilty of "absence without leave," forfeits the reward of thirty dollars paid for his arrest.[5]

The deposits of soldiers with paymasters, under the act of Congress of May 15, 1872, are forfeited by desertion.[5]

Sec. 1998 Revised Statutes provides that every person who hereafter deserts the military service shall be liable to all the penalties and forfeitures of Sec. 1996. These penalties are a voluntary relinquishment and forfeiture of the rights of citizenship, and incapability forever of holding an office of trust or profit under the United States, or of exercising any rights of citizens thereof. This pro-

[1] G. O. 4, A. G. O. Jan. 12, 1874.
[2] G. O. 88, A. G. O, Sept. 3, 1873. [3] Opinions J. A. G. p. 139.
[4] Ibid, p. 364. [5] Endorsement of Sec'y of War, Nov. 23, 1874.
[6] Revised Statutes § 1305.

vision not being positive, in order to make it effective, courts-martial would have to embody it in their sentence.[1]

Time of War. In time of war, insurrection or rebellion, the jurisdiction of courts-martial is extended to a large class of crimes when committed by persons in the military service, not triable in time of peace, and the punishment in any of these cases is not to be less than the punishment provided for the like offenses by the laws of the state, territory or district, in which such offense may have been committed.[2] Courts-martial ordinarily would limit themselves to the punishments provided; but in cases where severer punishments have been awarded they have been held legal and approved.

Corporal Punishment. Certain of the articles require the infliction of *corporal* punishment.[3] By reference to the 17th article it will be seen that *confinement* is regarded as a corporal punishment, and would doubtless most frequently be resorted to under these articles.

The old corporal punishments of flogging, branding, marking or tattooing on the body, are prohibited by the 98th Article of War. In view of this abolition the Judge-Advocate General says that courts-martial must needs often draw upon the customs of the service for a penalty which shall insure the description of a corporal punishment. Thus, the accused may be adjudged to carry a loaded knapsack for a certain time, stand on a barrel, or suffer any other ignominy which would naturally result in a degree of bodily pain or fatigue, provided the same were not excessive and physically injurious.[4]

Punishments Prohibited. Courts-martial in our service have sometimes awarded sentences which have been disapproved on account of their nature.

[1] This results by operation of law in the Articles of War recently proposed.

[2] See Article 58. [3] Articles 17. [4] Opinions J. A. G. p. 16.

Where a soldier was sentenced to do a certain amount of guard duty, the Secretary of War said, "The attention of courts-martial and of reviewing officers is called to the danger of associating with the honorable and important duty of guards any idea of punishment or degradation. These remarks are called forth in disapproving the sentence of a court-martial directing that a prisoner shall do guard duty every other day for a year."[1]

Where a court-martial sentenced a soldier for absence without leave "to serve one year after his present term of enlistment expires," the following remarks were made,— Courts-martial are reminded that "additional service" is not mentioned by regulations, or by any text writer, as one of the punishments proper to be inflicted by them. Sentences for "absence without leave" cannot be supported by analogy to cases of "desertion," for the reason that the service required in cases of desertion is not by virtue of the sentence, or dependent upon it, but results by operation of law in fulfillment of a contract. The military service of the United States has always been considered honorable. It does not therefore comport with the honor, dignity, or security of the service to use it as a punishment for an offender. Such use will go far to destroy the *esprit de corps* which is so essential to the efficiency of an army.[2]

Where a court proceeded to direct that an officer tried should be discharged from arrest and returned to duty with his regiment, the commanding general held that "this was an entire transcending of the province of the court."[3]

[1] G. O. 3, A. G. O. Jan. 2, 1864. G. C. M. O. 7, A. G. O. May 19, 1871.

[2] G. C. M. O. 329, A. G. O. Oct. 19, 1864. But in 1865 "absence without leave" was placed in this respect on the same footing as "desertion," as previously stated in this Chapter.

[3] G. O. 18, A. G. O. Jan. 18, 1862.

CHAPTER XIII.

SENTENCE.

THE court having come to a finding, proceeds to a sentence. If the finding is "not guilty," they should acquit the accused, but if the finding is "guilty" they should award a sentence.

The punishments in the Articles of War are of two general classes, *mandatory* and *discretionary*. Under a mandatory article, in a finding of guilty, the court are obliged to award the punishment named in the article, no matter what their ideas may be as to its justness for the offense in question. The power which creates the court—Congress—has decided what are the appropriate penalties for the offenses named under these articles, and, in so doing, has placed the matter entirely beyond the decision of the court.

Under a mandatory article a court cannot give a greater punishment than the articles prescribe.[1] Where an officer was charged with and found guilty of "conduct unbecoming an officer and a gentleman" under the articles of war,[2] and sentenced, "to be dishonorably dismissed the service of the United States, to forfeit all pay and emoluments that may now be, or become due him, and to be utterly disqualified to hold any office or employment whatever in the service of the United States," the sentence was disapproved, on the ground that it exceeds the penalty pre-

[1] G. O. 163, A. G. O., April 15, 1854. [2] Art. 61.

scribed by the Article of War[1] for the offense of which the officer was convicted.

Mandatory. In the following cases the sentences are mandatory,

Art. 5. Knowingly, mustering persons not soldiers.

Art. 6. Taking money, etc., by way of gratification on mustering.

Art. 8. Making false returns.

Art. 13. Signing false certificate.

Art. 14. Making false muster.

Art. 15. Allowing military stores to be damaged, lost, etc.

Art. 17. Soldier losing and spoiling accoutrements.

Art. 18. Commanders laying a duty on victuals, etc.

Art. 25. Using reproachful speeches.

Art. 26. Sending challenge.

Art. 27. Allowing persons to go out and fight duels.

Art. 28. Upbraiding an officer or soldier for refusing to fight a duel.

Art. 37. Non-commissioned officers conniving at hiring of duty.

Art. 38. Officer drunk on duty.

Art. 50. Knowingly receiving and entertaining deserter.

Art. 52. Misconduct at divine service.

Art. 53. Using profane oaths.

Art. 57. Forcing a safeguard.

Art. 58. Larceny, robbery, etc., in time of war.

Art. 59. Refusing to deliver offender to civil authority.

Art. 61. Conduct unbecoming an officer and a gentleman.

Art. 65. Breach of arrest.

Sec. 1343.[2] Lurking as a spy.

In all other cases courts-martial have a discretionary

[1] 61st. [2] Revised Statutes.

power as to punishments, but must remember their oath to be guided by the provisions of the rules and articles of war, and, where a doubt arises not explained by those articles, then by their consciences, the best of their understanding, and the custom of war in like cases.

Voting on Sentence. Each member is required to vote upon a sentence, and, even though a member may have voted "not guilty," if the majority of the court (or two-thirds where the death penalty is involved) vote "guilty," it is his duty to vote an appropriate punishment: and where the offense falls under an article mandatory as to punishment, to vote for such sentence. There has been much difference of opinion upon this point, but the rule above given seems to be the accepted one in this country. While at first glance it may seem improper for a member who believes an accused innocent to vote to punish him, yet, this comes from the twofold character—as judges and jurymen—in which the members act. In the latter capacity they vote on the finding, in the former on the sentence. The same thing happens in civil cases where a judge, having heard all the evidence, and believing the prisoner innocent, is nevertheless obliged to declare a sentence on the finding of the jury.

Manner of Voting. The manner of voting in a discretionary punishment is as follows:—Each member of the court or such members as see fit, write out a sentence; these are collected by the judge-advocate who reads them to the court, and then proceeds to take its vote commencing with the lightest recommended. If this is rejected he takes the next lightest in order, and so on till one is agreed to by the proper number. Where an agreement cannot easily be reached, it is suggested that a vote first be taken on the kind of punishment best to be awarded; for instance, whether it shall be confinement, or forfeiture or both combined. This being agreed upon, the amount can more easily be settled.

If the members of the court are unable to agree upon a sentence, which would rarely ever happen, all that can be done is for the reviewing officer to adopt the same course as prescribed in failure to agree upon a finding.

Changing Sentence. Courts-martial, at any time during their sitting, may reconsider any judgment or sentence rendered by them, and alter it as seems to them proper. This was first illustrated in our service in the case of Peter Williamson, a soldier tried for desertion. He was sentenced "to confinement at hard labor with ball and chain." On the ensuing day, at the suggestion of a member, the said sentence was reconsidered and the court substituted the following :—"that the said Peter Williamson be shot to death." The question of the power of the court to so act was referred to Attorney General Wirt who said,—"In courts of civil jurisdiction when sitting even in criminal cases, the court is not concluded by an opinion which they may have expressed in any one day of its session, the whole subject being completely within its control until the end of the term, and I am not apprised of any difference in the powers of the two courts over the subjects which severally belong to them during the continuance of their respective terms.

"If a civil court of criminal jurisdiction, therefore, may lawfully reconsider and alter during the term, any opinion which it may have pronounced on a previous day of the same term; so, in like manner, I conceive may a court-martial * * * A general court-martial convened for general purposes, continues a court with full powers while it has any business to do, of which it alone is the judge; and while it so continues a court, its power of judicial deliberation and decision over all the subjects which may have been brought before it is as full on the last day of its sittings as on any preceding day. I am of the opinion that the court had the power to alter the opinion they had expressed on the preceding day, and that their final opinion is regularly and legally pronounced."[1]

The question again came up in 1844, but was complicated, as it involved the right of a *mutilated* court to change a former judgment or sentence. A General Order from the War Department published the following decision:

"However it may be asserted that the usage and laws of courts-martial may sanction the right of the court to amend and entirely change their positive decision at any time before their final adjournment, yet it is a right that should be cautiously exercised, and only on obvious and extraordinary occasions. In the present instance, a full court acquitted the prisoner, and upon the next day a mutilated court, one member being absent, undertake to rescind the judgment of the previous day, and to pronounce the accused guilty and sentence him to punishment. To justify such reversal, the court should be as full and constituted precisely as it was, when the first judgment was pronounced. In consequence of this irregularity, the proceedings of the court are disapproved." [2]

If, however, a mutilated court, on revision, can alter its sentence as is now held to be the case, there is no reason why such alteration should not be made during the original proceedings.[3]

It frequently happens that there are circumstances connected with a case which lead courts to award a milder punishment than they ordinarily would for similar offenses. Thus age, inexperience, length of service, aggravating

[1] I. Opinions Att'y Gen'l, Aug. 29, 1819.
[2] G. O. 40, A. G. O. Oct. 14, 1844. [3] See Chapter XIV. page. 192.

causes, etc., may be reasons for such action. In these cases it is well for the court to add something to indicate its reasons for so doing. Without it, their action may appear inconsistent to the reviewing authority and have a bad effect upon the discipline of the service. The following form is frequently used : "The court is thus lenient on account of the previous good character of the accused as shown in evidence." Any reason, of course, may be assigned.

Some doubt has arisen as to whether a court in awarding a sentence could take into consideration previous confinement, or whether this was purely a matter for the reviewing authority. On this point, the Secretary of War in 1874 said,—"It appears in evidence that the prisoner was in confinement some time before his trial; but the court, having the power to fix the sentence, could take this into consideration, and adjust the punishment accordingly."[1]

Recommendations to Clemency. As it may often happen, especially in mandatory sentences, that the punishment for the particular case tried is greater than the members deem appropriate, recommendations to clemency are made by all or part of the members, setting forth reasons to induce leniency on the part of the reviewing authority. It is well settled that such recommendations are no part of the judicial proceedings or record of the court; it is merely the personal act of the parties signing it. The recommendation should be signed by all the members making it, but they should be careful not to indicate to the reviewing authority the particular mode in which he should exercise his clemency.

Such recommendations should not be embodied in the proceedings, but attached to, or forwarded separately

[1] G. C. M. O. 62, A. G. O., Aug. 10.

with them.[1] Recommendations to mercy should be made with care. Where six members of a court recommended an accused (found guilty of drawing money on fraudulent discharge final statement papers) to clemency on account of previous good character, the Secretary of War said, "The officers recommending the accused to clemency are admonished as to the impropriety of such recommendations in favor of convicted forgers, which can only tend to lower the standard of honesty and trust-worthiness in the military service, and bring courts-martial into low esteem."[2]

Forfeiture of Pay. In forfeiting a soldier's pay, courts-martial frequently except the just dues of the laundress. This is not necessary, as it has been held that so much of the pay of a soldier as is required to satisfy the certified claims of a laundress cannot be diverted from that object by sentence of a court-martial.[3]

Sentences of forfeiture of pay cannot apply to the "deposits" of an enlisted man under the act of 1872.

Meaning of Word Month. The word *month* as used in common parlance, and in ordinary business transactions, means a calendar and not a lunar month, and in the case of a sentence by court-martial it is to be so construed.[4]

[1] The members making recommendations to clemency are required to state on the record their reasons for such recommendations, in the Articles recently proposed.

[2] G. O. 342, A. G. O., Oct. 19, 1863.

[3] Regulations, ¶ 1329.

[4] Opinions J. A. G., p. 344.

CHAPTER XIV.

CONFIRMATION.

No sentence of a court-martial can be carried into execution until the proceedings shall have been approved by the officer ordering the court, or by the officer commanding for the time being.[1]

To this end the judge-advocate should forward the authenticated proceedings as expeditiously as possible to the officer having authority to confirm the sentence. Whether he will forward the proceedings of each case as soon as finished, or retain and forward all the cases tried at the end of the session, will depend upon circumstances. The latter is the ordinary custom, but, when there is a probability of a court sitting for several days, it is better to forward each case, thus doing as little injustice as possible.[2]

The reviewing authority must state his decisions and orders on the proceedings in each case.[3] The orders and decisions should properly be written *in* the record *at the end* of the proceedings, and, though the case may require the action of a higher authority, these "orders, etc.," should appear. A mere reference or forwarding of the record in such cases is not expressive of any "decision" or "order" thereon, and does not fulfill the requirements of the law.[4] He should formally act on it and note his

[1] Art. 104.

[2] Proceedings should be forwarded with a letter of transmittal; the charges and papers connected therewith being enclosed.

[3] Regulations, par. 896. [4] Opinions J. A. G., p. 318.

approval or disapproval. This action of the reviewing authority is a legal act on his part, which is required before the sentence can be executed; and, as the law requires a particular person to perform the act, it cannot be delegated. The Judge-Advocate General advises that the approval or disapproval of the reviewing officer should be attested by his personal signature, and that the custom of impressing his name by a stamp, or having it affixed in his name by his Adjutant General, should be discountenanced.[1]

This power conferred upon the reviewing officer is of great importance. By his approval he may, with some few exceptions, decide that the punishments awarded shall be inflicted, and, unless such approval is given, it cannot be executed. By his disapproval he may render the proceedings nugatory and thus terminate any future proceedings in the case,[2] and this whether he has the power of final approval or not.

Neither the President or Secretary of War have power to approve or disapprove a sentence of a court-martial in a case where it may lawfully be carried into execution on the confirmation of the officer ordering the court.[3]

The power of confirmation includes the right to approve of certain parts of the proceedings, to disapprove of others; to send the case back to the court for reconsideration or revision; to comment on the action of the court, the judge-advocate or accused, or any portion of the record; and this is not only the right, but the duty of the reviewing officer. He should be careful that no fatal defects in the record are overlooked; should call the attention of the

[1] The personal examination of proceedings by reviewing officers and the indorsement of their approval of the sentence, upon the record, over their own signatures is required by the Articles of War recently proposed.

[2] G. O. 209, A. G. O. July 7, 1863.

[3] XI Opinions Attorney General, June 20, 1865.

court in the orders promulgating the proceedings to any irregularities; in fact should make a careful and thorough revision of the case, and be governed in his decisions by the rules of law.

In a *circular* issued from the War Department in 1874, commanders, in reviewing the proceedings of courts-martial, are requested to be careful not to omit to note the date of their action in the proper place of each record. The history of the case, as it should fully appear, is imperfect without such date.

Proceedings may be confirmed but not approved.[1]

If the finding upon two or more charges be "guilty," the reviewing officer may disapprove the finding on one of these, and, approving the other, direct the sentence to be executed, provided it is appropriate to the offense under the approved charge. The same would be true in a single charge where he disapproves of portions of the testimony, or of the proceedings; he may approve the sentence, provided the parts disapproved do not affect the validity of the proceedings.

The reviewing officer could not disapprove the proceedings in a case, and then direct that the sentence be executed, or order it executed in a mitigated form. When the proceedings are disapproved there is no legal sentence which can be executed.

In 1874 a soldier convicted of desertion was sentenced, "to be dishonorably discharged the service of the United States, etc., and to be confined in such military penitentiary as the commanding general may direct." There being no such place as a "military penitentiary," and confinement in any penitentiary for a purely military offense being illegal, the reviewing officer held that "when a sentence is divisible into distinct parts, and one of these

[1] G. O. 54, A. G. O., Aug. 19, 1843.

is contrary to law, it is within the power of the reviewing authority to give effect to that which is legal, setting aside the illegal part. * * * On the other hand, a sentence conforming to law cannot be substituted by the reviewing authority for one which is contrary to law. The substitution of one punishment for another can only be resorted to in exercise of the power of mitigation, but a sentence cannot be mitigated until it has been confirmed, and its confirmation rests upon its legality. It is accordingly neither within the power of the reviewing authority to confirm the illegal part of a sentence for the purpose of giving it a legal effect by mitigation, nor to supply this absence of power by confirming the sentence with the exception of the illegal part, substituting for the latter a punishment which would have been legal. When a sentence, or part of a sentence, is contrary to law, it (or so much of it) is void, and, unless amended on a reassembling of the court, must be disapproved.[1]

The question has arisen as to the power of a reviewing officer to suspend a sentence, the suspension to be dependent on the future good behavior of the parties. In a case in which this was done, the Judge-Advocate General said: "However beneficial to the interests of the service the plan adopted by Col. M. may be, about which I refrain from expressing an opinion, I know of no authority, either in statutes or in the customs of the service for the practice originated by him."[2] Such a suspension was however made by the Secretary of War in 1866 in the case of certain cadets.[3]

Approval of Secretary of War. It had long been considered settled that the Secretary of War, "as the

[1] G. O. 101, Hdqrs. Mil. Div. of the Atlantic, Dec. 31, 1874, approved by the Judge-Advocate General, Dec. 22, 1874.

[2] Bureau of Military Justice, Feb. 25, 1870.

[3] G. C. M. O., A. G. O., Feb. 10, 1866.

regular constitutional organ of the President," had the power of acting upon court-martial proceedings requiring the President's approval."[1] Where it was objected in a sentence of dismissal of an officer that the sentence was published as confirmed "by order of the Secretary of War," and that the requirements of Article 106, "requiring the confirmation of the President," had not been complied with, the Judge-Advocate General held that such objection could not be sustained.[2]

In the case of Major Runkle, however, notwithstanding the proceedings were laid before the President (Gen. Grant) and approved as mitigated by him, yet, because his signature was not attached to the record but signed by the Secretary of War, President Hayes decided that he was improperly dismissed, revoked the order of dismissal, and disapproved the proceedings and sentence, reinstating him in the army.[3] His case came before the Senate for decision, upon the legality of the latter action, and is still undecided.

In the similar case of Capt. Armes, the Senate Committee on Military Affairs held that the President's duty in this regard (*i. e.* as reviewing officer) is judicial, and therefore cannot be performed by any one save the President himself. The record of *his* judgment, of *his* "decision and orders" may, of course, like any ministerial act, be performed by another hand, but the judgment, the decision, the orders in the case, must result from the operations of his mind and conscience.[4]

Article 104 directs that the proceedings be approved by the officer ordering the court, *or by the officer commanding for the time being.* Where the officer who convened a

[1] Opinions Attorney-General, p. 330. U. S. *vs.* Eliason, 16 Peters 291, Wilcox *vs.* Jackson, 13 Peters 498.

[2] Opinions J. A. G., p. 25.

[3] S. O. 166, A. G. O., August 4, 1874.

[4] Senate Report 121, 45th Congress, 2d Session.

court-martial has ceased at the date of the sentence and termination of the proceedings to exercise the command to which the accused belongs, the proceedings must be reviewed by his successor in such command. And where the regiments and companies of a number of enlisted men at the date of their conviction, had been separated from the command of the general who convened the court, the Judge-Advocate General held that the proper reviewing officer in each case was the officer commanding the division, etc., to which the company or regiment of the accused was attached.[1]

Some question has arisen as to who is the proper reviewing officer in cases tried by courts convened by a department commander, when such commander is absent from the department. For a long time department commanders have been accustomed to act on proceedings, even when thousands of miles away from their department. This was done on the ground that they are appointed as such by the President, and that the right remains in them until regularly relieved, and that the next in command, unless so designated by the President, is not the department commander so as to allow him to act on court-martial proceedings. In the late case of Capt. Campbell, Sixth Cavalry, where the proceedings were confirmed by a department commander, on leave of absence some 1500 miles beyond the limits of his department, the proceedings were disapproved on this ground.

The Superintendent of the United States Military Academy has power to convene courts-martial for the trial of cadets, and to execute the sentences of such courts, except the sentences of suspension and dismission, subject to the same limitations and conditions now existing as to other general courts-martial.

[1] Opinions J. A. G., p. 24.

In those cases, however, where the power of final confirmation and execution resides in a higher authority, the original reviewing officer—that is, the officer ordering the court,—has an absolute power by disapproval to render the sentence nugatory. In forwarding such proceedings, however, if he approves them, he should always subscribe a *formal approval*.[1]

No officer can review the proceedings of a court upon which he sat as a member. Should an officer, sitting as a member of a court-martial, succeed the convening officer in command before the proceedings are forwarded for approval, he cannot review them as "commanding officer for the time being," but must forward them to his proper superior.

Approval of President. There are certain cases in which the sentences of courts-martial cannot be executed without the approval of the President. These are:

1st. Death sentences.

The Articles[2] direct that no sentence of a court-martial, inflicting the punishment of death, shall be carried into execution until it shall have been confirmed by the President. To this there are some exceptions *in time of war*, in the case of persons convicted as spies, mutineers, deserters, murderers, or guerilla maurauders convicted of robbery, burglary, arson, rape, assault with intent to commit rape, or of violations of the laws and customs of war. In these cases the sentence of death may be carried into execution, upon confirmation, by the commanding general in the field, or the commander of the department as the case may be.

2d. Dismissal of an officer in time of peace.[3]

In time of war, while the sentence of dismissal of an officer does not require the approval of the President,

1 Opinions J. A. G., p. 55. [2] Art. 105. [3] Article 106.

Art. 107 provides that no sentence of a court-martial, appointed by the commander of a division, or of a separate brigade of troops, directing the dismissal of an officer, shall be carried into execution until it shall have been confirmed by the general commanding the army in the field to which the division or brigade belongs.

In this connection Article 111 should be read. "Any officer who has authority to carry into execution the sentence of death, or of dismissal of an officer, may suspend the same until the pleasure of the President shall be known, and, in such case he shall immediately transmit to the President a copy of the order of suspension, together with a copy of the proceedings of the court."

3d. Sentences respecting general officers.[1]

With these exceptions all sentences of a court-martial may be confirmed and carried into execution by the officer ordering the court, or by the officer commanding for the time being.

Regulations formerly authorized a superior military commander to the officer confirming the proceedings to suspend the execution of the sentence, when, in his judgment it was void upon the face of the proceedings, or when he saw a fit case for executive clemency.[2] In 1853, it was held to be not only within the authority, but the duty of every commander attentively to inspect and supervise the proceedings of courts-martial within his command.[3] In 1874, the Secretary of War held that this portion of Par. 889 of the Army Regulations (after first clause) as legally inoperative, because inconsistent with the 65th and 89th Articles of War,[4] in authorizing a commander not contemplated by those articles (viz. a superior military commander to the officer confirming

[1] Art. 108. [2] Regulations 1863, par. 899.
[3] G. O. 22, A. G. O., Aug. 23, 1853. [4] Present 109th and 112th.

the proceedings) to "suspend" and "prohibit" the execution of sentences. G. O. 22, Aug. 23d, 1853, above quoted, so far as conveying a contrary view, was therefore revoked.[1]

This order, in 1874, was held by the Judge-Advocate General to apply only to the proceedings of *general* courts-martial, and not to prohibit a department commander from suspending the execution of the sentence of a *garrison* court approved by the post commander.[2]

The proceedings of the minor courts-martial must be transmitted without delay by the garrison or other commander to the department headquarters for the supervision of the department commander.[3]

Such a commander is authorized to set aside the proceedings of such courts, so forwarded to him, without reference to the War Department.[4] By this is not meant power to set aside proceedings not invalid in themselves, but only such as are illegal in some particular. This is implied from a decision of the Judge-Advocate General since the publication of the Digest, which was approved by the Secretary of War.[5]

Field Officer's Court. The 110th Article directs that no sentence of a field officer, detailed to try soldiers of his regiment, shall be carried into execution, until the whole proceedings shall have been approved by the brigade commander, or, in case there be no brigade commander, by the commanding officer of the post.

In reviewing these cases, the regularity of the proceedings, and the adaptation of the punishment to the offense of which the party has been found guilty, are the only questions on which the reviewing officer can be enabled to pass

[1] G. O. 72, A. G. O., July 7, 1873.

[2] Bureau of Military Justice, Dec. 27, 1873.

[3] Regulations, par. 898.

[4] Opinions J. A. G., p. 28.

[5] Letter from A. G. O., Dec. 28, 1873.

a judgment. It could not have been contemplated that he should inquire into the sufficiency of the testimony to sustain the sentence. Had this been intended it would have been necessary to spread upon the record the evidence in all its details in each case, and such a record it would often be out of the power of the "field officer" to prepare.[1]

Revision. It is not within the power of the reviewing authority to enlarge the punishment awarded by a court-martial, nor change it except by way of mitigation, which will hereafter be discussed. If he deems the sentence inadequate, or if he finds portions of the record defective which can properly be corrected, he should reconvene the court, or, if in session, return the proceedings with such suggestions as he deems proper. If the court has been dissolved by order of the reviewing officer, it cannot be reconvened, but if not, it is still a legal court.

Procedure. When a court is reconvened for a *substantial* amendment to its record, the reconvening order should be spread upon the record, which should show that at least five members of the court, the judge-advocate, and the accused were present, and that the amendment was then made to conform to, and express the truth in the case.

A mere *clerical* error can be corrected without having the accused present, and of course where the question for reconsideration touches the finding or sentence, the court would sit with closed doors.

The correction of a clerical error in the material averment of the swearing of the court, etc., effected by means of a simple interlineation upon the record, is not sufficient in law. The authority by which the correction is made must appear, and the record must show that the court was duly reassembled and the correction regularly made at a

[1] Opinions J. A. G., p. 176.

formal session. If the court has been dissolved, the record corrected only by such formal interlineation in the particular referred to, is invalid, and the sentence inoperative.[1]

A reviewing authority has no power to compel a court-martial to alter its sentence. He can only recommend certain action upon reconvening it, and, if the court disagree with him, it may adhere to its original finding and sentence. It would be proper for a court, in adhering to its original findings and sentence, to state its reasons for so doing, although this is optional with the court.

Number of Revisions. In 1843 the Secretary of War held that, as there was no restriction in our rules and articles, proceedings may be remanded for revision as often as the superior authority shall deem necessary for attaining the purposes of justice.[2] There is nothing said in our articles on the subject of revision, but the rule which obtained in the English service at the time of adoption of our articles has, by custom of the service, it is believed, obtained in ours. In that service the proceedings can be sent back but once.[3]

Receiving New Testimony. It is the general rule of law that no new testimony can be legally taken before a reconvened court. In 1872, however, the Judge-Advocate General held "that when a court has erred in its rulings in the rejection of a witness for supposed incompetency, or in rejecting offered documentary evidence, or in not permitting a proper and legal question to be put to a witness, the reviewing authority should reconvene the court for a reconsideration of its action, with suggestions for its guidance, and that the court may, therefore, should it concur in the views submitted, proceed to remedy the error or errors pointed out.

[1] Opinions J. A. G., p. 317. [2] G. O. 2, A. G. O., Jan. 13, 1844.
[3] See VI. Opinions Attorney General, p. 204.

"No witness not previously called can legally be examined before a reconvened court.

"In cases where courts are reconvened, and their attention called to such errors of ruling as have been herein referred to, and they become convinced of their error, they may, it is true, modify or completely change their findings; but, if this is done without having before them the excluded witness or document, or hearing the response to the rejected question, it is obvious that the ends of justice may not be accomplished.[1]"

The prisoner and his counsel should be present under such circumstances, and it may be necessary for him to call witnesses in rebuttal of statements made at such time.

In 1874 a court improperly refused to call a witness for the accused. Upon this fact being submitted to them (the court being reconvened) by the reviewing authority, the court still refused to call the witness on the ground that, not having been summoned and put upon the stand, he had not been "called" in the sense of the above order. This view was held erroneous by the reviewing authority and his opinion confirmed by the Judge-Advocate General. The latter said, —"Under a fair interpretation of the record, the witness in this case must be treated as having been 'called' so far as it was practicable for the accused to call him."[2]

Revision by Mutilated Court. A question of considerable importance has arisen as to the power of a mutilated court to revise its proceedings upon being reconvened. A general court-martial assembled at West Point in 1853, for the trial of two cadets, and was reconvened by the Secretary of War to revise its sentence. On re-assem-

[1] G. O. 82, A. G. O., Aug. 29, 1872.

[2] G. C. M. O. 55, Hdqrs. Dept. of California, Dec. 13, 1875, approved by Secry. of War, Nov. 29, 1875.

bling two of the original members were absent, and the question as to the power of such a court to revise its sentence was referred to the Attorney-General, who held that the absence of the two members at the re-assembling of the court did not impair its jurisdiction, or otherwise affect its power to revise the sentence; and that it was the same continuous and competent court as when it first assembled under the order of the Secretary.[1]

Such remains the law as expounded by the Attorney-General and adopted by the War Department; but, insomuch as apparent injustice at least might be done an accused by a mutilated court changing its finding or sentence, its members should well consider the matter before taking such action.

"Although a court-martial, on revision, is competent to amend any defect which has resulted from its own decision, not connected with questions of legality of procedure, it yet nevertheless cannot amend any illegality as to the constitution of the court, or any defect in its composition; nor can any illegality in the charge be so remedied. Such deficiencies must be fatal to all the proceedings, and any sentence or opinions rendered by them be innoxious to the prisoner."[2]

The President may direct a court-martial to reconsider their judgment in cases where his previous sanction is necessary for the execution of such judgment.[3]

PARDON AND MITIGATION.

By the Constitution of the United States the President has power to grant reprieves and pardons for all offenses against the United States, except in cases of impeachment.[4]

Every officer who is authorized to order a general

[1] VII. Opinions Att'y-Gen., p. 338 *et seq.* Published in G. O. 19, A. G. O. Nov. 12, 1855.
[2] De Hart, p. 207.
[3] IV. Opinions Att'y-Gen. April 20, 1842.
[4] Art. II. § 2.

court-martial has power to pardon or mitigate any punishment adjudged by it except the punishment of death, or of dismissal of an officer.

Every officer commanding a regiment or garrison in which the minor courts-martial may be held, has power to pardon or mitigate any punishment which such court may adjudge.[1]

Definitions. A *pardon* is an act of grace proceeding from the power invested with the execution of the laws, which exempts the individual on whom it is bestowed from the punishment the law inflicts for a crime he has committed.[2]

Pardons are of various kinds: They may be *absolute* or *conditional*,[3] *full* or *partial*, of a *general* nature or granted to a *single* individual.

Absolute. An absolute pardon frees the person without any condition, but this cannot reach an *executed* sentence which has been regularly imposed by a competent court.

If a sentence has been executed in part, the remainder may be remitted. Thus, where a sentence imposes imprisonment and dishonorable discharge at the end, a pardon, after a portion of the imprisonment had been executed, would entitle a soldier to an honorable discharge.

The pardoning power is co-extensive with the power to punish. It includes the power of remission of fines, penalties, and forfeitures which are imposed by law as punishment for offenses.

The power, however, does not go to the length of making restitutions of fines, penalties and forfeitures after

[1] Article 112. [2] U. S. *vs.* Wilson, 7 Peters, 150.

[3] I. Opinions Att'y-Gen'l March 30, 1820, V. Ibid May 10, 1851, U. S. *vs.* Wilson, 7 Peters 150, Ex parte Wells, 18 Howard 307, Ex parte Garland, 4 Wallace, 333–380.

they have been actually paid into the Treasury.[1] An officer's or soldier's pay is regarded as in the Treasury until delivered to him.[2] A pardon by the President could not therefore restore forfeited pay.

Conditional. A conditional pardon annexes a condition which must be performed before the pardon can take effect—for instance, the President might pardon a military officer under the sentence of death, on the previous condition of resigning his commission.[3] If the conditions are not complied with, or not accepted, the pardon is null and void. The Supreme Court of the United States has decided that "a pardon is not complete without acceptance. It may be rejected by the person to whom it is tendered, and we have discovered no power in a court to force it upon him."[4]

Full. A full pardon has the effect generally to restore a party to all his rights. There is an exception to this, however, in the case of perjury. A pardon will not qualify a person to be a witness at any time afterwards.[5]

Partial. A partial pardon is, as its name implies, a condoning of a portion of the punishment. It is authorized in case of sentences to two kinds of punishment, the one pecuniary and the other corporal.[6]

General. A general pardon extends to a class of individuals, or a distinct class of offenses. *Example.* The proclamation of the President as to deserters of March 11, 1865.

Special. A special pardon applies to a single individual.

There is a difference between a general and a special

[1] II. Opinions Att'y-General, March 17, 1830, VIII. Ibid Jan. 1, 1857, XII. Ibid Nov. 2, 1866.

[2] Opinions J. A. G., p. 261. [3] I. Opinions Att'y Gen'l, March 30, 1820.

[4] U. S. *vs.* Wilson, 7 Peters, 150. [5] Sec. 5392 Rev. Statutes.

[6] XI. Opinions Att'y-General, p. 35.

pardon, in the manner in which they are brought to the notice of a court. The court takes judicial cognizance of the former, while the latter must be brought specially to its notice.

The pardoning power may be exercised at any time after the commission of an offense, as well as before legal proceedings are taken, or while they are pending, as after conviction and judgment.[1]

In 1874 *Congress* relieved a number of persons from the proceedings, findings, and sentence of a court-martial held in 1865, and wherein the parties were severally convicted of mutiny; setting aside and revoking the proceedings, findings, and sentence, and restoring the said persons in all respects to the same rights and privileges to which they would have been entitled if said proceedings, findings, and sentence had not been had or rendered.[2]

Mitigation. In addition to the power of pardon, the power to mitigate is conferred on the reviewing officer. Mitigation, generally speaking, is making a punishment less in degree, preserving the same species.

Some question has arisen in past years, as to whether the power of mitigation includes that of commutation—*i. e.*, to substitute a different punishment. As the sentence of *death* and *dismissal* admit of no technical mitigation, the question is of much importance. In the case of Private William Bansman this point was involved. Attorney-General Wirt, to whom the case was referred, said: "The only question is whether the power of mitigating a punishment includes the power of changing its species, or whether it means anything more than *lessening the quantity*, preserving nevertheless the *species of the punishment*," and held "that a power of mitigation, in *general terms*, leaves the manner

[1] Ex. parte Garland, 4 Wallace 333–380, VI. Opinions Attorney General April 15, 1853, VII. Ibid, p. 20.

[2] G. O. 51, A. G. O., June 4, 1874.

of performing this act of mercy to himself; (the President) and if it can be performed in no other way than by changing its species, the President has, in my opinion, the power of adopting this form of mitigation. Such is precisely the case under consideration. A sentence of death cannot be mitigated in any other way than by changing the punishment. To deny him the power of changing the punishment in this instance, is to deny him the power of mitigating the severest of all punishments, while you leave open to him the comparatively insignificant power of mitigating the milder class of punishments: or in other words to refuse mercy in the case in which, of all others, it is most loudly demanded."[1]

This opinion is upheld in several other decisions of different Attorneys General.[2]

The same views have been held on the subject of *dismissal.* In the case of Surgeon Guillon, U. S. A., the Attorney-General held that the President has ample power to mitigate the sentences of courts-martial by commuting sentences of dismission from the service to suspension without pay or emoluments for a limited time. For as dismission deprived the officer of his pay forever, the suspension of his office and his pay for one year only is an inferior and milder degree of the punishment decreed by the court.[3]

The Statutes of Congress recognize the fact that the President under certain circumstances can commute sentences of courts-martial.[4]

As a *commutation* is virtually a conditional pardon, the party must accept it, or otherwise even the President can-

[1] I. Opinions Attorney General January 4, 1820.

[2] IV. Ibid, March 18, 1842; Ibid Sept. 18, 1845; Ibid Oct. 16, 1845; V, Ibid Oct. 12, 1848.

[3] V. Opinions Attorney-General, Oct. 12, 1848.

[4] Article 99, § 1229, Revised Statutes.

not commute a sentence. In 1843 Capt. Ramsay, of the navy, was sentenced by a court-martial "to be suspended from all rank and command in the navy of the United States, for and during the period of five years." The President ordered that the sentence be commuted "to suspension for six months without pay." The Attorney-General decided that Capt. Ramsay was entitled to his pay during the six months suspension, notwithstanding the terms in which the President commuted his sentence. He said,—"It does not appear that the commutation of the sentence was made at Capt. R.'s request, or that the condition was accepted by him. The executive has no power, while an officer retains his commission and is not sentenced by a court-martial to that effect, to take from him the pay which the law gives him."[1]

Reviewing officers, other than the President, have no authority under the general power of *mitigation* to commute a sentence.

Reviewing officers cannot pardon or mitigate the sentences of death or of dismissal of an officer.[2]

Any officer who has authority to carry into execution the sentence of death or of dismissal of an officer, may suspend the same until the pleasure of the President shall be known; and, in such case he shall immediately transmit to the President a copy of the order of suspension, together with a copy of the proceedings of the court.[3] This does not confer the power of commutation.[4]

In general, it may be said, in the language of a General Order, that "the powers and duties of a commander in acting on the proceedings of a court-martial are fixed by the articles of war. As to any particular punishments

[1] IV. Opinions Attorney-General, Oct. 16, 1845.

[2] Article 112.

[3] Art. 111.

[4] VI. Opinions Attorney-General, Sept. 20, 1853. G. O. 198, A. G. O., June 30, 1863.

imposed by a sentence approved by him, he must either execute the same as imposed or else pardon or mitigate it. Beyond this the articles give him (in time of peace) no discretion."[1] In this case a reviewing officer had postponed the time of a dishonorable discharge required by a sentence to be imposed at once, to the end of an imposed confinement. It was held that this was not an executing of the sentence as it stood, nor was it a form of pardon. Further, it was not a mitigation, since it did not substitute for the particular penalty a lesser degree of punishment of the same species (which is that in which mitigation consists, as defined by the Attorneys-General) but merely defers its enforcement while retaining it unchanged in kind and quality. Such a postponement was thus regarded as not coming within the statutory authority of a reviewing officer.

General Observations. The successor of a reviewing authority has no power to review proceedings approved by his predecessor. He may exercise the power of pardon, or mitigation, if he deems proper.

An order on duty and command of a person under sentence of suspension, is an *express* remission, not of the whole sentence, but of the unexecuted residue of the sentence.

An order to attend as witness at a court-martial does not operate as a constructive pardon.[2]

During the war a practice grew up of setting aside approved sentences of dismissal awarded by courts-martial and giving to such remission the effect of a restoration. The law now provides that no officer of the army who has been or may be dismissed from the service by the sentence of a general court-martial, formally approved by the proper

[1] G. O. 71, A. G. O., July 10, 1875.
[2] VI. Opinions Attorney General, Sept. 12, 1854.

reviewing authority, shall ever be restored to the military service, except by a reappointment confirmed by the Senate.[1]

Section 6 of General Orders No. 12, 1877, establishing a military prison, authorizes and directs the Secretary of War to remit, in part, the sentence of those convicts who by their obedience, honesty, industry, or general good conduct earn such favor, and to give them an honorable restoration to duty in case the same is merited.

Animadversions. The reviewing authority may animadvert upon the action of the members, judge-advocate, prisoner, witnesses, officer preferring charges,[2] or any person whose name is connected with the charges.[3]

New Trial. The 102d Article directs that no person shall be tried a second time for the same offence. When a court-martial has regularly come to a finding and sentence, and forwarded the proceedings to the reviewing authority, that constitutes a trial. The reviewing officer cannot upon disapproval, or because he thinks the sentence inadequate, set aside the proceedings and order a new trial. In only one case—*i. e.* where the court had no jurisdiction, would he be authorized to so act.

This does not prevent the ordering of a new trial on the application of the accused. In 1818 Captain Hall applied to the President for a new trial, on the ground that the court had refused to receive certain evidence which was both legal and material to the defense. Attorney General Wirt, to whom the matter was referred, held that the President of the United States had the power to order a new trial for the benefit of the accused. "It is very apparent," he said, "that the whole of Article 87 (present 102d) is designed *for the benefit* of the party accused, not

[1] Revised Statutes, Sec. 1228. [2] G. O. 42, A. G. O. July 24, 1851.
[3] G. O. 36, A. G. O. Jan. 10, 1851.

for his prejudice. * * The plea *is his* (the prisoner's) *privilege*, which he may either use or waive at his pleasure, and if he does not use it, however the fact may be, the court will not take notice of it so as to bar the trial.[1]

In the case of Captain Van Bokkelen, owing to certain irregular action of the court, the accused was allowed to say whether he would stand by the verdict, or claim a new trial. He requested the latter, which was granted him.[2]

Several cases have arisen where officers, whose sentences have been executed, have applied for new trials on the ground of irregularities in the proceedings of the court. The decisions of several of the Attorneys-General have been opposed to such right. In the language of Attorney-General Legare, "It is a vain conceit that, because the proceedings are irregular, and fatally irregular (if the exception be taken at the proper time) the judgment once suffered to be entered up is void.[3]

Attorney-General Cushing held that after the sentence of a court-martial dismissing an officer has been approved and acted on by the President, it cannot be revised except for suggestion of absolute nullity in the proceedings, as for instance *coram non judice*, or, for other cause absolutely void *ab initio*.[4]

The cases here referred to were cases in which the President was called on to revoke sentences of former Presidents, but Attorney-General Bates held that a President could not revoke his own action.[5]

[1] The right to order such trial is given in terms in the Articles of War recently proposed.

[2] G. O. No. 18, A. G. O., May 8, 1861.

[3] IV. Opinions Attorney General, April 3, 1843.

[4] VI. Ibid, March 13, 1854, and June 5, 1854. See also III. Ibid, April 27, 1840, IV. Ibid, Nov. 6, 1843, V. Ibid, June 23, 1851, X. Ibid, June 13, 1861.

[5] XI. Ibid, March 12, 1864.

The Judge-Advocate General maintains that the President has no authority to order a new trial for the accused, except in a case of which he is the reviewing authority, without whose approval the sentence cannot be carried into effect; (as where the court was convened by his immediate authority, or where the execution of its sentence has been suspended for his action under the provisions of the 89th[1] Article of War) and where the sentence on the ground of irregularity or error in the proceedings, or because the findings are not deemed to be sustained by the evidence, is formally *disapproved* by him. That a new trial can in no case be granted by the Executive where the proper reviewing military authority has duly confirmed and ordered the execution of the sentence of the court, the judgment of which is thus made final.[2]

[1] Present 111th. [2] Opinions J. A. G., p. 246.

CHAPTER XV.

EXECUTION OF SENTENCE.

After a sentence is confirmed by the proper officer it only remains to promulgate the proceedings and execute it. The graver sentences of courts-martial are executed with considerable ceremony, in order that the example may aid in deterring others from committing similar offenses.

The sentence of death is executed either by shooting with musketry, or by hanging.

Shooting. The following custom, taken from the English service, is observed where the criminal is to be put to death by shooting. An execution party, consisting of ten or twelve men, commanded by a sergeant, is usually ordered from the prisoner's regiment, and placed under the order of the provost marshal. The troops to witness the execution are drawn up on three sides of a square, in two lines, with an interval between the lines. The provost marshal heads the procession, followed by the band of the prisoner's regiment, drums muffled, playing the dead march; the execution party comes next; then four men, bearing on their shoulders the prisoner's coffin; and immediately after follows the prisoner, usually attended by a chaplain,—the escort being in rear.

The procession passes down the front of the three faces of the square, the lines facing inward. On the procession's arriving at the flank of each regiment, the band of that regiment plays the funeral march, and continues until the procession has cleared its front. On arriving at the open face the music ceases; the prisoner is placed on the fatal spot marked by his coffin; the charge, finding, sentence, and order for his execution are read aloud to him; the chaplain, having engaged in prayer with the condemned, retires; the execution party forms at six or eight paces from the prisoner, and receives the word from the provost marshal.

When the firing party forms, the escort moves by the right flank and takes position in rear of that party, at ordered arms. Should the fire not prove instantaneously fatal, it is the duty of the provost marshal, or of a file or two which have been reserved for duty, under the direction of the provost marshal, to complete the sentence. The execution being over, the troops break into column by the right and move past the corpse.

Hanging. Less ceremony is observed in this case. The prisoner is brought on the ground by the provost marshal and escort. The troops to witness the execution are formed in a square, with the gallows as a centre. The charge, finding, sentence, and order of execution are read, and the executioner, under the direction of the provost marshal, performs his office. The execution being over, the troops march off the ground, the provost marshal with the escort remaining until the body is taken down.

If the sentence of the court in capital cases fixes the day or hour of its execution, and these happen to pass without the sentence being executed, the court should be reconvened, if not dissolved, and another day and hour appointed, or, what is better, the execution of the sentence ordered on a day or hour, and at a place to be designated by the commanding general. Nevertheless the time named not being properly a part of the sentence, but directory merely to the officer charged with its execution, if the direction is not from any cause complied with, it would seem that the general power which belongs to the proper commanding officer to enforce the sentence would remain, and that he could exercise it at will.

Where, however, the time is fixed by the *general*, and not by the court, and it passes without the sentence being executed, the case is simply one of an order not obeyed, and the right to renew and modify it at the pleasure of the commanding general is unquestionable.[1]

Commencement of Sentence. By direction of the Secretary of War, in cases where the sentence of a court-martial involves confinement for a definite period, the confinement shall be considered as commencing at the date of the promulgation of the sentence in orders (if the person sentenced is in custody at that time) unless the time for its commencement is otherwise expressly fixed by the sentence of the court, or in the order promulgating the proceedings.[2]

A sentence to confinement, with or without forfeiture of pay, should not, in terms, be made to commence at a date prior to the confirmation of the proceedings of the court.

Under date of September 26, 1872, the Judge-Advocate General rendered the following opinion: "A sentence can only take effect from the date of its promulgation, and the power of the reviewing authority does not extend retroäctively, but only to action on a sentence as it appears of record, which, unless it provides for a forfeiture of antecedent pay in express terms, can only be held to affect a period subsequent to the date of its promulgation."

It sometimes happens that considerable delay in the review and confirmation of a sentence of imprisonment

[1] Opinions J. A. G., p. 349. [2] G. O. 21, A. G. O., Feb. 17, 1870.

takes place. This period cannot legally be credited to the prisoner on account of the term imposed by the sentence. If it is proper to take into consideration the length of confinement to which the prisoner has been subjected previous to such confirmation, it may be done by the mitigation of the sentence, so that its term from the date of approval shall not extend beyond the period contemplated by the court or by the reviewing officer.

Place. Courts-martial should not generally name the place of execution of a sentence, leaving this to the discretion of the reviewing officer. The place of confinement may have to be changed, and, if the place is fixed by the court, this cannot be done except by the President. The right of the Executive to transfer military prisoners from one place of confinement to another has never been questioned.[1]

When a change of the place of confinement is made, the time occupied in effecting the change would be counted. If the sentence was solitary confinement on bread and water diet, the prescribed number of days according to the judgment of the court should be fulfilled.

If a soldier is sentenced to close confinement, and sickness requires his removal to the hospital, he may, on recovery, be returned to imprisonment. The time of his continuance in hospital should be counted as part of the time of his imprisonment.

Where a soldier, sentenced to be imprisoned for the balance of his term of service, escaped while under sentence, and was not apprehended till after his term had expired, the Judge-Advocate General held that he could not still be imprisoned under the sentence, the period of his punishment, which was limited by a certain event, which had happened, having expired.[2]

Dismissal. If no time is named in the order promul-

[1] Opinions J. A. G. p. 348. [2] Ibid, p. 350.

gating the sentence of a dismissal or discharge, it takes place at the time of publication, and the accused is entitled to his pay and emoluments up to that time.

Forfeiture. In sentences of forfeiture of pay the term "now due" is frequently used. The Judge-Advocate General regards this as referring to the date of the sentence imposed by the court, and not to the date of the order promulgating the proceedings.

Drummed out. Soldiers are sometimes sentenced to be drummed or bugled out of the service. This is executed as follows: The troops are assembled; the man about to be discharged brought forward under charge of a guard; the charge, findings, sentence, and order for his dismissal from the service are read; the buttons, facings, etc., of his dress are stripped off, and he is marched down the ranks and trumpeted or drummed, as the case may be, out of the camp or post.

CHAPTER XVI.

RECORD.

EVERY court-martial is required to keep a complete and accurate record of its proceedings.[1]

This record is kept by the judge-advocate, or the recorder of the court, and should contain a copy of the order convening the court and all orders modifying the detail; it should show the members present and absent at the commencement of each trial, and at each day's proceedings, and, if any member is absent during any portion of the trial, it should likewise appear; it should contain a copy of the charges and specifications, and must show that the court was organized as the law requires; that the court and judge-advocate were duly sworn in the presence of the prisoner; that he was previously asked whether he had any objection to any member, and his answer thereto, and that the witnesses were duly sworn; it must also contain the "statement" of the accused, if any is made, and the reply of the judge-advocate.

In addition to this the record should set forth the entire proceedings of the court upon a trial, or in any session; all orders, motions, votes, or rulings of the court itself—all motions, propositions, objections, arguments, statements, etc., of the accused and judge-advocate, the entire testimony of each witness given in his own language, and as nearly verbatim as possible; and, in short,

[1] Regulations, par. 891.

every part and feature of the proceedings, material to a complete history of the case, and to a correct understanding of every point of the same by the reviewing officer—should be recorded at length.[1]

The record must be clearly and legibly written; and, as far as practicable, without erasures or interlineations; the pages should be numbered with a margin of one inch on the left side of each page, and at the top of the odd and bottom of the even pages: through this last margin the sheet should be fastened together.[2 & 3]

All papers received in evidence, and other exhibits, should be securely attached to the record, but in such a way that they can be freely read, in the order in which they are received, and distinctly numbered so as to facilitate reference to them.[4]

Control of Record. Every court has control over its own record, and may determine whether any portion of its proceedings shall be recorded or not. For a court-martial to order any part of its proceedings to be expunged from the record would be an irregular and exceptional act, although such act—unless it involved the striking out of testimony (or other material part of the trial) against the consent of the accused or judge-advocate—might not fatally affect the validity of the final judgment. Whenever a court has determined on such expunging, the entire action connected therewith, including the motion to expunge, the arguments on the subject, if any, alike of the judge-advocate and the defense, the order made, etc., should be recorded at length. Although a court-martial has full control over the form of its record, it is not authorized to suppress or withhold any portion of its action, in

[1] Opinions J. A. G., p. 316.

[2] Regulations, par. 893.

[3] The ordinary legal cap paper, is generally used.

[4] G. C. M. O. 80, A. G. O., Oct. 30, 1875.

the course of a trial or during any session, from the reviewing officer, who, in the absence of a complete history of all the proceedings, cannot certainly be enabled to act intelligently thereon.[1]

Fair Copy. The judge-advocate or recorder is required to write up each day's proceedings, if practicable, in order that they may be submitted to the court, upon its reassembling, for its approval or alteration. The latter and not the rough draft made by the judge-advocate during the trial, are the original proceedings.

Reading over Proceedings. Each day's proceedings should, upon the reassembling of the court, be read over by the judge-advocate. He should read from the fair copy and not from the original draft. The best plan is for some member of the court to verify the judge-advocate's copy as he reads by comparing the original notes. These proceedings should be read over in the presence of the prisoner and his counsel, in order that he may call the attention of the court to any error. An accused has an undoubted right to be present at the reading over of the previous day's proceedings.[2]

The court might, if it deemed it advisable, dispense with the reading of the proceedings, but this should not ordinarily be done.

Separate Record. Whenever the same court-martial tries more than one prisoner, the proceedings in each case must be made up separately.[3] Each record must be complete in itself; so complete that, if the records of all other cases were lost or destroyed, the reviewing officer could act with perfect knowledge upon the one remaining.

Authentication. The proceedings of every case before a court-martial must be authenticated by the signa-

[1] Opinions J. A. G. p. 169. [2] G. C. M. O. 35, A. G. O., June 3, 1867.

[3] Regulations, par. 892.

tures of the president and judge-advocate or recorder, who are required, in like manner, to certify the sentence pronounced by the court in each case.[1]

The custom of the service is for the judge-advocate to authenticate each day's proceedings, and for the president and judge-advocate to sign the proceedings of each case immediately after the sentence, and also the final adjournment.[2]

It is not absolutely necessary that the judge-advocate, even, should authenticate each day's proceedings.

Where a judge-advocate dies or is disabled pending a trial, another may be appointed in his stead; but where he dies after the conclusion of the trial, and before authenticating the proceedings and certifying the sentence, the record cannot be completed by the signature of his successor, and the sentence is inoperative.[3]

Regimental and Garrison Courts. The record of these courts is kept by the recorder, and is made up as has been described for the general court, the president and recorder authenticating the record, etc.

Field Officer's Court. A field officer is required to keep a record of his proceedings in each case, but, as the proceedings are necessarily summary, it is more brief than the ordinary court-martial record. It should, however, set forth the order detailing him as a court, the names of the offenders, the offenses with which they are charged, with the time and place of commission, the pleas, the findings, and the sentences imposed. The character and circumstances of the offense in each case should so far appear, that the reviewing officer may be able to determine

1 Regulations, par. 891.

2 Unless some military exigency, such as the movement of troops in campaigns, prevents; the record must be completed before final adjournment and signed by the president and judge-advocate or recorder in the presence of the court, in the Articles recently proposed.

3 Opinions J. A. G., p. 208.

whether the court kept within its proper jurisdiction. The record should also show that the accused was present before the court, and that the charges were investigated. But the testimony, except under very peculiar circumstances, need not be recited, nor need it be set forth that the accused had an opportunity to introduce evidence, or make a statement. Though it is preferable that the record of each case should be made up separately, it is not a fatal irregularity if the proceedings in a number of cases are united, and accompanied by a single copy of the order detailing the court instead of repeating it in each case.

It is not deemed *essential* to the validity of a field officer's court that the accused should appear from the record to have had an opportunity to challenge. It is advisable, however, if any valid objection to being tried by the field officer detailed as the court is presented by the accused, that such objection should be set forth in the record as a fact for the information of the reviewing officer.[1]

Revision. Where a court is reconvened for amendment or alteration of its action, the proceedings should be recorded with the same formality as before; authenticated in the same way; and submitted for the orders of the reviewing authority. The order reconvening the court should appear upon the record, which should also show the members present and absent, the presence of the judge-advocate, accused and counsel, and the action taken by the court.

Lost Record. Where the record of a court-martial is lost before any action is taken upon it by the reviewing authority, it is held that the proceedings against the accused are terminated, unless the court could be reconvened and a new record could be made out from extant

[1] Opinions J. A. G., p. 175.

original notes of the proceedings, and could be duly authenticated by the signatures of the president and judge-advocate. Where the proceedings have been confirmed and afterwards lost, this constitutes no legal obstacle to the enforcement of the penalty. Where the record was lost *in transitu* to the President, in a case where the execution of the sentence was suspended to await his action under the 111th Article of War, the President could not review or act upon the proceedings, unless possibly the history of the case could be supplied from original papers made out by the judge-advocate, and duly authenticated by him. In the absence of any such the President would be justified in withholding his approval from the proceedings, and declaring the sentence inoperative.[1]

Transmittal of Proceedings. The judge-advocate, or recorder, is required to transmit without delay the original record of the proceedings, findings, and sentence, duly authenticated, to the officer having authority to confirm the sentence.[2]

The original proceedings of all *general* courts-martial after the decision thereon of the reviewing authority, and all such proceedings requiring the decisions of the President, should be forwarded directly to the Judge-Advocate General of the Army, in whose office they are required to be carefully preserved.[3]

The proceedings of the *minor* courts are required to be transmitted without delay, by the garrison or other commander to the department headquarters, for the supervision of the department commander;[4] and, after having been filed at these headquarters for two years, these records may be destroyed.[5]

Party entitled to Copy. Every party tried by a

[1] Opinions J. A. G. p. 216. [2] Regulations, par. 896. [3] Art. 113.
[4] Regulations, par. 898. [5] G. O. 28, A. G. O. March 29, 1877.

general court-martial, upon demand thereof, made by himself, or by any person in his behalf, is entitled to a copy of the proceedings and sentence of such court.[1&2]

The Judge-Advocate General holds that by the reading of the law, an accused would not be entitled to be furnished with a transcript of any recommendation to mercy which may have been signed by the members upon the conclusion of the trial, as this is merely an informal private communication addressed to the reviewing officer.

A copy of the record may be furnished to a party other than the accused, and not applying in his behalf, by order of the Secretary of War. It remains for him to decide in what cases such action would be proper.[3]

Fatal Defects in Record. Great care is necessary in making up the record of court-martial proceedings. The following errors and omissions will be fatal to the validity of the sentence, unless they are corrected upon a reassembling of the court:

1. Where the record does not contain a copy of the order appointing the court, or copies of all orders modifying the detail in any manner.

The record of each case must contain a copy of these orders.

2. Where, in a court of less than thirteen members, the copy of the order in the record does not contain the statement that "no other officers than those named can be assembled without manifest injury to the service."

3. Where the copy of the order in the record does not show by what officer the court was convened.

4. Where the record does not show that the court met pursuant to the order constituting it.

[1] Art. 114.

[2] He is also entitled to a copy of the reports thereon to, and the action of the reviewing authorities, in the Articles recently proposed.

[3] Opinions J. A. G. p. 252.

5. Where the record does not show that the court was organized as the law requires.

To state in the record, "The court being in session proceeded," etc., does not sufficiently set forth the organization.

6. Where the record does not show how many members were present each day and took part in the trial, or how many were present at a re-assembling for revision.

7. Where the record of a *general* court-martial shows that less than five members conducted the trial.

8. Where the record does not show that the judge-advocate was present during the trial.

9. Where the record does not show that the order convening the court was read in the presence of the accused, or that he had opportunity of challenge afforded him, either to a member then sitting, or to one who subsequently took his seat.

10. Where the record does not show that the members of the court were severally duly sworn by the judge-advocate in the presence of the accused.

11. Where it does not show that a member who subsequently took his seat was thus sworn.

12. Where the record does not show that the judge-advocate was duly sworn by the president in the presence of the accused, or that a new judge-advocate who subsequently took his seat was similarly sworn.

13. Where the record does not contain a copy of the charges and specifications upon which the accused is tried.

14. Where the record does not show that the accused was allowed to plead, or shows that he was tried without pleading to the merits, or does not contain his entire plea.

15. Where the record shows that the accused was arraigned and pleaded prior to the organization of the court.

16. Where the record does not show that the witnesses were sworn.

That they were not sworn in the presence of the accused would not constitute a fatal defect.

17. Where it does not set forth the testimony of the witnesses.

It is not sufficient to set forth a summary, or such portion as the judge-advocate deems material. The full testimony of the witness in his own language should be given.

18. Where the record does not show that a clerk, or reporter, who recorded the proceedings of the court, was sworn to a performance of his duties.

19. Where it does not show that an interpreter was so sworn.

If an interpreter was called to interpret the testimony of a single witness, and the record did not show that he was sworn, it would not be a fatal defect; *provided*, there was sufficient evidence to convict without the testimony of this witness.

20. Where the record shows affirmatively that the court commenced its sessions before eight o'clock A. M., or continued in session after three o'clock P. M., and sets forth no authority therefor from the officer appointing the court.

It will be presumed, in the absence of evidence to the contrary, that a court did not sit beyond the prescribed hours.[1]

21. Where the record does not show that the court was closed for deliberation on findings and sentence.

22. Where the record does not contain the findings and sentence.

23. Where there is a fatal variance between the name

[1] Opinions J. A. G. p. 34.

of the party in the specification, and in the finding or sentence.

24. Where, in the case of a capital sentence, the concurrence thereon of two-thirds of the members of the court does not appear from the record.

25. Where the proceedings are not authenticated by the signature of both the president and judge-advocate.

When proceedings are not signed by the president of the court, and the court is dissolved, the sentence is, wholly invalid, and the order approving it must be revoked.[1]

The record of a trial by a military court is furthermore, incomplete and insufficient where the reviewing officer fails to state his "decisions and orders" at the end of the proceedings. And it is not sufficient to state such decisions, etc., at the end of a series of cases passed upon by the same reviewing officer; it must be stated independently at the end of each case. To annex a copy of the general order promulgating the proceedings to a collection of records is not deemed a compliance with the law.

Defects not Fatal. The following defects, though they are to be avoided, would not render the finding or sentence invalid :—

1. Where the record does not show that a member who was challenged withdrew during deliberations on the challenge.

2. Where it does not show that the court was closed for deliberation on points arising during the trial.

3. Where it does not show that a witness was for the prosecution or defense.

4. Where it does not contain a note of the close of the prosecution.

5. Where it discloses the vote on the findings or sentence.

[1] Letter A. G. O., Feb. 7, 1874.

6. Where the record does not show that proceedings were read to court.

7. Where the record stated that there was a finding of guilty on the *second* charge and specification when the prisoner was only arraigned upon *one*.

Endorsement. Every record of the proceedings of a military court should be endorsed on the first fold[1] by the judge-advocate or recorder of such court, with name of the place where the court is held; the date when the proceedings were signed; the designation of the order convening the court; the names of the presiding officer, judge-advocate, and of the prisoner tried, according to a prescribed form.[2&3]

[1] Legal cap paper should be folded in four equal folds parallel with the writing. The left hand fold of the outer page is the first fold.

[2] G. O. 29, A. G. O. March 18, 1871.

[3] For Form see Appendix.

CHAPTER XVII.

BUREAU OF MILITARY JUSTICE, JUDGE-ADVOCATE'S CORPS, AND DUTIES OF JUDGE-ADVOCATES.

By the act of June 20th, 1864, a Bureau of Military Justice was established to exist during the continuance of the rebellion. This was afterwards made permanent and exists as part of the Military peace establishment of the United States.

Organization. By the act of June 23d, 1874, the Bureau of Military Justice is to consist of a Judge-Advocate General, and the law also provides for a certain number of Judge-Advocates of the Army with the rank of Majors of Cavalry.[1]

Duties of Judge-Advocate General. The Judge-Advocate General is to receive, revise, report upon, and cause to be recorded the proceedings of all courts-martial, courts of inquiry, and military commissions, and perform such other duties as have been performed by the Judge-Advocate General of the army.[2]

All communications pertaining to questions of military justice, or to the proceedings of military courts and commissions, throughout the armies of the United States, must be addressed to the Judge-Advocate General,[3] and commanding officers are enjoined to furnish promptly to the Bureau of Military Justice all proceedings of courts-mar-

[1] Revised Statutes, § 1200. [2] Ibid, § 1199.
[3] G. O. 270, A. G. O. 1864.

tial, military commissions, and courts of inquiry, together with the orders promulgating decisions thereon.

Such report as the Judge-Advocate General may make on cases requiring the action of the President will be addressed to the Secretary of War, and forwarded, through the Commanding General of the army, for such remarks and recommendations, as he may desire to make.[1]

He reports at once for the action of the Secretary of War, illegal and unusual punishments, and all fatal irregularities. But when a case has been disposed of, it cannot be reopened without instructions from the President.

Duties of Judge-Advocates of the Army. The Judge Advocates of the Army are stationed at the headquarters of divisions and departments, serving with officers having power to convene general courts-martial. Their duties are to supervise charges forwarded for trial, and to review and report upon such proceedings of military courts as may be submitted to them by the commander.

They are required to forward to the Judge-Advocate General at the end of each month a list of all cases tried and to be tried within their jurisdiction.[2]

A Judge-Advocate on duty at division or department headquarters is liable to detail by the commanding officer, as judge-advocate of a general court-martial, court of inquiry, or military commission.[3]

Judge-Advocates of Courts-Martial. Officers who may appoint a court-martial are competent to appoint a judge-advocate for the same;[4] and without such judge-advocate a *general* court-martial is not regarded a legal court.[5]

[1] G. O. 39, A. G. O., 1877. [2] G. O. 270, A. G. O., 1864.

[3] Decision Adjutant General, Aug. 11, 1870. [4] Article 74.

[5] The power of appointing judge-advocates is restricted to *general* courts-martial in the Articles of War recently proposed.

The law does not say who may be appointed as judge-advocates, and cases have occurred in our service where civilians have acted in this capacity. While there is no law or army regulation precluding the appointment of judge-advocates from civil life, the usage of the service and of the government is opposed to the employment of civil judge-advocates, except in special cases requiring in the prosecuting officer such legal knowledge and experience as are not often found in a military man.[1] As a rule, therefore, he should be an officer of the army.

He must be appointed as such by the authority convening the court-martial; the mere fact that he is the Judge-Advocate of the department would not authorize him to take any part in the proceedings unless formally detailed.

The court cannot appoint a judge-advocate, nor can it authorize or empower its junior member to act as such during the absence of the regular judge-advocate, or when he has been relieved without a successor being appointed in his place, and when one is so appointed and acts temporarily, the proceedings are irregular and the sentence void.[2]

Even the convening authority cannot authorize one of the members of a court to act as the judge-advocate, without formally relieving him as a member and appointing him as judge-advocate. Where a reviewing authority reconvened a court for revision of sentence, and added in the order,—"Should the judge-advocate be prevented from attending, the junior member of the court will act in his stead," it was held, the junior member so acting, that the proceedings upon the reassembling of the court were void in law.[3]

The convening officer cannot detail a single officer to

[1] Opinions J. A. G. p. 207. [2] Ibid. [3] Opinions J. A. G., p. 206.

act as judge-advocate of all courts under his command, although the same officer might be specially detailed on every court.

Duties of the Judge-Advocate. The judge-advocate has some duties preliminary to the trial. When it is decided to try a person, the charges are sent to the judge-advocate with directions to bring the party to trial before the court-martial of which he is appointed judge-advocate.

In the case of an officer, a copy of the charges must be furnished him within eight days after his arrest; and, though not required by the Articles of War, such copy should be furnished by the judge-advocate to a soldier before calling upon him to plead; and this in time to allow him properly to defend himself. In lieu of a copy, it is customary, especially where the offender is to be tried by one of the minor courts, for the judge-advocate to read over to the accused, sometime previous to the trial, the charges and specifications. At the same time he is asked how he intends pleading, and whether he desires any witnesses for his defense. If he should still desire a copy of the charges, it should be furnished him.

By finding from the accused how he intends pleading, the judge-advocate is often saved the trouble and expense of summoning unnecessary witnesses. An accused, however, could not be forced to divulge his plea.

Judge-advocates should exercise great care in advising prisoners how to plead.

Summoning Witnesses. The accused furnishes the judge-advocate with a list of his witnesses to enable him to summon them. As this knowledge might give the prosecution some advantages, the question naturally arises as to whether the accused can require the list of witnesses for the prosecution. The accepted rule is that it is not necessary that the copy of charges furnished the accused should contain a list of the witnesses, nor can the accused demand as a right such list. The only reason the judge-advocate can call for the list for the defense is to enable him to summon them. Unless there is danger of the witnesses being tampered with, there seems no good reason why such list should not be furnished the accused on application.

The judge-advocate must exercise a discretion in summoning witnesses, especially where they reside away from the post, and ordinarily summon them before the assembling of the court in order to prevent delays. He is not to summon any witness at the expense of the United States, nor any officer of the army, without the order of the court, unless satisfied that his testimony is material and necessary to the ends of justice.[1]

The same nicety of form is not necessary in the summoning of military as in the case of civilian witnesses. Great care is needed in the latter case, and, to prevent the evil results that might arise from incorrect forms, it is suggested that the form given in the Appendix be strictly adhered to.

By an order from the War Department it is strictly enjoined upon judge-advocates of courts-martial, who may find it necessary to subpœna witnesses, to send the subpœna whenever it is possible through the proper military channels.[2] If to an officer residing within the department, it should be sent to him through the post commander; if to a soldier, to his post commander. If the party resides without the department, it should be sent through the department commander. The scope of this order was in 1872 enlarged so as to include in its provisions *all* courts, boards, or other tribunals, civil and military, competent to

[1] Regulations, par. 890. [2] G. O. 97, A. G. O., Dec. 12, 1866.

issue subpœnas to witnesses; and, hereafter, orders from competent military authority will be required for the movement of all officers and enlisted men, summoned to leave their posts as witnesses before such tribunals in accordance with the requirements of the said General Order No. 97 of 1866.[1]

For securing the attendance of civilian witnesses *duplicate* subpœnas should be sent to the nearest post commander for service, if the witness resides within the department, or else to department headquarters, unless otherwise specially directed by the department commander.

Service is made under the laws of the United States by delivering the subpœna to the witness; and *proof* of service by returning the duplicate original to the judge-advocate with an affidavit endorsed to the effect that, on such a day, date, and place, the affiant personally served the within named witness, by delivering to him a subpœna of which the within is a complete copy.

Any military person, or civilian of competent discretion, can serve the subpœna, but service by mail is *not* a legal service.[2]

If the judge-advocate declines to summon as a witness an officer of the army, because not satisfied that it is proper to do so under paragraph 890 of the Regulations, the court may still order the summons to be issued, if it disagrees with the judge-advocate.[3 & 4]

Writs of Attachment. The law provides for the failure of witnesses to appear upon being duly summoned. It authorizes every judge-advocate of a court-martial to issue like process to compel witnesses to appear and testify,

[1] G. O. 59, A. G. O., June 28, 1872.

[2] See Gardner's Practical Forms, p. 40. [3] Opinions J. A. G., p. 390.

[4] Courts-martial are expressly authorized to summon of their own motion and at any stage of the proceedings any witness whose testimony appears material to the case, by the Articles of War recently proposed.

which courts of criminal jurisdiction within the State, Territory, or district where such military courts shall be ordered to sit, may lawfully issue.[1 & 2]

The Attorney-General has decided, that the power to issue such process includes also the power to execute it through some officer who shall be especially charged with its execution.[3]

General Orders from the War Department present the mode to be pursued.[4] Judge-advocates of military courts who may hereafter issue such process to compel the attendance, as witnesses, of persons not in the military service, shall formally direct the same, by name, to some military officer who shall be designated by the department commander as available for the purpose, and the nearest military commander will thereupon furnish a sufficient force for the execution of the process whenever such force shall be actually required. It will be noted, however, that whereas a process of attachment can only be enforced as herein directed, the preliminary summons or subpœna may be served by any person whatever.

Every officer serving such process of attachment should see that it is technically accurate, otherwise he lays himself liable in arresting a civilian witness to a suit in damages for trespass.

It should properly contain:

1st. A copy of the order convening the court. 2d. A copy of the charges. 3d. A copy of the subpœna with proof of service. 4th. It should show that the party has failed and neglected to appear; that he is a necessary and material witness; and that no just excuse has been offered for his neglect.

[1] Rev. Stat. § 1202.

[2] This power is given to courts-martial and military commissions instead of to judge-advocates, in the Articles of War recently proposed.

[3] XII. Opinions Att'y Gen'l, p. 501.

[4] G. O. 93. A. G. O., 1868.

The court must judge whether the particular case justifies the resort to this process.

Subordinate military courts cannot compel the attendance of civilian witnesses unless a judge-advocate is appointed for such court.[1]

The service of a subpœna upon a witness ought always to be made in reasonable time before trial. In the United States the reasonableness of the time is generally fixed by statute, requiring an allowance of one day for every certain number of miles distance from the witness's residence to the place of trial; and this is usually twenty miles. But at least one day's notice is deemed necessary, however inconsiderable the distance may be.[2]

In cases before courts-martial a witness present in the court-room can be required to testify though he has not been summoned.

It is not necessary in a subpœna issued from a court-martial that there should be a tender of fees. Citizen witnesses, duly summoned, however, are paid the actual cost of their transportation or travel fare to and from the court, together with the per diem for the time necessarily occupied in attendance upon the court, and in making the journeys.[3] The judge-advocate should give a certificate in duplicate of the fact of such attendance.[4]

Judge-advocates of courts-martial, courts of inquiry, and military commissions will insert the names in full in all certificates of attendance given to persons summoned as witnesses, or employed as interpreters, and, in the case of an officer, his rank and regiment.[5]

Rooms and Stationery. The judge-advocate should sufficiently early apply to the post quartermaster for an

[1] Opinions J. A. G., March 15, 1873, January 25, 1876.

[2] Greenleaf on Evidence, Vol. I., p. 373.

[3] See G. O. 97, A. G. O., September 8, 1876.

[4] For form, see Appendix.

[5] G. O. 154, A. G. O., Oct. 20, 1865.

appropriate room in which to conduct the trial; and for the necessary stationery, which for military courts and boards will be furnished on the requisition of the recorder, approved by the presiding officer.[1]

Duties of Judge-Advocate during Trial. The judge-advocate should carefully supervise the order convening the court and note any irregularity. Such supervision will often prevent proceedings by illegally constituted courts. Any grave irregularities, such, for instance, as regular officers being named in the order for the trial of militia troops, should be brought to the notice of the convening authority, if there is time, before the assembling of the court. If not, the attention of the court should be brought to that fact.

The duties of the judge-advocate in conducting a trial are of an important character, and too much care cannot be exercised by the convening authority in selecting officers qualified to perform the duties required. In the English service special care is taken in selecting the judge-advocates. "It appears to be usual in England to select a civilian, one who is professionally a lawyer, to conduct the duty of Deputy Judge-Advocate."[2] How much more important in our service to select a qualified person, where the judge-advocate, in addition to the functions of the English Deputy Judge-Advocate, acts as prosecutor.

The English Article provides that, "No person acting as prosecutor, or being a witness for the prosecution, shall also act as judge-advocate at a trial.[3]

The 90th Article of War gives in outline the judge-advocate's duties. It says, the judge-advocate shall prosecute in the name of the United States, but when the prisoner has made his plea, he shall so far consider himself

[1] Regulations, par. 1133.

[2] Hughes, Duties of Judge-Advocates, p. 2.

[3] Article 159.

counsel for the prisoner as to object to any leading question to any of the witnesses, and to any question to the prisoner, the answer to which might tend to criminate himself. In addition to these he has, by regulations and custom, other quite as important functions. I shall therefore consider his duties under the following heads :—

1st. **As Conductor of the Trial and Recorder.** The judge-advocate conducts the trial, and takes care that it proceeds smoothly and without unnecessary delay. His practical duties as conductor of the trial are outlined in Chapter IX.

If the judge-advocate, when the court meets, is not ready to proceed, he may properly make a request for delay. Such motion may also be made at any stage of the trial. The court is the judge of the reasons and of the time of adjournment. In the case of Major Porter, 4th Artillery, the court refused to admit on their record an argument of the judge-advocate, objecting to an application by the defense for delay. The Secretary of War held that it was the duty of the judge-advocate to make the objection, and the argument by which he sustained it was very proper. It was a part of the proceedings which ought to have been entered on their record.[1]

Oath. He administers the prescribed oath to the members, and also takes the oath required of the judge-advocate. He may be affirmed at his own request. It is necessary that the judge-advocate should be sworn (or affirmed) and, where it did not appear upon the record of a court that he was so sworn, the Attorney-General held the proceedings irregular and void.[2]

He administers the oaths to witnesses, reporters and interpreters.[3]

[1] G. O. 5, A. G. O., May 23, 1857.

[2] III. Opinions Attorney-General, p. 396, *et seq.*

[3] See Chapter VIII. on Oaths.

He is required to keep the record and authenticate the proceedings.[1]

2d. **As Prosecutor.** In his capacity as prosecutor the judge-advocate is required to look out for the interests of the government. He is its counsel for the time being. In fulfilling these duties, however, he should bear in mind the object for which the court is assembled; that its purpose is to arrive at the exact truth of the matter in question, and to administer simple justice. Erroneous views are sometimes held by judge-advocates upon this point; they suppose that their duties as prosecutor require the conviction of the accused, and that they will be regarded by the convening authority as inefficient if they fail to secure such conviction. This is incorrect. They are simply required to produce such affirmative testimony as they can procure, and, confining themselves to legal methods, prove, if possible, the allegations set forth in the specifications.

In important cases it may be appropriate for the judge-advocate to state the facts which he intends proving, thus giving to the court a clearer insight of the case. Of the necessities for this he must be the judge.

At the appropriate time he calls his witnesses for the prosecution, examines and re-examines them, and, if objection is made to any question he thinks proper to ask, he should, if possible, show his right to ask it.

The judge-advocate has the right of a closing address.[2]

3d. **As Counsel for the Accused.** The 90th Article of War specifies that the judge-advocate shall so far consider himself as counsel for the prisoner as to object to any leading question to any of the witnesses, and to any question to the prisoner, the answer to which might

[1] For his duties as Recorder see Chapter XVI. [2] See Chapter IX. p. —.

tend to criminate himself. He should therefore object to such questions, by whomsoever asked, even though by a member.

Ordinarily questions are written out by a member, handed to the president, who passes them to the judge-advocate. The latter, before asking any such question, should interpose any objection he desires to make. It remains entirely in the discretion of the court to decide whether the question shall be asked or not, and, if it decides affirmatively, the judge-advocate has no right to object further.

Justice and the best practice do not restrict the judge-advocate to the mere statutory obligation of Article 90, in his duties as counsel for the accused. When the accused is ignorant or inexperienced and without counsel—especially when he is an enlisted man—it is deemed to be the duty of the judge-advocate to take care, generally, that the accused does not suffer upon the trial for any ignorance or misconception of his legal rights, and has full opportunity to interpose such plea and make such defense as may best bring out the facts, the merits, or the extenuating circumstances of the case.

For the judge-advocate to counsel the accused (a soldier) to plead guilty, is ordinarily improper and a thing not to be done. But where such plea is voluntarily and intelligently made, the judge-advocate should still inform the accused of his right to offer evidence in explanation or extenuation of his offense, and, if any such evidence exists, should assist him in securing it; and where no such evidence is attainable in the case, the judge-advocate should still see that the accused has an opportunity to present a "statement," written or verbal, to the court, if he has any desire to do so.[1]

[1] Opinions J. A. G. p. 205.

4th. **Other Duties of the Judge-Advocate.** It is the duty of the judge-advocate to watch the proceedings of the court and call its attention to any illegal steps on its part. If the court persists in its course he is not entitled to protest against its action, nor could he insist that his opinion should be entered upon the record. The better plan in such cases is for the court to allow his opinion to be recorded, the better to bring the point before the reviewing authority.

The Judge-Advocate General says: "It is strictly the more proper practice for a judge-advocate not to give his opinion upon a point of law arising upon a military trial, unless the same may be required by the court. This practice, however, is often departed from, and the opinions of judge-advocates are generally received and entertained by the court without objection, whether or not formally called for. But where the court *does* object to the giving an opinion by the judge-advocate, he is not authorized to attempt to give it, and, of course, not authorized to enter it upon the record. Whether the *fact* that the opinion was offered and objected to by the court shall be entered upon the record, is a matter for the court alone to decide. It is, however, certainly the better practice that *all* the proceedings, even those that are irregular, which transpire in connection with the trial, should be set out in the record for the inspection of the reviewing authority." [1]

Maj. Gen. Kennedy, in speaking upon this point, says, "The opinions offered by the judge-advocate form an essential part of the proceedings, and that, without their insertion the record does not exhibit a true and faithful account of all that took place during the trial; and, consequently, that the approving officer becomes called upon,

[1] Opinions J. A. G., p. 208.

without being apprised of the circumstances, to decide upon the merits of a case which has not been fully and correctly submitted to him. For the judge-advocate, however, it must be a matter of perfect indifference whether his opinions are inserted on the face of the proceedings or not, because he has always the means of bringing them to the notice of the approving officer; and thus, in excluding them, a court-martial would merely deprive itself of the opportunity of explaining its reasons for having acted contrary to the judge-advocate's advice."[1]

Right of Court to Judge-Advocate's Opinion. The court, without doubt, has a right to the judge-advocate's opinion upon any point of law, and, when called upon, he should give it. The value of such opinion, however, will depend upon the particular person acting in that capacity. It frequently happens in our service that the judge-advocate has not the experience or knowledge of court-martial proceedings which most of the members possess; his opinion therefore would be of little value to them.

Responsibility for Opinion. There has been a diversity of opinion among English writers, as to the responsibility of the judge-advocate to a civil court for opinions given by him to a court-martial. Whatever may be the responsibility in English courts-martial, where this officer is, as before stated, generally a civil lawyer, such responsibility does not obtain in this country—nor should it. Few officers add to their other military knowledge an extensive knowledge of military and criminal law, and to make them responsible in damages for an erroneous opinion would be an absurdity.

During the deliberations on the finding and sentence the duties of the judge-advocate are of an especially important nature. The court may labor under erroneous

[1] Hughes' Duties of Judge-Advocates, p. 123.

ideas as to the evidence, or may proceed to an illegal or irregular finding; it might by oversight give a discretionary punishment where the law is mandatory, or sentence to capital punishment where less than two-thirds had voted guilty. In cases of that kind it is the duty of the judge-advocate to call the fact to the notice of the court. He should, however, abstain from any remark by which his opinion as to the guilt or innocence of the accused may be ascertained.

How far under the Orders of the Court. The judge-advocate is in some cases under the orders of the court, and in some cases not. In his character as prosecutor he cannot be interfered with. He is not under their control as to the manner of conducting the trial. He may examine such witnesses as he deems necessary, and no others; or refuse to call any witnesses for the prosecution; he may call his witnesses in the order he desires.

The court may order him to summon witnesses, but it cannot compel him to examine them.

It cannot interfere with his right of an opening and closing address, or his right of argument, upon points arising during the trial, where the interests of the prosecution are involved.

In his character as recorder, he is under the orders of court, and yet, for a refusal to obey such orders the court cannot punish him, nor could it place him in arrest. Its proper course is to note any insubordination on his part, and report it to the reviewing officer.

Responsibility. The judge-advocate, as the prosecutor for the government, is responsible for his manner of conducting the trial, and, for failure to perform his functions properly, is liable to the censure of the reviewing officer, and even to trial for willful wrong doing.

Witness. The judge-advocate may be a witness,

although it is deemed the better practice not to detail a person as judge-advocate who may be called on to testify. Where he does testify, however, the President of the court should administer the oath, and the testimony be recorded by the clerk or a member, or he may record it himself.

It is at all times competent for the officer convening a court-martial to relieve the judge-advocate first detailed, and to substitute another in his place. This course, however, when resorted to pending a trial, tends to embarrass the prosecution, and should not be pursued except in extreme cases.[1]

Recorders of courts-martial have duties corresponding to those here given for judge-advocates.

[1] Opinions J. A. G., p. 207.

CHAPTER XVIII.

CONSTRUCTION OF ARTICLES OF WAR.

False Returns. Article 8 provides for the case of an officer knowingly making a false return to the Department of War, or to any of his superior officers authorized to call for such returns, of the state of the regiment, troop or company, or garrison under his command, or of the arms, ammunition, clothing, or other stores belonging thereto.

Where an officer was charged with making a false return of company funds, and found guilty under this article, *held,* that the article did not apply to return of funds.[1]

False returns, made by a commissary or quartermaster, are not offenses cognizable under this article.[2]

False Certificates. Art. 13 relates to the signing of false certificates relating to the absence or pay of an officer or soldier.

An officer in 1859 was charged with "conduct unbecoming an officer and a gentleman," and convicted of "*signing a false certificate of transportation,*" but acquitted of signing the same "*knowingly.*" The court found him not guilty of "conduct unbecoming, etc.," but guilty of "conduct to the prejudice of good order and military discipline." The War Department held the finding entitled to an acquittal, and is in legal effect an acquittal and therefore avoids and omits the sentence. "It is not neces-

1 G. C. M. O. 36, A. G. O., April 11, 1877.

2 G. C. M. O. 12, A. G. O., May 17, 1872. G. C. M. O. 19, A. G. O., July 24, 1872. G. C. M. O. 47, A. G. O., Aug. 22, 1870.

sary in military charges," it was held, "to allege that the acts were done 'maliciously,' or 'wilfully,' or 'knowingly.' A specification of fact is good without such expressions, but if they are alleged and negatived by the court in their verdict, then the inference from the fact fails, and the accused, being acquitted of intention, is acquitted of the offense. That is certainly the legal effect and meaning of such finding.

"What other meaning was in the minds of the court? They find that the accused did not 'knowingly' sign, meaning, probably, that he did not know that the certificate was false. Then did he sign it in good faith, to the best of his knowledge and belief? or in such ignorance and disregard of what he certified as made the certificate an act of bad faith? In that finding of the specification it sustains the charge. But the court negative the charge, and therefore reject that sense of the specification. The court probably find only a due want of care and accuracy a neglect of duty."[1]

In 1869 the Secretary of War in a general order stated that "the practice of drawing pay twice for the same time and refunding at some subsequent period has lately been of such frequent recurrence, and is perpetrated under such circumstances, as to preclude the supposition of inadvertence or mistake, but rather of deliberate intention. * * Every officer's pay account contains the certificate that the officer has not already received pay for the same period. If, therefore, an officer signs two sets of pay accounts for the same month, one set must be false, and if the name and facts reach the Headquarters of the Army, as they surely will through the Paymaster-General, the officer will be tried by a general court-martial under the 14th (present 13th) Article of War."[2]

[1] G. O. 28, A. G. O. Dec. 31, 1859. [2] G. O. 61, A. G. O., Aug. 7, 1869.

Accountability for Stores, etc. Article 15 directs that any officer who, willfully or through neglect, suffers to be lost, spoiled, or damaged, any military stores belonging to the United States, shall make good the loss or damage, and be dismissed from the service.

The loss or damage may be assessed by a Board of Survey with the approval of the commanding officer;[1] or it is presumed, by the court-martial trying him. The former would seem to be the better way.

In referring to losses occasioned by neglect of company commanders, the Secretary of War holds that the pecuniary responsibility cannot be transferred to enlisted men. It is the duty of the commander to attend personally to its (the property's) security, and either to himself superintend the issues, or cause it to be done by a commissioned officer. The plea that the keys of the rooms or chests, and the making of issues, were entrusted to enlisted men, or to civilians, without direct proof of vigilance on the part of the responsible officer, and a resort to every reasonable precaution, including frequent personal inspections, intended to prevent loss or damage, will not be accepted by Boards of Survey as relieving such officer from liability. Evidence must be demanded, showing clearly the circumstances of the loss and all the means and precautions taken to guard against it; and reviewing officers, in examining the proceedings of Boards of Survey, will apply the principles set forth in this order and be governed by them in affixing their approval.[2] These remarks should be borne in mind by courts-martial, in trying offenses under this article.

Losing Accoutrements. Article 17 provides that any soldier who sells or, through neglect, loses or spoils his horse, etc., shall suffer such stoppages, not exceeding

[1] Under par. 1027 Regulations. [2] G. O. 66 A. G. O., June 24, 1874.

one-half of his current pay, as a court-martial may deem sufficient for repairing the loss or damage, and shall be punished by confinement or such other corporal punishment as the court may direct.

General Orders from the Adjutant-General's office direct that in future, the amount, charged against an enlisted man on muster and pay rolls for indemnification for loss or damage to government property, will not exceed the value of the article alienated, or the amount of damage, or the cost of repairs, and such charges will be made in conformity with paragraphs 1027 and 1028 Revised Regulations for the Army of 1863. The soldier will be informed, at the time for signing the roll, that his signature will be regarded as an acknowledgement of the justice of the charge set against his pay ; but, in case he objects to signing the rolls and demands a court-martial, and in cases of loss from stealing, selling, gross neglect, or other illegal disposition of or damage to public property, such as should subject the offender to punishment, in addition to making good the loss to the United States, he will be proceeded against as provided for in the 16th and 17th Articles of War, Revised Statutes of the United States. In these cases the stoppages imposed by a garrison or regimental court-martial—or in time of war a field officer's court—is not limited to one month's pay, but only to the amount necessary to reimburse the government, and the conditions imposed in said 17th Article of War.[1]

In 1877 a soldier was tried for violation of this article in unlawfully disposing of his great-coat. The court failed to make any stoppage, and on being re-convened, adhered to their action on the ground that, the great-coat having been issued to the soldier and charged against him, the government had sustained no loss or damage which it was

[1] G. O. 110, A. G O., Dec. 1, 1876.

in the power of the court to assess. The convening officer held the conclusion of the court erroneous, both as to the fact of actual loss or damage, and as to the legal relation of the prisoner and government as to ownership. The actual cost for care and transportation of clothing to any particular station forms no part of the value as stated in the price-list, and there is, in such respect, an actual ascertainable loss to the government, resulting both from the wrongful sale of clothing in the first instance, and usually from the necessity of replacing the articles at places of issue. The legal right of the soldier to the clothing issued to him is a qualified right, that of use only, whilst he is in service, and is still public property within the intent of the 17th Article of War, so far as the right of disposition is concerned.[1]

Where a soldier came into possession of articles of government clothing by purchase or gift from soldiers discharged, the Judge-Advocate General held, that selling such clothing to citizens constituted an offense under Sec. 23 of the Act of March 3, 1863, the same being construed as not intending to restrict the offense denounced to a selling by the identical soldier to whom the clothing was originally issued.[2]

The Judge-Advocate General holds, that the imposition by sentence of certain stoppages of pay for violation of this article is, in all cases, mandatory upon the court.[3]

The punishment for offenses under this article is limited to *corporal* punishment, confinement being regarded as such.

Disrespect. Article 20 refers to an officer or soldier behaving with disrespect toward his *commanding* officer.

Every officer entitled to require the obedience of an-

[1] G. C. M. O., 31, Headq'rs. Dept. of the South, April 17, 1877.
[2] Bureau of Military Justice, Nov. 24, 1873. [3] Opinions, p. 13.

other, for the time being, is to the latter his commanding officer.

Disrespectful language used towards his captain by a soldier, when detached from his company and serving at the hospital, to the surgeon in charge of which he was ordered to report, was held not properly charged "as disrespect towards his commanding officer"—the surgeon, not the captain, being his commander at the time. The offense should, under these circumstances, have been charged as "conduct to the prejudice of good order and military discipline."[1]

Striking Superior Officer and Disobedience of Orders. Article 21 provides that any officer or soldier who, on any pretense whatsoever strikes his superior officer, or draws or lifts up any weapon, or offers any violence against him, being in the execution of his office, or disobeys any lawful command of his superior officer, shall suffer death, or etc.

Three things are necessary to make an act an offense under this article:

First. The violence mentioned must be against a *superior* officer; the term "superior" being interpreted to mean any commissioned officer superior in rank to the accused.

Second. It must be shown, in evidence, that the superior officer was in the execution of his office.[2]

Third. If the offense charged is "disobedience of orders," the order disobeyed must be a *lawful* command of a *superior* officer.

The fact that any stated duty is enjoined in regulations, or orders, does not in itself render a non-performance of such duty a disobedience of orders, in violation of the 21st Article; but, to support this, it is essen-

[1] Opinions J. A. G. p. 4. [2] G. C. M. O. 2, Army of the Potomac, Jan. 2, 1865.

tial that there should be shown such an intentional disregard of authority, as is evinced by a willful refusal or omission to comply with the specific command of a superior officer.[1]

The Article, it will be seen, does not provide for the punishment of disobedience of an unlawful order. On the contrary, it is well settled that an officer or soldier is justified in disobeying such order. It may become his imperative duty to do so, for obedience of such an order may often render him liable in damages, the same as if it was committed of his own free will and accord. Thus, in the case of *Mitchell vs. Harmony*, the United States Supreme Court held that upon principle, independent of the weight of judicial decision, it can never be maintained that a military officer can justify himself for doing an unlawful act, by producing the order of his superior. The order may palliate, but it cannot justify.[2]

Disobedience of orders, however, is one of the severest offenses known to the military code, and is made punishable in all armies by the severest penalties. Prompt, unhesitating obedience is the very root of discipline, without which the efficiency of an army would instantaneously be impaired. How can we reconcile the two? What will justify an officer or soldier in disobeying an order? May he pause to consider, and obey or not as the order appears to him legal or illegal?

In the case of *McCall vs. McDowell*, it was said, "If every subordinate officer or soldier were at liberty to question the legality of the orders of the commander and obey them or not as they may consider them valid or invalid, the camp would be turned into a debating school, where the precious moment for action would be wasted

[1] G. C. M. O. 26, A. G. O., Aug. 31, 1872.
[2] 14. Howard, p. 137.

in wordy conflicts between the advocates of conflicting opinions." [1]

To the same effect the U. S. Supreme Court in the case of *Martin vs. Mott*,[2]—"While subordinate officers or soldiers are pausing to consider whether they ought to obey, or are scrupulously weighing the evidence of the facts upon which the commander-in-chief exercises the right to demand their service, the hostile enterprise may be accomplished without the means of resistance."

The rule to be adopted from the weight of authority seems to be this:—

Unless an order is *manifestly* and *clearly illegal,* it is the duty of the subordinate to obey it, and failure on his part will render him liable under this article.

As held by the judge in *McCall vs. McDowell*,—"Except in a plain case of excess of authority, where at first blush it is apparent and palpable to the commonest understanding that the order is illegal, I cannot but think that the law should excuse the military subordinate when acting in obedience to the orders of his commander; otherwise he is placed in the dangerous dilemma of being liable in damages to third parties for obedience to an order, or to the loss of his commission and disgrace for disobedience thereto."

Verbal Orders. Several cases have arisen in our army where officers have refused to obey *verbal* orders because not properly delivered.

In 1778 Col. Hall was tried, for refusing to obey an order of his commanding officer directing him to impress certain horses; the order being conveyed to him through the hands of a quartermaster. The court held that the order was not military, and not conveyed through a military channel, and found the accused not guilty; but the

[1] I. Abbott 213–245, Reported also in Scott's Digest, p. 428.

[2] 12. Wheaton, p. 19.

commander-in-chief disapproved this decision, and held that the order was regular and obligatory.[1]

In 1827 Lieut. B. was found not guilty of disrespect to his commanding officer, for refusing to obey an order delivered by a soldier. In so deciding, they stated that they had been governed by a paragraph of existing regulations which said, "verbal orders addressed to officers will be transmitted by officers." The commanding general held that the regulation was not applicable to the case, —"It more appropriately applies to commands in the organization of which 'staff officers' are a necessary and constituent part—as divisions, brigades, and possibly a single regiment—but to the limited sphere of company commands, within the jurisdiction of company officers only, and *limited* to official intercourse between the captain and his subalterns (as illustrated in this trial) the rule would seem devoid of any application.[2]

Again, in 1869 Bvt. Major K. was tried for "disobedience of orders," the specification alleging that,—"Having been informed by his 1st Sergt. that he had been directed by the Sergeant-Major of the post, to inform Bvt. Major K., that the commanding officer of the post had ordered that wagoner ——, of said battery, was to be excused from inspection the next morning, he did say to the said 1st Sergt., that he would not obey any order transmitted in that way, and did order 1st Sergt. ——, not to excuse said wagoner from said inspection." The commanding general in commenting on the case said,—"The manner of communicating orders, brought in question by the proceedings in this case, is one that is fully established by long continued custom and is sanctioned by the regulations (par. 443). It is the substitute in part for the 'officer's

[1] Revolutionary Orders of Washington, p. 48.

[2] G. O. 4, A. G. O., Jan. 16, 1827.

call,' and works mainly to the convenience of company officers, by relieving them from the duty of reporting in person, to receive the daily details and unimportant orders, and it has always been held customary, proper, and sufficient."[1]

Mutiny. Articles 22 and 23 provide punishments for engaging in, or failing to resist, mutiny or sedition.

Mutiny and sedition are, by some, considered as convertible terms, and perhaps properly so; but, by military men, *mutiny* is rather understood to imply extreme insubordination, as *individually* resisting by force, or *collectively* rising against or opposing military authority; and *sedition* is supposed to apply to deeds of a treasonable or riotous nature, directed rather against the government, or civil authorities, than military superiors, though necessarily involving or resulting in insubordination to the latter.[2]

The resistance may be *active* or *passive.* O'Brien cites the case of Col. Parish, who, in 1836, ordered Lieut. Ward of the Volunteers, to be arrested. The latter refused to obey the arrest, and threatened to shoot any one who should attempt to arrest him. No one would attempt it. He was then shot down by Col. Parish.[3] Here are examples of active and passive resistance, both of which constituted mutiny.

The question as to whether *mutiny* requires for its commission more than one person has been a subject of discussion. O'Brien holds the affirmative,[4] De Hart[5] and Benét,[6] citing Samuel,[7] the negative.

The facts by which it is intended to substantiate mutiny (or sedition) should be set forth in the charge; it

[1] G. O. 133, Hdq'rs. 1st Mil. Dist. Richmond, Va., Dec. 11, 1869.
[2] G. O. 77, A. G. O., Dec. 21, 1877.
[3] O'Brien's Courts-Martial, p. 76.
[4] P. 71. [5] P. 348. [6] P. 258. [7] P. 257.

must be proved by facts, not by words alone, or by words at all, except in connection with facts.[1]

When a mutiny or sedition partakes of the character of a conspiracy, the rule applies that any act committed by one of the conspirators is considered the act of all. Thus, if murder result from the action of one of the conspirators, this is murder by all.

Quelling Mutiny. The following order of General Scott as to the manner of quelling a mutiny, deserves careful consideration. "But it may be said, in the case of mutiny, or conduct tending to this crime, that it is necessary to cut down on the spot, the exciter or ringleader. *First.* Order him to be seized. If his companions put him into irons or confinement, it is plain that there is no spread of the dangerous example. But should *they* hesitate; or should it be necessary in any case of disobedience, desertion, or running away, *the object being to secure the person for trial,*—as always to repel a personal assault, or to stop an affray—in any one of these cases any superior may strike and wound, but only to the extent clearly necessary to such lawful end. Any excess, wantonly committed beyond such measured violence, would, of itself, be punishable in the superior. No other case can possibly justify any superior in committing violence upon the body of any inferior, without the judgment of a court, except that it may sometimes be necessary, by force, to iron prisoners for security, or to gag them for quiet."[2]

Challenges. Articles 26 and 27 refer to the sending of challenges, or allowing persons to go out to fight a duel.

In 1858, Col. S. sent the following communications to General H.:

1 Simmons, p. 268 (2d. Ed.)

2 G. O. 53. Hdq'rs. of the Army, Aug. 20, 1842.

WASHINGTON, D. C., FEBRUARY 15, 1858.

SIR: As more than twenty-four hours have passed since my note to you of yesterday, I have a right to presume that you do not intend to answer it. I have therefore to invite you to leave this city with me to-morrow morning, to go to any place you may designate.

I send this note privately to avoid committing any friend as long as possible. An early answer is requested.

I am, with due respect,
E. V. S——
Col. 1st Cavalry.

Brevet Brig. Genl. W. S. H.
Col. 2d Dragoons.

WASHINGTON, D. C. Feb. 16, 1858.

SIR: I received with great surprise your note of last evening, and have only to say to you; that a man who could insult a brother officer from an official covert, and afterwards refuse to apologize, or to give him that satisfaction which he had a right to demand, is utterly unworthy of any further notice from me.

I am, &c.
E. V. S——
Col. 1st Cavalry.

Brevet Brig. Gen. W. S. H.
Col. 2d Dragoons.

Colonel S., was tried under two charges.

First. For sending a challenge to fight a duel. *Second.* In upbraiding General H——, for refusing to fight a duel. The specifications were contained in the above communications.

The court acquitted him of both charges and their specifications.

In reviewing the proceedings the Secretary of War said,—"Colonel S———'s note of the 15th February is a challenge within the meaning of the Article of War. The military authorities and the decisions of courts-martial are clear in this regard. They lay down, what indeed is the necessary doctrine to give effect to the law, that '*no particular phraseology, no set form, is necessary to a challenge;*' nor '*a formal invitation to fight;*' but '*a mere hint or suggestion* is sufficient, and even '*such defiance as casts the burden on the other party.*' As challenges are in violation of law, ingenuity is not uncommonly exercised to avoid a plain expression of their purpose. But these are artifices to defeat the law, which courts of law will never favor, and when the meaning is so clear as to be intelligible to the party who receives the challenge, it answers the purpose, and is intelligible to the tribunal which tries it. In this case, however, the challenge is plainly expressed; even if it were not conclusively interpreted by the rest of the correspondence, and expressly as '*a demand for satisfaction.*'

"The doctrine of the findings in this case would render the article of war void and inoperative, by indicating a mode of doing without breach of the law what it is the exact purpose of the law to forbid.

"A rigid enforcement of strict discipline in the army is the most essential requisite for its honor and efficiency. If the bonds of discipline are loosened, it is only a question of time when the army will become a mob, and public opinion will ascribe to it that character, even before it would fairly be entitled to it."[1]

The 25th Article of War covers cases of challenge by word of mouth, or where a written challenge is handed personally by the challenger to the party challenged.[2]

[1] G. O. 2, A. G. O., March 10, 1856. [2] Opinions J. A. G., Aug. 14, 1872.

Redress of Wrongs to Officers. Article 29 provides the mode to be pursued by officers for redress when they deem themselves wronged.

The Article, by its terms, is limited to wrongs committed by the commanding officer of his (the officer's) regiment. The course marked out, however, is appropriate when an officer thinks himself wronged by any superior officer.

First. To make due application to the officer.

Second. If redress is refused, to make complaint to the officer superior to the latter, and, in extreme cases, when all other means of justice fail, appeals may be made to the Secretary of War.

The right, in charges and appeals, is not to be made in any mode or style the subordinate pleases, but with some reasonable circumspection, and in good faith, and in subjection to the controlling law of discipline which, to sustain military authority, requires obedience, and forbids disrespect to commanding officers. Under cover of charges or appeals a subordinate has no right to avail himself of the opportunity to behave with contempt to his commanding officer. Where such case is alleged in the specification, a court-martial will entertain and try the charge.[1]

Drunk on Duty. Article 38 provides that any officer who is found drunk on his guard, party, or other duty, shall be dismissed the service. Any soldier who so offends shall suffer such punishment as a court-martial may direct.

This Article is not applicable to simple cases of drunkenness, but to cases where the accused is *drunk on duty*, and in such manner it must be charged.

Where an officer was charged with "*drunkenness*," the

[1] G. O. 1, A. G. O., Jan. 11, 1856.

specification alleging "*drunkenness on guard*," found guilty, and sentenced "*to be cashiered*," it was held that the failure to express the charge in the terms used in the 38th Article was fatal to the validity of the proceedings.[1]

Difficulty has ever obtained in determining what con stitutes being "*on duty*," so as to make an offense cognizable under this article. A few citations from cases in our own service will illustrate the doubts that have arisen.

In 1843 a court-martial held, in the case of Capt. D., that "being drunk while in command of Detroit Arsenal," did not constitute an offense under this article; this particular article, in their opinion, having reference solely to matters of *detail*.[2]

The Judge-Advocate General holds, however, that a post commander, while present and exercising command as such, is deemed to be *at all times* "on duty" in the sense of this article, and so legally liable to a charge of a violation of the same if he become drunk and incapable to properly perform the duties of such command.[3]

In the case of Major P., in 1853, the court found him "guilty" of being "*drunk in the actual execution of his office*," but not "*drunk on duty*."

The Secretary of War, in reviewing the proceedings, said,—"The Department cannot discover any just ground for the distinction, which is even expressed by a contradiction. The Article of War must be taken to use its words in their plain meaning. If it be the idea of the court, that because certain duties are specified in this article, its province is limited to those and like duties, they impose a restriction on the general words that follow the specification, which the words themselves do not carry, and which is inconsistent with the policy and history of

[1] G. O. 264, A. G. O., Aug. 3, 1863. [2] G. O. 59, A. G. O., Oct. 11, 1843.
[3] Opinions J. A. G., p. 16.

the statute. If by specifying 'guard or party,' only like duties of special detail are meant, the law is greatly defective, and disregards the most important occasions of military service, where the whole are under arms, as parade, review, drill, or battle. The former statute specified 'guard, party, or other duty under arms.' The omission of the words 'under arms,' removed one restriction without introducing a new one. The specification and the general expression, each has its appropriate office; for example, the case specified is that of an officer of the guard being drunk during his tour, even when engaged in no act of duty; and the general words provide for actual occasions of duty."[1]

In the case of Captain I., charged with being "drunk on duty," the specification alleged that "the accused was found drunk while on duty in command of company D," the said company being at the time engaged in an expedition against hostile Indians. The court threw out the charge. The department commander disapproved this action, holding that "the nature of the service and the safety of the command certainly constitutes this a *duty* within the meaning of the 38th Article; but if the court had any doubt of that fact, it was competent to find the accused guilty of a criminal disorder under the 62d Article of War."[2]

The following General Order gives the views which have been maintained at the War Department. "In one sense 'on duty' is in contradistinction to 'on leave of absence.' But the expression appears to have a narrower meaning in the 38th Article of War. The old law in this matter ran in these words, 'guard, party, or other duty under arms.' The omission of the words 'under arms' from the present law, with intention to include descrip-

[1] G. O. 5, A. G. O., May 23, 1857. [2] G. C. M. O. 9, A G. O., Jan. 27, 1875.

tions and circumstances of duty, yet still leaves excepted those other occasions in camp or garrison, when the officer is, in the ordinary language of the service, 'off duty.' It is unnecessary to add that drunkenness 'off duty,' according to the circumstances, may be cognizable by a court-martial, but not under the 38th Article of War. What then are the conditions which bring the offense under this article? It is difficult to make a general definition which shall be precise and accurate. The law leaves it, as other general words of statutes, to judicial interpretation in the particular case. In one of these cases the court find that an officer, drunk at a dancing party, when engaged in no act of duty, was drunk on duty, because it was during his tour as officer of the day; and the same court find in the other case, that an officer is not drunk on duty, when, being sent to execute a duty requiring his attention from day to day, he gets drunk after he has commenced it, and is thus rendered unable to continue it; or when, having received an urgent and peremptory order, calling for immediate execution, he is unable to execute it because of his drunkenness. The department holds that all these cases are cases of drunkenness on duty."[1]

The Secretary of War in 1872, referring to the misconduct which should be brought under this article, held:

1st. A soldier on drill is on duty within the meaning of the 45th (present 38th) Article of War.

2d. It is manifestly wrong to order upon duty a soldier who is known to be at the time unfit for duty, whether this unfitness is caused by the fault of the soldier or not.

If the unfitness is the result of misconduct on the part of the soldier, the 99th (present 62d) Article of War provides for his punishment.

[1] G. O. 7, A. G. O., June 18, 1856.

The officer who orders upon duty a soldier whom he knows to be unfit for duty from any cause commits a grave offense.[1]

Some difficulty has also arisen with courts as to what constitutes "*drunkenness.*"

In the case of Lieutenant N., United States Volunteers, the commanding general said: "The court has gone out of its way to make a difficulty of a rather ludicrous nature. The prisoner is acquitted of being '*drunk,*' but found guilty of being '*intoxicated.*' It is not easy to find words more accurately synonymous than those between which the court-martial has attempted to make a distinction. When a man is *intoxicated* he is *drunk*. When he is under the influence of intoxicating liquors so as to cloud his faculties, or render his gait and motions unsteady, *he is drunk;* and if this occurs when he is on duty he must be *cashiered.* Nothing can be more erroneous than to suppose that as long as an officer is not drunk to insensibility—a condition, moreover, in which he is far less apt to do mischief, than when he is simply drunk enough to be indiscreet—he is not drunk at all. Whatever the court-martial may think of the matter, the fullest possession of his faculties, by every officer, is necessary to fit him to 'discharge his duties properly.'"[2]

In the case of Lieutenant H., the court struck out the words in their finding "did become drunk," and substituted the words "did become under the influence of intoxicating liquor." The Secretary of War, in reviewing the case, stated that—"The object of the law is manifestly to enforce that measure of sobriety which is essential to the full and calm control of both the mental and physical faculties, and thus to protect the military administration from

[1] W. D., A. G. O. March 4, 1872.

[2] G. O. 98, Army of the Potomac, March 8, 1862. G. O. 53, Army of the Potomac, Feb. 15, 1862.

the great mishaps to which it might be liable from the blunders and excesses of officers attempting to perform their duty under the influence of drink. Any such intoxication, therefore, as is sufficient to sensibly impair the rational and free exercise of the mental or physical abilities, is drunkenness within the meaning of the law. And should the condition of an officer accused of this offense not have partaken of this description, it is better that he should be acquitted, than that courts, by endeavoring to mark degrees of drunkenness, should encourage such a nice discrimination as, if grown into practice, would tend to defeat in great measure the purpose of the article.[1]

Relieving the Enemy. Article 45. This Article permits the trial of *all* persons by courts-martial, whether in the army or not, for relieving the enemy with money, etc.

The meaning of the word *enemy*, as used in this article, is that adopted by international law. All persons residing in the enemy's country are generally enemies, unless detained by force within the borders when desirous to escape.[2]

The Supreme Court has decided that this rule applies equally to civil and to international war.[3]

"When parties are engaged in supplying ammunition to Indians in open and notorious hostility to the United States, who properly come within the description of public enemies, in that case they would seem to be amenable to trial and punishment by courts-martial under the 45th Article of War. This applies to persons who are not, as well as to persons who are, in the military service."

The view in this particular case was given on the assumption that "there exists such a state of hostility on the part of the Indians as amounts to war. This state, in

[1] G. C. M. O. 33, A. G. O., May 12, 1875.

[2] Woolsey's International Law, p. 459.

[3] 2 Wallace, p. 419.

our peculiar relations with Indian tribes, is perhaps not susceptible of an exact definition. It is not necessary to the existence of war that hostilities should have been formally proclaimed. When any Indian tribes are carrying on a system of attacks upon the property or persons, or both, of the settlers upon our frontiers, or of the travelers across our territories, and the troops of the United States are engaged in repelling such attacks, this is war in such a sense as will justify the enforcement of the articles of war against persons who are engaged in relieving the enemy with ammunition, etc." [1]

Corresponding with the Enemy. Article 46. The same rule applies as to the trial of all persons by courts-martial for corresponding with the enemy, as laid down under Article 45.

The following Order was issued upon this subject at the commencement of our late war. "Public safety requires strict enforcement of this article. It is therefore ordered that all correspondence and communication, verbally or by writing, printing or telegraphing, respecting operations of the army or military movements on land and water, or respecting the troops, camps, arsenals, entrenchments, or military affairs within the several military districts, by which intelligence shall be directly, or indirectly, given to the enemy, without the authority and sanction of the General in command, be and the same are hereby absolutely prohibited, and from and after the date of this order, persons violating the same will be proceeded against under the 57th (present 46th) Article of War." [2]

Under this article it is essential only that correspondence should have been commenced. It is not necessary that the letters should have reached their destination.

[1] XIII. Opinions Attorney-General, July 19, 1871.
[2] G. O. 67, A. G. O., Aug. 26, 1861.

During the late war the government never regarded correspondence between citizens of the loyal and rebel States, when strictly confined to merely domestic affairs, as within the purview of this article.[1]

Desertion. Article 47 provides for the case of an officer or soldier deserting the service of the United States, and prescribes the punishment.

By desertion is meant the absenting of an officer or soldier from his regiment, battery, troop or company with intent not to return. The gist of the offense is the *intent*, and, no matter how long the absence, if the intent was to return, it is not technically desertion.

In order to decide whether the soldier left with the *intent not to return*, all the circumstances connected with his leaving, absence, and return, (whether compulsory or voluntary) must be considered together. Each case must be governed by its own particular facts, and no general rule on the subject can be laid down.[2]

As to whether escaping from confinement is desertion, the Judge-Advocate General in 1874 said, "This Bureau, having had occasion to reconsider its published opinion on the subject of escape from confinement, has considered that the same has not been sufficiently carefully expressed in the Digest. Its view simply is, that where a soldier escapes from an imprisonment under sentence after his term has expired, as, for instance, when he has been first discharged under the same sentence, he is guilty then of escape only. But that where he escapes from an imprisonment while still in the service, he is guilty *prima facia* of an escape only, but may be treated as guilty of a desertion, if the facts connected with his escape indicate the *animus* to separate from the service, and not to return to it, which is necessary to constitute desertion.[3]

[1] Opinions J. A. G. p. 19. [2] Opinions J. A. G., p. 138.
[3] Bureau of Mil. Justice, April 4, 1874.

Officers Deserting. The President is authorized to drop from the rolls of the army for desertion, any officer who is absent from duty three months without leave; and no officer so dropped shall be eligible for re-appointment.[1]

Where an officer was *dropped for desertion*, and afterwards captured, and tried for "desertion" with other charges, the proceedings were held void *ab initio* on this charge, as he was not in the military service of the United States.[2]

Good Order. Article 54. Every commanding officer is required by the provisions of this article to keep order in his command, and, to the utmost of his power, to redress all abuses or disorders which may be committed in quarters, garrison, or on the march by any officer or soldier under his command.

Under this article it is made the duty of commanding officers to see reparation made to the party or parties injured, from the pay of the soldiers who are guilty of abuses or disorders committed against citizens. Upon proper representation by any citizen of wanton injury to his person or property, accompanied by satisfactory proof, the commanding officer of the troops will cause the damage to be assessed by a board of officers, the amount stopped against the pay of the offenders, and reparation made to the injured person.

This proceeding will be independent of any trial or sentence by court-martial for the criminal offense.[3]

Delivery of Military Offenders to Civil Authority. Article 59. This Article provides for the delivery over to the civil authorities, of officers or soldiers accused, in time of peace, of a capital crime, or of any offense

[1] Rev. Statutes, Sec. 1229.
[2] G. C. M. O. 16, A. G. O., August 30, 1871.
[3] G. O. 35, A. G. O. July 3, 1868.

against the person or property of any citizen of the United States.

The duties of commanding officers under this article, are a matter of importance.

The subordination of the military to the civil authority is an axiom of this government; but it was never meant by this axiom to place the military entirely at the mercy of any individual who might call for the surrender of offenders under this article.

Referring to this question, Attorney-General Wirt remarked,—"You will discover that the case in which the article raises this duty on the commanding officer, etc., is when the person called for has been accused of some offense, such as is 'punishable by the known laws of the land.' The commanding officer owes a duty to the men under his command; he owes them the duty of protection so long as they continue in the faithful discharge of their duty. This duty is first in point of time, and highest in point of obligation. This 33d[1] Article gives him no authority to withdraw that protection, and deliver over his men to others, except in the case it describes,—where they are accused of such an offense as is 'punishable by the known laws of the land.' To justify him in delivering them up, he must see that the case described by the article has arisen. He is required by his duty to exercise his judgment upon the case. It is not enough to tell him that *some* offense has been committed; he must know what the specific offense is, in order that he may see whether it is an offense 'punishable by the known laws of the land.' The application according to the article, must be duly made to him, and, in my opinion, no application is duly made which does not state the specific offense, so as to enable the commanding officer to see dis-

[1] Present 59th.

tinctly that the case contemplated by the article has arisen. In the present instance, the demand made by Mr. Thompson did not state the specific offense. It is addressed to the commandant of Fort Delaware, Lieut. G. W. Gardiner; and then states that 'Lieut. Joseph Strong and John Farley are charged before me, on oath, with having violated the known laws of the land, and especially of the State of New Jersey; you are therefore requested, etc.' Mr. Thompson ought to have furnished the commanding officer with the specific charge, and with the name of the injured party; a copy of the affidavit ought to have accompanied the demand; and then, if as special as an affidavit ought to be to warrant an arrest, it would have given all the information that was necessary on the occasion. On such a demand as this before me, I am of the opinion that the commanding officer would have acted unjustifiably in delivering the men; and hence, that there is nothing to punish or to censure in his refusal."[1]

Speaking upon the same question, Attorney-General Cushing said: "Questions may arise on the Article of War, as to the precise circumstances under which an officer or soldier, having violated the law of the land, is to be delivered up to the civil magistrate. According to the express tenor of the articles, it is 'upon application duly made by, or on behalf of, the party or parties injured.' The law does not give the civil magistrate any right of voluntary and officious interference in these matters.

"Suppose, however, that a soldier stationed at Boston or New York perpetrates an act of murder, rape, robbery, or burglary upon the person or property of a person not in or attached to the army; can there be any doubt in such case that the law of the land, through the public prosecutor or the grand jury, represents and takes the place of a

[1] II. Opinions Attorney-General, Oct. 5, 1825.

private party injured? I conceive not; for in such a case the entire society is the party injured. A commanding officer would scarcely hesitate, in such a case, to surrender the criminal to the public authorities of the State.

"Suppose, again, that the act is internal to the army, as that an officer on duty kills a superior officer. Beyond all doubt, as we have seen, that act, though military by the ordinary law martial, would still be murder by the ordinary law, and so triable as such by the civil magistrate.

"There, also, the whole society is a party injured, and the public prosecutor may justly demand that the criminal shall be held amenable to the aggrieved majesty of the law of the land, either with or without a technical conformity of proceeding to the letter of the Article of War."[1]

In the case of Sergeant Gunther, a soldier stationed at Sidney Barracks, Nebraska, in 1876, and charged with shooting and wounding another soldier, the State sheriff, upon his own information and motion, and not on application made by or in behalf of the party shot, procured a warrant from a State court of Nebraska for the arrest of Gunther, and called on the commanding officer to deliver him up. The commanding officer refused to surrender him on the ground that "he is now a prisoner in the hands of the military authorities for an offense similar to that stated in the warrant, and for which he is being prosecuted by the United States government; he, of course, must be held until the United States has been satisfied." The sheriff then attempted to take Gunther, and was resisted by the commanding officer. A warrant was then procured against him for resisting a sheriff in the execution of his office; the grand jury found an indictment against him, and the case came on for trial before the District Court of the State of Nebraska.

[1] VI. Opinions Attorney General April 7, 1854.

The judge decided that had the warrant been procured by, or in behalf of the party shot, in accordance with the provisions of the 59th Article, the commanding officer would have been liable for refusing to give him up; but that, as the arrest was attempted at the instigation and motion of the sheriff, and not upon application made by or in behalf of the party shot, the commanding officer was not only justified in refusing to surrender Gunther, but under the circumstances would have rendered himself amenable to the military authorities therefor, under the 69th Article of War, had he so done.[1]

The surrender of officers and soldiers under this article, on warrants issued from the civil authorities, is somewhat complicated by our dual form of government.

Congress is authorized to exercise exclusive legislation, in all cases whatsoever, over all places purchased, by the consent of the legislature of the State in which the same shall be, for the erection of forts, arsenals, magazines, dock-yards, and other needful buildings.[2] These lands are ordinarily ceded by the State, with the reservation of the right to execute all civil and criminal process issued under the authority of the State. This reservation, however, does not give a jurisdiction to the State courts over offenses committed therein.[3]

The commanding officer should, therefore, only surrender offenders on such lands to the United States authorities. If, however, the jurisdiction has not been ceded by the legislature of the State, no matter how long the United States may have occupied it,[4] or an officer or soldier commits an offense outside the limits of a post, then, the

[1] The State of Nebraska *vs.* Capt. O. W. Pollock, reported in Army and Navy Journal, Sept. 5, 1877.

[2] Constitution, Sec. VIII. Article I.

[3] U. S. *vs.* Cornell, 2 Mason (R. I.) 60–91.

[4] The People *vs.* Godfrey, 17 Johns, (N. Y.) p. 225.

commanding officer should surrender on a warrant from the State court, as those courts have the jurisdiction of such offenses.

"Whether or not the jurisdiction of the State is concurrent with that of the general government over the locality where the officer or soldier is stationed, it is in no case competent for the civil official to proceed in the first instance to seize his person and carry him away by virtue of the warrant alone. On the contrary, it is from the commanding officer of the regiment, post, etc., that the delivery of the accused is to be sought and obtained; and it is only upon application duly made to such commander that any arrest of a military person when on duty can legally be affected. The course to be pursued for the purpose of such arrest is clearly pointed out in the article cited, which, though in terms directory upon the military commander only, at the same time indicates in general language the method proper to be adopted by or in behalf of the injured party."[1]

As a farther illustration of the course to be pursued under this article, the case of Private Bright is cited. In February, 1874, Frederick Bright, a private soldier of the United States Army, and stationed at Camp Douglas, came into Salt Lake City. He was arrested by the police while he was in the city, taken to the police court, tried upon a charge of violating a city ordinance against drunkenness, found guilty and sentenced to pay a fine of five dollars. In default of payment thereof he was committed to prison until said fine should be paid, time of imprisonment, however, not to exceed five days. While so confined a writ of *habeas corpus* was sued out by Colonel H. A. Morrow, Commander of Camp Douglas, for his release. On hearing, McKean, C. J., ordered Bright to be dis-

[1] II Opinions Attorney General, p. 14.

charged, and on appeal to the Supreme Court of the Territory the order was affirmed. McKean, C. J., delivering the opinion, said the law governing the case was to be found in the 33d[1] Article of War, and after discussion, arrived at the following conclusions :—

1st. That a soldier of the national army can be demanded by and surrendered to the civil authorities, to be tried and punished by them, only when he is charged with an offense, in time of peace, "such as is punishable by the known laws of the land," that is, by the laws of the United States, or of a State or territory.

2d. That a city by-law or ordinance is not in this sense a law of the land; but that a soldier who, when off duty, violates the ordinance of Salt Lake City forbidding drunkenness and disorderly conduct, may, in the absence of a provost guard, be arrested in the act and restrained by the civil authorities, but may not be tried and punished by them.

3d. That in case of such arrest and restraint, it is the duty of the civil authorities to deliver over such soldier to the military authorities, on the demand of the latter; and the duty of the military authorities to enforce against him the law military forbidding such offense.

4th. That if the civil authorities, after arresting such an offender, refuse to deliver him over on such demand, or proceed to try and punish him, the military authorities may take him by force.

5th. That if, instead of resorting to force, the military authorities present a petition to a federal court or judge of the territory, the prisoner must be discharged from the custody of the civil authorities by the writ of *habeas corpus.*[2]

[1] Present 59th. [2] Ex parte U. S. ex rel. Morrow, reported in American Law Register, Sept. 1874.

In two opinions[1] the Judge-Advocate General held the same views, and farther said,—"Where the party is not accused and his surrender is not applied for as contemplated by the statute, he cannot legally be taken or delivered into the custody of the civil authorities. Whether or not the application is duly made, is devolved upon the commander, and him alone, to decide. He may, therefore, refuse to surrender the accused, if the application is not in such form and so presented as to secure his confidence in its having been made in good faith and upon reasonable grounds. If it fails to identify the accused, or to fully state the offense charged, or to show that it is an offense against the person or the property of a citizen of the state or territory, or to make it clear that it is an offense punishable by the laws of the state or territory, or of the United States, or by the common law as recognized in the state or territory,—for this, in the opinion of the Bureau, is evidently the meaning of the term 'punishable by the known laws of the land,'—the commander may properly and legally decline to accede to the application. So, although it is not expressed in the article that the application shall be sworn to, the commander may nevertheless require it to be in the form of an affidavit, if he has any doubt of the *bona fide* character of the demand. * * *

"Such being the intent and effect of the 33d[2] Article, the duty of the commanding officer, and of the military authorities under it, is plain. If an officer or soldier is arrested or seized in the absence of a proper application, or without any application at all, it is incumbent upon the commander, without listening to any discussion or paltering on the part of the civil officials, simply to proceed to liberate the prisoner. In so doing he is entitled and required to use such force as may be necessary." In

[1] May 1, 1874, and July 14, 1874. [2] Present 59th.

explanation of this latter statement the Judge-Advocate General said, "It was therefore incumbent on the military authorities, if they desired to assume the custody of the soldier, to send a guard for him and request that he be delivered up. A decent respect for public order, as well as the simplest courtesy, would have suggested this course of action. To have proceeded at once, without any demand whatever, to break into the place of confinement and seize the prisoner by force, would have been wholly uncalled for and grossly disorderly."

Frauds. Article 60. This Article provides for the punishment of crimes of fraud against the United States, when committed by persons in the military service of the United States.

It gives jurisdiction to courts-martial of a class of civil offenses, *i. e.*, theft, embezzlement, perjury, subornation of perjury, and forgery in the particular cases named in the article.

It often happens in charges under this article, that officers undertake to excuse themselves by throwing the blame on their clerks or assistants. In this connection may well be read the following General Order from the War Department: "The principal cannot absolve himself from responsibility for the actions of his agents, unless it be clearly proven that they were beyond his control, or could not have been prevented by the exercise of proper vigilance in the execution of his duties. An officer cannot lawfully do for another, or permit to be done by those under his control, what the law forbids him to do himself, and any act of permission or commission on the part of an officer of the government, which tends to dishonor its credit, impeach the integrity of its officers, or bring scandal on the service, is misconduct in office which merits the severest reprobation."[1]

[1] G. O. 130, A. G. O., March 30, 1864.

Conduct unbecoming an Officer and a Gentleman. Article 61. The question as to what constitutes "*conduct unbecoming an officer and a gentleman*," is one upon which much difference of opinion has existed.

In a case tried in 1862 the commanding general of the Army of the Potomac said,—"Conduct unbecoming an officer and a gentleman is a phrase to which a technical meaning has been attached, and in that technical sense it is used in the articles of war. In one sense, every impropriety, every indecorum, is unbecoming an officer, and equally so to a gentleman. But this is not the signification that the words have when employed in framing charges."[1]

And again, in another case, "These words imply something more than indecorum, and military men do not consider the charge sustained unless the evidence shows the accused to be one with whom his brother officers cannot associate without loss of self-respect."[2]

In still another case that came up in that army it was held that "this article should only be used when the offense is such as to disgrace an offender—to make him an unfit associate for officers and gentlemen, and to render his expulsion from the society of such, necessary to the preservation of the respect due them as a class. That such is the nature of the unbecoming conduct contemplated by the 83d[3] Article of War is plainly deducible from the fact that dismissal is the prescribed and certain punishment. To draw the line less rigidly would subject every officer in the army to dismissal by a court whose notions of propriety were more stringent than, or even different from his own, and lead to the anomaly presented by the foregoing case, in which a number of officers request to

[1] G. O. 97, Army of the Potomac, March 8, 1862.
[2] G. O. 111, Army of the Potomac, March 25, 1862.
[3] Present 61st.

have returned to them as a companion, one whom they have just pronounced guilty of conduct for which the Article of War brands him as unfit to be among them."[1]

In the case of Surgeon Stone a court rendered a verdict of "not guilty" of "*conduct unbecoming an officer and gentleman*," and, upon being reconvened for a reconsideration of their finding, adhered to it, stating that they did not "justify such conduct, or sanction such acts; but they are not of that enormity (scandalous and infamous) which, in their opinion, is contemplated by the article in question, such as degrades a man from the association of gentlemen." The Secretary of War held that it was not necessary for conduct to be "*scandalous and infamous*" to secure conviction under this article; that, while the corresponding article of the code of 1776 had contained these words, in the revision of 1806 they had been dropped *ex-industria*, and this was held by him equivalent to a declaration by Congress that it should no longer be necessary, in order to bring an officer within the scope of this article, that the act charged should be "scandalous and infamous," provided it were unbecoming an officer and a gentleman. He further said,—"An officer of the highest merit may, from indiscretion or thoughlessness, or from momentary excitement, do an act which all right minded persons would consider as highly unbecoming a gentleman, and yet, if it involved nothing dishonorable or morally wrong, he would not thereby forfeit his character as a gentleman.

"Assuming the facts found by the court to be true, the attack by Dr. Stone upon Lieut. Schrœder, was attended with many aggravating circumstances which distinguished it from an ordinary assault and battery. The court have found that it was premeditated and without good and suffi-

[1] G. O. 45, Army of the Potomac, Nov. 17, 1864.

cient cause; that Dr. Stone struck Lieut. Schrœder while he was looking in the opposite direction, and not prepared for an assault, and this in the view of ladies, citizens, and soldiers. Conduct like this would be considered highly reprehensible if committed by any one in civil life; and the Department does not consider that either the character or the interests of the army would be promoted by lowering the standard of propriety in the service, and converting conduct improper in itself—whether committed by an officer or by anyone else—into a mere breach of military discipline.

"The court may possibly have considered, that the punishment prescribed by the 83d[1] Article, was disproportioned to the offense committed by Dr. Stone, but that question was not submitted to them. The law in this case affixes the punishment, and it is the province of the reviewing power, and not that of the court, to mitigate it according to circumstances." [2]

In 1856, Lieutenant Smith was tried for "conduct unbecoming an officer and a gentleman." The court found him "not guilty" of the charge, but "guilty" of conduct unbecoming an officer, and to the prejudice of good order and military discipline."

In commenting on this case the Secretary of War held that,—"There is no such offense known to the articles as 'conduct unbecoming an officer.' The unbecoming conduct of a commissioned officer of which the law takes notice, and authorizes a court-martial to take cognizance, is 'conduct unbecoming an officer and a gentleman.' There is no minor indecorum, no unbecoming conduct, not unbecoming an officer and a gentleman, that the law submits to the jurisdiction of a court-martial, and the court in pronouncing the conduct of Lieutenant Smith 'not unbecoming an

[1] Present 61st. [2] G. O. 41, A. G. O., Dec. 11, 1852.

officer and a gentleman,' acquitted him of the legal charge before them. At the same time they give judgment under the 99th[1] Article of War. He was not charged with any offense under that article. If charges are drawn up so as to bring them expressly and exclusively under particular articles of war, a court-martial cannot convict under other articles. The sentence of the court-martial in this case is therefore *void*."[2]

The latter part of this decision has been overruled, and it is proper now to find a person, charged under a specific article, where the evidence does not prove an offense under that article, "not guilty," but "guilty" of "*conduct to the prejudice, etc.*"

Conduct Prejudicial to Good Order and Military Discipline. Article 62. In 1869 the question was raised,—"Does a specification alleging that a soldier filled up a blank check on the assistant treasurer of the United States, signed thereto the name of a paymaster of the army, and negotiated or used the same as money, charge a military offense of which a general court-martial can take cognizance?" The Judge-Advocate General held the offense one properly charged under the 99th[3] Article, inasmuch as, in the forging of the name of an army officer, his military superior, and in availing himself of the forged signature in the manner set forth, the soldier was guilty of a criminal act, necessarily prejudicial to good order and military discipline.[4]

Under this article all offenses not capital are cognizable by courts-martial, provided they affect the good order or discipline of the service. But where a crime, not specially brought within the jurisdiction of a military court by some other article of war or other statute, does

[1] Present 62d.

[2] G. O. 8, A. G. O., July 23, 1856.

[3] Present 62d.

[4] Bureau of Mil. Justice, Oct. 23, 1869.

not affect, or prejudice, military order or discipline, it can be taken cognizance of, in time of peace, only by the State or local criminal courts.[1]

It is not absolutely necessary that the words "to the prejudice of good order and military discipline" be added, to make an offense cognizable by courts-martial. If the offense, as derived from the charge and specification, is contrary to good order and military discipline, the court will have jurisdiction whether the words are added or not. The Judge-Advocate General so held in the case of a soldier charged with "assault with intent to kill," the specification alleging that the offense was committed by a fellow soldier.[2]

[1] Opinions J. A. G., p. 44. [2] Bureau of Mil. Justice, April 8, 1869.

CHAPTER XIX.

COURTS OF INQUIRY.

Courts of Inquiry are courts established by law for the purpose of examining into the nature of any transaction of, or accusation or imputation against, any officer or soldier of the army.

Constitution. They may only be ordered in one of two ways:—

1st. By the President at his option, or on demand.

2d. By a commanding officer upon application of the party desiring the court.

The 115th Article provides that as courts of inquiry may be perverted to dishonorable purposes, and may be employed in the hands of weak and envious commandants, as engines for the destruction of military merit, they shall *never* be ordered by any commanding officer, except upon a demand by the officer or soldier whose conduct is to be inquired into. The term "commanding officer," as used in this connection, is interpreted to mean such superior officer as might properly convene a court-martial for the trial of the accused.[1]

The question arising in 1874, as to the right of a regimental commander to convene a court of inquiry, the Judge-Advocate General held, that if the charges to be inquired into are beyond the jurisdiction of a regimental court, then it is believed that the regimental

[1] Opinions J. A. G., p. 42.

commander would not be the proper commanding officer to order the court of inquiry, and this whether the party demanding the court be a commissioned officer or enlisted man. It is the offense charged which should give the jurisdiction, and not the status of the party in the service.[1]

Composition. A court of inquiry consists of one or more officers, not exceeding three, and a recorder[2] thereof.

As in the minor courts-martial, the presence of all the members for purposes of business is necessary.

The recorder is not a member; his position and duties correspond closely to those of a judge-advocate of a general court-martial.

A new member may be appointed and take his seat after the court has been in session;[3] but previous testimony should be read over to him.

The accused is permitted to be present, and should be allowed counsel, but the court would have the same right to object to an improper person as on a court-martial.

The law authorizes the appointment of a reporter, who shall record the proceedings of, and testimony taken before such court, and may set down the same in the first instance in short hand. Before entering upon his duty he is to be sworn (or affirmed) faithfully to perform the same. The rule as to appointment prescribed for courts-martial governs all military courts.

Courts of inquiry, and the recorders thereof, have the same power to summon and examine witnesses as is given to courts-martial and the judge-advocates thereof.[4]

The recorder was in 1863,[5] given power to issue like

[1] Letter A. G. O., Sept. 22, 1874.

[2] The term "Judge-Advocate" is substituted for the term "Recorder" in the new Articles recently proposed.

[3] Howard Court of Inquiry. [4] Article, 118.

[5] Sec 25, March 3, 1863.

process to compel the attendance of witnesses before such court, as is issued by the local courts of criminal jurisdiction in the State, Territory or district where the court is sitting, but has not this power now.[1]

Depositions may be taken and read in evidence under the circumstances named in Article 91.

Procedure. The Articles of War are not specific as to the mode of procedure to be adopted by courts of inquiry, and the question has arisen as to "what rules are to govern the court in those numerous incidents of its constitution and mode of action, concerning which the statute rules do not speak; such as the place and time of sitting, the publicity or not, the admission or exclusion of evidence, the allowance of counsel, the privacy of votes, and sundry matters of practice and procedure." In answer to this question which Attorney-General Cushing propounded, he himself replies,—"I apprehend there is but one possible answer to these questions, namely, that the court is to be governed by the general principles of military law, applying the analogies of a court-martial where these are applicable, and recurring to adjudged cases, precedents ruled, authoritative legal opinions, and approved books of legal exposition, where there is no pertinent paramount statute rule."[2]

This is the rule which has been adopted in practice. The mode of procedure will differ somewhat, depending on the character of the question to be examined into.

For instance, the President may order a court of his own will, to examine into a question where no accusation is made against any person, or where the question of fault is only remotely involved. In this case all attainable evidence would be submitted, the witnesses being examined by the court (or through its recorder) unless the

[1] Revised Statutes, § 1202. [2] VIII. Opinions Attorney-General.

interest of some party was involved and he demanded to be present. In 1831, such a court was ordered to inquire into the causes and circumstances which led to the burning of Fort Delaware. In 1836, a similar court was instituted to inquire and examine into the failure of the campaigns of that year in Florida against the Seminole Indians, under the command of Major-General Gaines and of Major-General Scott.

Again, a court may be ordered on demand, or by order of the President, to inquire into the nature of some transaction of an officer or soldier.

The accused not only has the right to be present with counsel, but should take advantage of this right. In 1831, Lieut. Thomas failed to attend a court of inquiry appointed to examine into his failure to settle his accounts as a disbursing officer, and was in consequence dismissed by the President.[1]

The better practice would seem to be in this case to allow the recorder to conduct the case for the government, leaving the accused to conduct his defense; the court asking such questions as it may desire, and summoning new witnesses if deemed necessary.[2]

In the case of General Howard, this was the mode adopted. After the testimony was concluded, the accused and the recorder were allowed to address the court. This manner of proceeding seems better than for the court to conduct the examination.

Finally, when a direct accusation is made by an officer against another, the best plan seems to be to allow both the accuser and the accused to be present and conduct the examination; the court summoning such witnesses of both

[1] O. 23, A. G. O., June 7, 1831.

[2] The judge-advocate of the court is required to submit all attainable evidence in the case, in the Articles of War recently proposed.

parties as it deems material. The *accuser* would then examine his witnesses, followed by any desired cross-examination, re-examination, or questions by the court; the *accused* would follow in the examination of his witnesses. Both parties should be allowed to make a statement, and the court would then close for deliberation.

In the Court of Inquiry of General Dyer in 1869, this was the practice pursued. The court in their report said, "The greatest latitude was allowed the accusers to produce both oral and documentary evidence in support of their charges. They were permitted to appear, and to be represented by counsel, several of them were also heard as witnesses in support of the allegations; and it is believed that no evidence offered has been excluded from the consideration of the court which could possibly have shed any light upon the question involved, or which could have affected the decision of the court."[1]

Oaths. The 117th Article requires the members of a court of inquiry to take a prescribed oath, after which an oath is administered to the recorder.[2]

Witnesses are required to take the same oath which is taken by witnesses before courts-martial.[3]

Challenge. The accused is allowed the right of challenge, for, although an examination by a court of inquiry is not a *trial* in the strict sense of the word, still its opinions may reflect upon the conduct of an officer, and biased or prejudiced officers should not be allowed to conduct such an examination.

The challenge must be for cause stated to the court, and the court will dispose of such challenges as prescribed in the case of courts-martial.

Jurisdiction. Courts of inquiry cannot take cogni-

[1] G. O. 51, A. G. O., May 15, 1869.
[2] See Chapter VIII, p. [3] Ibid, p.

zance of any case save upon specific orders from the proper authority. The same court may investigate by authority any number of cases. It must be organized, however, in each case, and render its report separately in each.[1]

Opinion when Given. A court of inquiry shall not give an opinion on the merits of the case inquired of, unless specially ordered to do so.[2] The order convening the court should therefore expressly state whether the court shall give an opinion upon the merits of the case or not. If not required to give such opinion, it simply reports the facts ascertained by evidence. A simple submission of the record and testimony in the latter case, however, is not deemed sufficient; the conclusions of the court as deduced from the evidence must be set forth.

Hours of Sitting. The limitation as to hours of sitting, imposed by the Articles of War on courts-martial, does not apply to courts of inquiry.

Statute of Limitation. The two years limitation does not apply to investigations by courts of inquiry. On this point Attorney-General Cushing says,—" Courts of inquiry are not limited in the terms of the Article of War; it is well settled that they are not limited by construction in Great Britain; the more general conclusion has been the same in this country; and that conclusion seems to me consonant with the general principles of law, and especially convenient in a constitutional government like the United States.[3]

Open or Closed Court. Courts of inquiry are inherently close courts, to which defendants generally and auditors and spectators occasionally have access, by permission, and not of right.[4]

[1] VIII. Opinions Attorney General, Jan. 31, 1857. [2] Art. 119.

[3] VI. Opinions Attorney General, p. 243; VIII. Ibid, p. 349.

[4] VIII. Opinions Attorney General, Jan. 31, 1857.

The wording of the 118th Article establishes without doubt the right of the accused to be present. Sir Charles Napier wrote that a "court of inquiry ought generally to be a closed court: no one allowed to enter but such individuals as are called for, and who, being privately examined, are sent out."[1]

Secrecy. There is nothing in the oath of the members or recorder requiring secrecy, but most authorities unite in the opinion that such secrecy as is required of members of courts-martial should be observed.

Record. A record of the proceedings must be kept, and should be made up in the same manner as the record of a court-martial. This must be authenticated by the signatures of the recorder and the president thereof, and delivered to the officer appointing the court, or his successor in office.[2]

The original proceedings, after the decision thereon of the reviewing authority, or where the proceedings require the decision of the President, are to be forwarded direct to the Bureau of Military Justice.

Not a Trial. As before stated, the investigation of a court of inquiry is not a *trial*, and, though an opinion upon the merits may have been given, it could not be pleaded in bar of trial before a court-martial. It is generally a preliminary investigation to aid in determining whether the accused shall be brought before a court-martial for trial. It corresponds somewhat to an investigation by a grand jury in civil cases.

Rules of Evidence. Courts of inquiry do not generally confine themselves to the exact rules of evidence which govern courts-martial; their province is to find out the truth of the matter in question, and they often allow much greater latitude than such courts. As the proceed-

[1] Clode's Military and Martial Law, p. 174. [2] See Art. 120

ings of a court of inquiry may be admitted as evidence by a court-martial in certain cases,[1] it would seem proper for them to adopt the same rules as govern courts-martial. Such proceedings need not necessarily be admitted. A court-martial must exercise a discretion upon this point. In a case where the record of a court of inquiry was not duly authenticated in accordance with the requirements of Article 120, it was held not admissible in evidence upon a trial before a military commission.[2]

Right to Court of Inquiry. An officer or soldier is not entitled of right to a court of inquiry, but where a request is made, especially by an officer against whom imputations are made, the convening officer ought to consider whether he will not do an injustice by refusing such application.

Where an officer is out of the service he is not entitled to a court of inquiry, though the President might, on his application, order such court if he deemed it advisable.

Contempts. Courts of inquiry, though not empowered by statute to punish for contempts, would without doubt be justified in ordering an officer in arrest, or a soldier in confinement, for any of the contempts which a court-martial may punish.

Copy of Record. The accused is not entitled by law to a copy of the record, but it may be furnished him on application to the Secretary of War.

[1] Art. 121. [2] Opinions J. A. G., p. 43.

CHAPTER XX.

MILITARY COMMISSIONS.

In times of war, whether foreign or a rebellion, we have seen that[1] a large number of offenses are committed by persons not in the military service, which must either be tried by special tribunals or go untried. It may be that the civil courts have been suspended, or have ceased to exist, or, if existing, have no jurisdiction of the offense. Again, cases may arise when the civil courts are in session, and have jurisdiction of the case, and yet there would be little or no hope of securing justice through them. Thus, during the Mexican war the soldiers of General Taylor's army were deliberately assassinated. How could these assassins be punished? Not by courts-martial, for these are courts of limited statutory jurisdiction, and are not authorized to take cognizance of such offenses: to have submitted the cases to the local Mexican courts would have been mere folly. It only remained in these cases to punish the offenders summarily, by which errors might be committed and great injustice done; or to submit them to a special tribunal, which could speedily try the case, decide as to the guilt or innocence of the accused, and award a suitable punishment. The latter course was pursued.

The character of such courts must depend upon the local laws of each particular country.

History. During our entire national existence we have had recourse to such tribunals. In the Revolution-

[1] Chapter I.

ary war frequent cases arose where persons, not in the military service, were tried, convicted, and sentenced by such tribunals, and their punishments executed. One or two cases will illustrate:—When Major André was captured, courts-martial had no jurisdiction, as now, to try the offense of acting as a spy. General Washington, therefore, convened a tribunal, styled "A Board of General Officers," to examine and report upon the charges. This, tribunal examined the case, and recommended that André be hung as a spy, which the Commander-in-Chief approved and had executed. Another case was that of Joshua Hett Smith, a civilian, at whose house Arnold and André met. He was tried for treasonable practices by a court-martial (properly a military commission) and this, notwithstanding the civil courts were open at that time.[1]

These tribunals were at that time differently styled—often improperly as courts-martial,—for they tried a class of cases over which courts-martial, in the accepted sense of the term, had no jurisdiction. They were likewise differently composed. The "Board" which tried André consisted of fourteen general officers and the Judge Advocate General; while some of them were composed of as many as twenty officers.

During the Mexican War General Scott resorted to such tribunals to govern the Mexican people within his lines, and enumerated the cases wherein they should have jurisdiction. They were styled by him *military commissions*. During our late war this court (military commission) was constantly resorted to, and formed one of the most important aids in the furtherance of justice.

As the legality of these commissions has been denied by many able jurists, it may not be improper to state that

[1] For other cases see Articles on Martial Law during the Revolution, by Col. Lieber and Major Gardner, in Magazine of American History for 1877.

all the departments of the Government have recognized them as legal. Congress has recognized them, in terms, in several of its acts;[1] the Executive department, under different executives, has sanctioned them in orders issued to the army, and approvals given to their sentences; and the Supreme Court in *Ex parte* Milligan,[2] while deciding that a military commission had no jurisdiction in that particular case, affirmed their legality under certain circumstances.

We may therefore consider the legality of such courts in this country as settled. The source from which they derive their jurisdiction was pointed out in Chapter I.

Military Commissions Defined. A military commission may be defined to be a tribunal composed of military officers, deriving its jurisdiction (in this country) from the express or implied will of Congress, and having power to try offenders against the common laws of war.

In *Ex parte* Vallandingham the Supreme Court said, that a military commission is not a *court* within the meaning of the 14th Sec. of the Judiciary Act of 1789, nor is it judicial in the sense in which judicial power is granted to the courts of the United States, but it involves discretion to examine, to decide, and sentence.[3]

Constitution. Any officer authorized to appoint a general court-martial may convene a military commission.

It would not be proper to authorize a general court-martial regularly to sit as a military commission. If deemed advisable to constitute the same members a commission they should be formally dissolved as a court-martial.[4]

Composition. The Statutes of the United States have not prescribed the manner in which military com-

[1] Act July 17, 1862, Chap. 201, § 5. Act March 18, 1863, Chap. 75, § 36. Resolution 18, March 11, 1862. Revised Statutes, § 1199, 1343 and 1344.

[2] 4 Wallace, 2, *et seq.* [3] I. Wallace, 243. [4] Opinions J. A. G., p. 129.

missions shall be composed, and, as those courts have grown out of the usages of war, we must look to those usages to determine the rules applicable to them. The principle has generally been adopted that the rules which apply to the convening, the constitution, and the proceedings of courts-martial should apply to them. An exception to this rule, however, has been adopted in the composition of these commissions, in fixing the minimum number at *three*. In important cases the Judge-Advocate General advised that the number should not be less than five. A judge-advocate is appointed, with the same duties as the judge-advocate of a general court-martial.[1]

The members are always commissioned officers of the army.

In the order convening a military commission it is not necessary to state, that "no other officers than those named can be assembled without manifest injury to the service."[2]

Where it appeared from the record of a military commission that it was constituted with less than three members; or that less than three members took part in the trial, or that there was no judge-advocate regularly detailed as such, the proceedings were held fatally defective.[3]

Jurisdiction. Congress has not in this country defined the jurisdiction of these courts, and it is a little difficult to lay down its exact limits.

As to *persons* it may be said:

1st. It has no authority to try persons in the military service of the United States, for purely military offenses, or for any of the civil offenses named in the 58th Article of War, but where a person in the military service commits a civil offense not named in the articles, and in a

[1] Opinions J. A. G., p. 222. [2] Ibid, p. 321. [3] Ibid, p. 320.

section of country where there is no civil court practicable to try him, a military commission has jurisdiction.[1]

2d. It has power to try persons in the service of the enemy for violation of the common laws of war.

Thus, during the Mexican war a number of Mexican officers were captured and released on parol; they were afterwards recaptured fighting against our army. General Scott very properly brought them before a military commission, which tried them, sentenced them to be hung, and they were executed.

It likewise has power to try persons in the enemy's service for the ordinary *civil* offenses, and would try them, especially when committed in a section of country where the ordinary criminal courts are closed by the fact of war.

3d. It has jurisdiction over citizens in certain cases, but the most difficulty arises in determining these cases.

In a military department under martial law, when the ordinary criminal jurisdiction both of the United States and State courts is suspended, or the offense is not cognizable by the courts in session, the military commission has jurisdiction. But in *Ex parte* Milligan, the Supreme Court in December, 1866, held that a citizen, not connected with the military service, and resident in a State where the courts are open and in the proper exercise of their jurisdiction, cannot, even when the privilege of the writ of *habeas corpus* is suspended, be tried, convicted, or sentenced otherwise than by the ordinary courts of law.[2]

The court, as we saw in Chapter I, went much farther than this, holding that it was not in the power of Congress to grant jurisdiction in such cases to a military commission; to which four of the nine judges dissented.[3]

[1] See G. O. 100, 1863. [2] 4 Wallace, 4.

[3] For their opinion see Chapter I.

This minority view, as we pointed out in Chapter I, seems to accord with the practice of the government. Under the act of Congress of March 2d, 1867—empowering district commanders to substitute in the rebel states, for the trial of *all* criminals, military commissions in the place of civil courts—one James Weaver, a citizen of Texas, was tried for murder in 1868, by a military commission, and sentenced to be hung; and this, notwithstanding the courts were in session, and an indictment pending against him before the state courts for the same offense. The question as to the jurisdiction of the military commission was submitted to the Attorney-General, who decided in the affirmative. He said, "The rights of war do not necessarily terminate with the cessation of actual hostilities. I have no doubt that it is competent to the nation to retain the territory and the people which have once assumed a hostile and belligerent character, 'within the grasp of war' until the work of restoring the relations of peace can be accomplished, and that it is for Congress, the department of the national government to which the power to declare war is entrusted by the Constitution, to determine when the war has so far ended that the work can be safely and successfully completed."[1]

Again, in 1873, the question arose as to the right to try certain of the Modoc Indians by military commission after the war had ceased. The Attorney-General held that it had jurisdiction; that although the war was practically ended, it was the right of the United States, as there was no agreement for peace, to determine for themselves whether or not any thing new ought to be done for the protection of the country, or the punishment of crimes growing out of the war.[2]

[1] XIII. Opinions Attorney-General, p. 65.

[2] XIV. Opinions Attorney General, p. 253.

In the case of the assassins of President Lincoln, the courts of the District of Columbia being open, the Attorney-General held that if the persons who are charged with the assassination committed the deed as public enemies, —and whether they did or not was a question to be decided by the tribunal before which they are tried—they not only can but ought to be tried by military commission.[1]

As to Place. The jurisdiction of a military commission, like that of a general court-martial, is not confined to the place of the commission of the offense, but is coextensive with the limits of the federal domain, and extends to any military department in which, on account of facilities for obtaining testimony or for other good reasons, it may be convenient to bring a case to trial.[2]

As to Time. It would seem, especially in the ordinary criminal offenses, that the two years' limitation prescribed for courts-martial should not apply to military commissions; but to subject military commissions partly to the laws and practice which govern civil courts, and partly to those which control courts-martial, would be to destroy the harmony between the two different military tribunals, and to embarrass the administration of military justice; the two years' limitation therefore applies.[3]

Procedure. The forms of procedure, as before stated, are the same as before courts-martial; formal charges are preferred; the accused has the right of challenge and of counsel; he has the right to cross-examine witnesses before the court; to produce witnesses of his own; and to make a statement.

Oath. The members and the judge-advocate take the oath prescribed for the same officers in a general court-martial.

[1] XI. Opinions Attorney General, p. 297.

[2] Opinions J. A. G., p. 225. [3] Ibid, p. 223.

Punishments. The punishments which military commissions can inflict are regulated by the laws and usages of war adopted by civilized nations. A two-thirds' vote is held necessary where a death sentence is inflicted, and such sentences would, under our present laws, require the approval of the President.

Record. The record is made up in the same way, and authenticated in like manner as court-martial proceedings.

Confirmation. The proceedings are forwarded to the officer who convenes the court, who is required to act upon them and has the same power over them as over court-martial proceedings. He may approve, disapprove, or order them back for revision.

Copy. The proceedings are filed in the Judge-Advocate General's office; and, while the accused is not entitled by law to a copy, it may be furnished by the Secretary of War on proper application.

Review by Civil Courts. The proceedings of a military commission are not subject to review by the civil authorities. In the case of Mr. Vallandingham, tried by a military commission and sentenced to be confined at a military prison during the war, the Supreme Court decided that, not being a judicial court within the meaning of the 14th Sec. of the Judiciary Act of 1789, it could not issue a writ of *habeas corpus ad subjiciendum* to review or reverse its proceedings, or a writ of *certiorari* to revise the proceedings of a military commission.[1]

Provost Judge or Court. During our late war general officers, commanding a department in which the ordinary criminal courts were suspended, appointed a provost judge or court for the trial of minor offenses.

This court consisted of a single person, sometimes a

[1] Ex parte Vallandingham, 1 Wallace, p. 243.

citizen and sometimes an officer, and derived its authority from the same source as military commissions.

The jurisdiction of these courts, says the Judge-Advocate General, should be confined to cases of police merely, to wit, such cases as are summarily disposed of daily by the police courts in our large cities, as, for instance, cases of drunkenness, disorderly conduct, assault and battery, and of violation of such civil ordinances and military regulations as may be in force for the government of the locality. The provost judge supplies the place of the local police magistrate in promptly acting upon the class of cases described, without, at the same time, being necessitated (as a formal military commission would be) to preserve a detailed record of the testimony and proceedings in each case. But he should not assume to take cognizance, on the one hand, of the offenses committed by soldiers in violation of any article of war, or of the regulations of the service; or, on the other hand, of the offenses of civilians of a strict military character, as for instance, those in violation of the laws and custom of war, and so properly triable by a military commission.[1]

[1] Opinions J. A. G., p. 303.

CHAPTER XXI.

RETIRING BOARDS.

OFFICERS of the regular army under certain conditions may be retired. Except in certain specified cases, however, no officer shall be retired from active service without a full and fair hearing before an army retiring board, if, upon due summons, he demands such hearing.[1&2] The right to such hearing he may receive or may forego by his own neglect. In neither case can he properly interpose an objection to a decision of the board, arrived at without such hearing or without his being personally presented before it.[3]

Constitution and Composition of Retiring Boards. The Secretary of War, under direction of the President, is required, from time to time, to assemble an army Retiring Board consisting of not more than nine nor less than five officers, two-fifths of whom shall be selected from the medical corps. The Board, excepting the officers selected from the medical corps, shall be composed, as far as may be, of seniors in rank to the officer whose disability is inquired into.[4]

A recorder is appointed to take down the testimony and record the proceedings, but is not a member of the Board.

Powers. A Retiring Board has to inquire into and

[1] At present officers may be retired by the President upon their own application after 30 years of service, or by reason of being 62 years of age, or of having served 45 years.

[2] § 1253, Revised Statutes.

[3] Opinions J. A. G., p. 329.

[4] § 1246, Revised Statutes.

determine the facts touching the nature and occasion of the disability of any officer who appears to be incapable of performing the duties of his office, and has such powers of a court-martial and of a court of inquiry, *as may be necessary for that purpose.*[1] The Board, therefore, has power to summon and compel the attendance of witnesses; and to make use of depositions in the same manner and under the same restrictions as courts-martial.[2]

Duties. The province of the Board is simply to determine the facts touching the nature and occasion of the disability of the officers examined. It has no authority to entertain any charge of a military offense, or to try an issue of fact involving the moral status of the officer. Its deliberations must be directed to his physical and mental capacity to discharge the duties incident to his rank and office; and its investigation is not limited to any particular period of time; for the length of service of the officer, and the duration and continuance of his disability are all material to be considered.[3]

Preliminaries. Prior to the Board's assembling the invalid officer should appear before the medical members of the Board, and undergo a careful mental and physical examination.

It is well also, to save time, for the recorder to notify the invalid officer to prepare his complete military history in writing and be prepared to swear to it, and, if he has asked to be retired, to state fully in writing the nature and cause of his disability.

Mode of Procedure. The proceedings of a Retiring Board assimilate closely to those of a court of inquiry, although the Board generally examines the witnesses.

The Board having assembled, and the officer whose case is to be determined upon being present, the recorder reads

[1] § 1248, Revised Statutes. [2] Opinions J. A. G., p. 330. [3] Ibid, p. 329.

the order convening the Board and asks the officer if he has any objection to any member present.

Challenge. The right of challenge should always be accorded. The statutes as to the formation of the Board intend a fair hearing and, without this right, great injustice might at times result.

Oaths. The members of the Board are required to take an oath to discharge their duties honestly and impartially.[1]

The recorder takes the same oath as the recorder of a court of inquiry.

The witnesses give their testimony on oath.[2]

Examination of Witnesses. The invalid officer is the first witness called and is asked to state his military history, and, if he has asked to be retired, the nature and occasion of his disability. If he has reduced his answers to writing he may sign them and submit them in that form, in which case they are read by the officer or recorder, and appended to the record. The Board should ask the officer if in his opinion, he is incapacitated for active field service, and such other questions as it may deem advisable.

The next witness should be the medical officers of the Board, in the order of their rank. They should be questioned as to their examination of the invalid officer. The results of this examination the medical officers should have reduced to writing, and signed, and they may submit it in that form, each officer referring to it as his answer when examined.

Other oral testimony, and documentary evidence from the Adjutant-General's office may then be introduced, with the right to the invalid officer of objecting to any improper evidence, and of cross-examining the witnesses called by the court.

[1] § 1247, Revised Statutes.

[2] For forms of oaths, see Chap. VIII.

After the Board has finished, the officer may produce such evidence as he deems necessary, and make such statement to the court as he may desire.

Benét gives the following rules as to the competency of evidence before Retiring Boards: [1]

(1) In a manifest and unmistakable case, the Board may take the evidence of their own senses as to the physical condition of a party, who, for instance, cannot walk into the room, or get up, or sit down without assistance. But generally, and in all questionable cases, they are to ascertain his condition, as in all judicial proceedings, by evidence.

(2) That the conduct and services of an officer are evidence of his fitness to exercise his commission; and that the reports of courts of inquiry, and the judgment of courts-martial, are competent evidence in inquiring into such conduct and services; and that the whole record of such court shall be admitted when required.

(3) That facts, by the testimony of officers, and their judgment on such facts witnessed by them, are also competent evidence in the same inquiry.

(4) That general professional reputation may also be given in evidence.

Finding. The Board is then closed for deliberation and is required to give an opinion as to whether the invalid officer is incapacitated for active service or not. When it finds an officer so incapacitated, it is further required to report the cause which, in its judgment, has produced his incapacity, and whether such cause resulted from an incident of service.[2] This conclusion of the Board is merely an opinion to assist the President in deciding the case.

Record. A complete and separate record of each case is kept by the recorder. This is made up in the same

[1] Page 241. [2] § 1249 Revised Statutes.

manner as the record of courts-martial proceedings. It must be authenticated by the president and recorder, and forwarded (through the Adjutant-General) to the Secretary of War.

A copy of the record may generally be obtained on application to the Secretary of War.

The Board sits with open or closed doors as they see fit, and are not limited as to the time of their sittings.

Revision. The Secretary of War is required to lay the proceedings and decision of the Board before the President for his personal examination, and approval or disapproval and orders in the case.[1]

When a Retiring Board finds an officer is incapacitated for active service, and that his incapacity *is* the result of an incident of service, (and such decision is approved by the President) said officer *shall* be transferred to the retired list.

When the Board finds that an officer is incapacitated for active service, and that his incapacity *is not* the result of any incident of service, and its decision is approved by the President, the officer *shall* be retired from the service, or wholly retired from the service as the President may determine.[3&4]

The retirement in these cases is upon the actual rank of the officer held at the date of retirement.

While the above clauses are mandatory, there should be read in conjunction with them the acts of Congress, passed, or which may be passed, limiting the whole num-

[1] § 1250 Revised Statutes. [2] Ibid., § 1251. [3] Ibid., § 1252.

[4] The corresponding clauses, as recently proposed to Congress, provide that if it be found that the incapacity results neither from an incident of the service nor from any vicious habit of the officer, he shall be transferred to the retired list or be discharged, as the President, upon the recommendation of the Board, may direct. But if it be found that the officer's incapacity is the result of intemperance, idleness, or other vicious habits, he shall be discharged.

ber of officers of the army on the retired list. Should the Board find that the officer is not incapacitated for active service, the President could not disapprove the proceedings and then retire him.

Status of Retired Officers. They are withdrawn from command and promotion, but are part of the army of the United States, and are borne on the Army Register. They are subject to the rules and articles of war and to be tried by courts-martial for any breach thereof.[1]

In view of the absence of the usual restraints in such cases, it is made the duty of all officers of the army who may become cognizable of flagrant violations of the military laws by any retired officer, forthwith to report the same to the Adjutant-General of the Army for the information of the General.[2]

They are entitled to wear the uniform of the rank on which they are retired.[3]

Residence. They may reside wherever they choose in the United States; may engage in private business; may change their residence or travel, at their pleasure, without further authority, except to go beyond the sea.

Civil Office. They may accept any civil office under the government of the United States, except an appointment in the diplomatic or consular service, without vacating their commission. Accepting an appointment in the latter services, however, is equivalent to a resignation.

If they hold a commission to a civil office under the United States, they are entitled to draw the pay of both offices.[4]

Professors of the Military Academy are on the same footing as other officers of the army as to retirement.

Retired officers may be assigned to duty at the Sol-

[1] § 1256, Revised Statutes.

[2] G. O. 2, A. G. O., Jan. 14, 1871.

[3] § 1256, Revised Statutes.

[4] Opinions Attorney-General, June 11, 1877.

diers' Home upon selection by the Commissioners approved by the Secretary of War. They may also be assigned to duty at any college or university entitled under the laws to the detail of an army officer.

They are not assignable to other duties than those here indicated, nor are they to receive any compensation from the government, other than their pay as retired officers, that is not expressly authorized by law.

CHAPTER XXII.

PROCEEDINGS AT LAW AGAINST OFFICERS.

When an officer is made a party to any action or proceeding in a civil court which may involve the interest of the United States; or when, by the performance of his public duty, he is involved in any action or proceeding in which he claims protection or indemnity from the United States, he shall promptly report the case (through the regular military channels, except in cases admitting of no delay) to the Adjutant-General to be laid before the Department of Justice.[1]

In ordinary cases, where an officer is called upon to show by what authority he holds a soldier in service, he can himself set forth the facts and need not employ counsel. In important cases, if counsel be necessary and there is not time to obtain the previous authority of the War Department, he should forthwith report the facts to the Adjutant-General.[2]

The cases are, however, rare where an officer would need to employ counsel before the proper authority could be obtained, and even in the most urgent cases, without such authority, he renders himself liable for payment of the services, as officers are forbidden to employ an attorney or counselor at the expense of the United States. If an officer is obliged by the necessities of the case to resort to counsel before he can obtain authority, he should, if possible, seek the assistance of the United States District-Attorney in preference to other counsel.

[1] G. O. 63, A. G. O., May 24, 1873. [2] Regulations, par. 1434.

It is not lawful for the Secretaries of either of the executive departments to employ attorneys or counsel at the expense of the United States, but such departments, when in need of counsel or advice, shall call upon the Department of Justice.[1]

Writs of Habeas Corpus. The most common proceedings in civil courts, with which officers will have to deal, are *habeas corpus* cases; and, as the preliminary measures in such cases are simple, officers should be conversant with the action to be taken without having recourse to counsel.

Definition. The writ of *habeas corpus* is that legal process which is employed for the summary vindication of the right of personal liberty when illegally restrained.[2]

By whom issued. The Supreme Court and the circuit and district courts have power to issue writs of *habeas corpus*.[3] The several justices and judges of the said courts, within their respective jurisdictions, have power to grant writs of *habeas corpus* for the purpose of an inquiry into the cause of constraint of liberty.[4]

The supreme and district courts of each Territory, and the respective judges thereof, except for Idaho and Montana, may grant writs of *habeas corpus* in all cases in which the same are grantable by the judges of the United States in the District of Columbia.[5]

Such writs may also be granted by the several State courts, depending upon the local law of the particular State.

In the United States courts the statutes provide that the writ shall in no case extend to a prisoner in jail, unless where he is in custody under or by color of the

[1] Act of June 22, 1870, § 17.
[2] Hurd on Habeas Corpus, p. 143.
[3] § 751, Revised Statutes.
[4] Ibid., § 752.
[5] Ibid., § 1912.

authority of the United States, or is committed for trial before some court thereof; or is in custody for an act done or omitted in pursuance of a law of the United States, or of an order, process, or decree of a court or judge thereof; or is in custody in violation of the constitution, or of law or treaty of the United States; or etc., or unless it is necessary to bring a witness into court to testify.[1]

Return. When a writ of *habeas corpus* is served upon an officer of the army, issued by a United States court or judge authorized to issue such writ, two things are required, *i. e.*, the production of the body, and a statement of the cause of caption and detention, which is called the *return* to the writ. The officer is required to make *due* return thereof within three days after service, unless the party be detained beyond the distance of twenty miles; and if beyond that distance and not beyond a distance of a hundred miles, within ten days; and if beyond the distance of a hundred miles, within twenty days;[2] and when the officer makes the return he is also required at the same time to bring the body of the party before the judge who granted the writ.[3]

When the writ is returned, a day should be set for the hearing of the cause, not exceeding five days thereafter, unless the party petitioning requests a longer time.[4]

The petitioner, or the party imprisoned or restrained, may deny any of the facts set forth in the return, or may allege any other facts that may be material in the case. Said denials or allegations shall be under oath. The return and all suggestions made against it may be amended, by leave of the court, or justice, or judge, before or after the same are filed, so that thereby the material facts may be ascertained.[5]

[1] § 753, Revised Statutes.
[2] Ibid., 756.
[3] Ibid., 758.
[4] Ibid., 759.
[5] Ibid., 760.

The court, or justice, or judge shall proceed in a summary way to determine the facts of the case, by hearing the testimony and arguments, and thereupon to dispose of the party as law and justice require.[1]

Writs of Habeas Corpus from State Courts. State judges and State courts, authorized by laws of their States to issue writs of *habeas corpus*, have undoubtedly a right to issue the writ in any case where a party is alleged to be illegally confined within their limits, unless it appears upon his application that he is confined under the authority, or claim and color of the authority of the United States, by an officer of that government. If such fact appear upon the application the writ should be refused. If it do not appear, the judge or court issuing the writ has a right to inquire into the cause of imprisonment, and ascertain by what authority the person is held within the limits of the State; and it is the *duty* of the marshal, or other officer having custody of the prisoner, to give, by a proper return, information in this respect. His return should be sufficient in its detail of facts to show distinctly that the imprisonment is under the authority, or claim and color of authority, of the United States, and to exclude the suspicion of imposition or oppression on his part. And the process or orders, under which the prisoner is held, should be produced with the return and submitted to inspection, in order that the court or judge issuing the writ may see that the prisoner is held by the officer in good faith under the authority, or claim and color of the authority, of the United States, and not under the mere pretense of having such authority.[2]

The enlistment contract, muster-roll, process, or order,

[1] § 761, Revised Statutes.

[2] Decision of the U. S. Supreme Court in the case of the U. S. *vs.* Tarble, 13 Wall, 397; Published in G. O. 16, A. G. O., April 16, 1872. See also Ableman *vs.* Booth, 21 Howard, 506.

as the case may be, under which the persons are held, should be produced with the return, and submitted to inspection of the court.

Since the State court has no authority to issue this writ when a person is held under the authority, or claim and color of authority, of the United States, an officer, while making respectful return, should not produce the body of the prisoner, nor allow it to be taken from him.[1] Upon this point Attorney-General Bristow said :—" And if the authority of a State, in the form of a judicial process or otherwise, should attempt to control the marshal or other authorized officer or agent of the United States in the custody of his prisoner, it would be his duty to resist it, and to call to his aid any force that might be necessary to maintain the authority of the law against illegal interference."[2]

Suspension of the Writ of Habeas Corpus. The constitution provides that the privilege of the writ of *habeas corpus* shall not be suspended, unless when in case of rebellion or invasion the public safety may require it. While strong arguments have been advanced to show that this power of suspending the privilege of this writ resides in the President, the accepted opinion is that Congress must take the initiative, and either suspend it by an act directly accomplishing the fact, or authorizing the President to do so.

Suspension of the privilege of the writ of *habeas corpus* does not suspend the writ itself. The writ issues as a matter of course; and, on its return, the court decides whether the applicant is denied the right of proceeding any further.[3]

[1] For form of Return see Appendix.

[2] XIII. Opinions Attorney-General, June 19, 1871.

[3] Ex parte Milligan, 4 Wall, 4.

When the privilege of the writ is suspended, an officer must nevertheless make respectful return.

Manner of obtaining Writ of Habeas Corpus. As it may often be necessary to obtain a writ of *habeas corpus*, the instructions contained in the Revised Statutes of the United States are given.[1]

Application for the writ should be made to the court, or justice, or judge authorized to issue the same by complaint in writing, signed by the person for whose relief it is intended, setting forth the facts concerning the detention of the party restrained, in whose custody he is detained, and by virtue of what claim or authority, if known. The facts set forth in the complaint shall be verified by the oath of the person making the application.

Such application would be appropriate in the case of a soldier, held in custody by the State authorities for an act committed under the authority of the United States; or to secure the attendance of a witness confined in jail, where it is desired to bring him before a court-martial to testify.

Officers Prosecuted in State Courts. In cases of officers and others, sued or prosecuted in State courts on account of acts done under the authority of the United States, it is ordinarily the first duty of the counsel employed for their defense to cause the removal of the action to the United States circuit court, if such removal is authorized by the acts of Congress on the subject. It has been the experience of the War Department that such a proceeding has in a vast majority of the cases insured a complete protection to the defendant; resulting in a verdict or judgment in his favor, or in a dismissal of the action—on the motion often of the plaintiff or prosecutor, who finds himself wholly thwarted in his scheme of retaliation or revenge.[2]

[1] § 754, Revised Statutes. [2] Opinions J. A. G., p. 126.

CHAPTER XXIII.

EVIDENCE.

As a text book on Military Law would be incomplete for practical purposes without something on the subject of Evidence, the author has added the following pages to meet that want. It is not his intent, nor within his ability, to write an elaborate treatise on this most important subject; nor is such a treatise necessary. The great principles and general rules of evidence meet all the requirements of the majority of cases in military practice. They have been gathered from the best writers on the subject, both in this country and England, and are presented to the reader as concisely as possible, without entering largely into the reasons of their adoption.

Rules of Evidence governing Courts-Martial. While Congress has authorized courts-martial, established their composition, jurisdiction, and rules of procedure, it has never prescribed the rules of evidence which shall govern their proceedings. Courts-martial, being courts alone of *criminal* jurisdiction, must therefore adhere to the rules of evidence of the United States criminal courts.[1]

These rules are the common law rules of evidence in criminal cases, except where Congress has prescribed otherwise. The only other exceptions which are permitted are those which are of necessity created by the

[1] II. Opinions Attorney-General, p. 344; Greenleaf, Vol. III, § 469.

nature of the service, and by the constitution of the court, and its course of proceeding.[1]

Definition. Evidence is that which (independent of all comment and argument) is legally submitted to a court or jury to enable them to decide upon the questions in issue.[2]

This term, and the word *proof*, are often used indifferently, as synonymous with each other; but the latter is applied by the most accurate logicians to the *effect* of evidence, and not to the *medium* by which truth is established.[3]

Divisions. Writers on Evidence make various divisions, which are to a great extent arbitrary. The subject, for convenience of discussion, will be arranged under the following heads :—

1. The Nature of evidence.
2. The Object of evidence.
3. The Instruments of evidence.

THE NATURE OF EVIDENCE.

As to its nature, evidence may be considered under the following divisions, (1) Primary, (2) Secondary, (3) Direct, (4) Circumstantial, (5) Hearsay.

Primary Evidence is that kind of proof which, under any possible circumstances, affords the greatest certainty of the fact in question.[4]

This may include written or unwritten evidence. *For example,* if the question is whether a person made a will, the production of the will is primary evidence : if the will is to be proved, the oral testimony of a subscribing witness is primary evidence.

[1] Greenleaf, Vol. 3, § 476.
[2] De Hart, p. 325.
[3] Greenleaf, Vol. 1, § 1.
[4] Ibid., § 84.

The law *generally* requires that *primary evidence—i. e.*, the best evidence—shall be produced. By this is not meant that the courts will require the strongest evidence of a fact, but it will not permit other evidence of a fact so long as primary evidence can be obtained. Thus, a will may be proved by one subscribing witness, even though the other may be present; but, so long as the subscribing witness can be obtained, other proof will be rejected.

Exceptions. There are certain exceptions to the general rule requiring production of the best evidence.

In the case of *enlistment* the best evidence is the enlistment papers; but, in view of the fact that it is difficult at times to procure these papers, it has become the practice to accept, as sufficient presumptive proof thereof, such facts as show on the part of an accused an acquiescence in the status of a soldier, as the receipt of pay, the doing of military duty, etc.[1]

In the case of *public officers* it is not necessary to produce their written appointment; all who are proved to have acted as such are presumed to have been duly appointed to the office until the contrary appears. So, where an accused is charged with disobedience of orders of a particular person, it is regarded as sufficient to show that this person had acted in the capacity of an officer.

Where the evidence involves the previous conviction of parties by general court-martial, it is not necessary to produce the original proceedings, but they may be proved by the *general orders* promulgating them.

Where from the nature of a *document* it cannot conveniently be produced before the court, the law will allow secondary evidence to be given. Thus, inscriptions on tablets, gravestones, etc., could be so proved.

Upon the trial of any indictment against any person

[1] Opinions J. A. G., p. 167.

for embezzling public money, it shall be sufficient evidence, for the purpose of showing a balance against such person, to produce a transcript from the books and proceedings of the Treasury.[1] This transcript must be certified by the Auditor and authenticated under the seal of the Department.[2]

Secondary Evidence. When for any reason primary evidence cannot be obtained, the law allows secondary evidence—*i. e.*, copies or parol evidence—to be given. In fact, such evidence becomes the best and may be produced under the general rule. This must be taken with the understanding that the evidence is legal, and inferior to the primary only as to the source from which derived. Thus, the copy of a copy of a destroyed or lost document is not receivable in evidence, even though, as it seems, the absence of the first copy has been satisfactorily explained.[3]

But, before secondary evidence will be admitted, it must be clearly shown that superior evidence cannot be obtained.

Secondary evidence refers chiefly to writings or documents, and the cases in which the law permits it to be received are:

First. Where the document has been lost or destroyed. In this case it must be shown that the document existed, that it has been lost or destroyed, and that sufficient search has been made for it. What will constitute sufficient search must be determined by the court; and, in deciding this point, much will depend on the character of the document. "Where a reasonable person would be satisfied that *bona fide* endeavors had been made to produce the document itself," seems a good guide.

Second. Where the document is in the hands of the

[1] § 887, Revised Statutes. [2] Ibid. § 886. [3] Best, Vol. II. § 483.

opposite party, and he has failed to produce it on due notice so to do.

This notice may be directed to the party or his attorney, and may be served on either; and it must describe the writing demanded, so as to leave no doubt that the party was aware of the particular instrument intended to be called for. This notice may be by parol or in writing. If the document is not produced, it simply permits secondary evidence of its contents to be received, but raises no inference against the party failing to produce it.

Where from the nature of the document the accused must be aware that he is charged with its possession, a notice to produce is unnecessary.

Third. Where the document is in the hands of a third party who is privileged to retain it and who refuses; or of a party without the jurisdiction of the court.

Failure to produce, on sufficient notice, in either of these cases, will justify the introduction of secondary evidence.

Admissions. Whether *verbal* admissions by a party of the contents of a document may be admitted against him, in lieu of the document, has been questioned. Greenleaf gives the rule:—"Where the existence, and not the formal execution of a writing, is the subject of the inquiry, or where the writing is collateral to the principal facts, and it is on these facts that the claim is founded, the better opinion seems to be that the confession of the party, precisely identified, is admissible as primary evidence of the facts recited in the writing; though it is not as satisfactory as the writing itself."[1]

Degrees of Secondary Evidence. In England the rule seems to be that there are no *degrees* of secondary evidence, that a party, once entitled to use this mode of

[1] Vol. I. § 96.

proof, may use any form of it. The American doctrine appears to be that if, from the nature of the case itself, it is manifest that a more satisfactory kind of secondary evidence exists, the party will be required to produce it; but that where the nature of the case does not of itself disclose the existence of such better evidence, the objector must prove that it was known to the other party in season to have been produced at the trial. The introduction of weaker secondary evidence, when better might be produced, gives rise to unfavorable inferences.[1]

In proving the existence of a document the primary evidence is the document itself; after which a copy should be produced; and, if there is no copy, then parol evidence of the contents of the document may be given.

It is sometimes difficult to say what is, and what is not primary evidence. In the case of *printed papers*, such as Orders issued from a Department, all the impressions are regarded as originals.

Direct and Circumstantial. All evidence may be classed again, according to its nature, into direct and circumstantial. As regards admissibility, direct and circumstantial evidence stand, generally speaking, on the same footing; still, the non-production of direct evidence which it is in the power of a party to produce is matter of observation to a jury, as indeed is the suppression of any sort of proof.[2]

Direct evidence is that which, if believed, establishes the truth or falsity of a fact in issue.

This evidence is derived from those who have acquired actual knowledge of the fact by their own senses; or from documents which prove the fact.

Circumstantial evidence is that which is not *direct*

[1] Greenleaf, Vol. I. § 34, Note 1.

[2] Best, Vol. I. § 295.

to the *principal* fact, but which the law deems sufficiently collateral to be received as evidence of it.

This is of two kinds, *conclusive* and *presumptive ;*

Conclusive. When the collateral part being proved, the principal fact *necessarily* follows. *Example*, Where a person charged with a crime proves an *alibi.*

Presumptive. When the collateral fact being proved, the principal fact does not necessarily follow, but is *probable* only.

Presumptive evidence is divided into *presumptions of law* and *presumptions of fact.*

Presumptions of law consist of those rules which, in certain cases, either forbid or dispense with any ulterior inquiry. Thus, the law presumes a man innocent until proven guilty; that a man intended the natural consequence of his act, etc.

Presumptions of fact consist of those inferences which *naturally* follow as to the principal fact from the proof of collateral facts.

It is impossible to lay down any fixed rule which shall guide courts-martial in deciding upon these presumptions. It may be said that presumptions of fact will be more or less strong according as the fact is a necessary, usual, or infrequent consequence of the fact or facts proved. Convictions, even in capital cases, constantly take place where the presumptions are of a strong nature. It must be remembered, however, that presumptions of fact, even though not rebutted, are not necessarily conclusive. Every case must necessarily be decided by the effect the collateral facts produce on the minds of the members of the court. It is sometimes said that "circumstances cannot lie," but even in the strongest cases the element of uncertainty enters. Gilbert cites the case of one being run through the body with a sword in a house, who instantly dies of that wound; and then another man is seen to come out with a bloody sword, and no other man was at that time in the house. "This," he says, "is a violent presumption that he is the murderer; for the blood, the weapon, and the hasty flight, are all necessary concomitants to such horrid facts; and the next proof to the sight of the fact itself is the proof of those circumstances that do necessarily attend the fact." But, as Best shows,[1] any of the following hypotheses will reconcile these facts with innocence of the man.

First, That the deceased, with the intention of committing suicide, plunged the sword into his own body; and that the accused, not being in time to prevent him, drew out the sword, and so ran out, through confusion of mind, for surgical assistance.

Second, That the deceased and the accused both wore swords; that the deceased, in a fit of passion, attacked the accused; and that the accused, being close to the wall, had no retreat, and had just time to draw his sword, in hope of keeping off the deceased, who, not seeing the sword in time, ran upon it and so was killed.

Third, That the deceased may in fact have been murdered, and that the real murderer may have escaped, leaving a sword sticking in or lying near the body, and the accused coming in may have seized the sword and run out to give the alarm.

Owing to this uncertainty, therefore, courts-martial should never find guilty on circumstantial evidence, unless the evidence produces moral certainty to the exclusion of every reasonable doubt. The proof ought to be not only consistent with the prisoner's guilt, but irreconcilable with any hypothesis of innocence.

Hearsay is the evidence of those who relate not what

[1] Vol. 1, § 317.

they perceived themselves, but what they have derived from others.

It is used in reference to that which is written as well as that which is spoken. For several reasons the law does not admit such evidence, the principal of which are:—*First*, the party originally stating the facts does not state them under the obligations of an oath; and *second*, the party against whom the evidence is given does not have an opportunity of cross-examination.

Courts-martial should be careful, however, not to confound *original* with *hearsay*. It does not follow because the writings, or words in question, are those of a third person, not under oath, that, therefore, they are to be considered as hearsay. On the contrary, it happens, in many cases, that the very fact in controversy is, whether such things were written or spoken, and not whether they were true; and, in other cases, such language or statements, whether written or spoken, may be the natural or inseparable concomitants of the principal fact in controversy. In such cases it is obvious that the writings or words are not within the meaning of hearsay, but are original and independent facts, admissible in proof of the issue.[1]

Informatoin. Thus, where a person acted on certain information derived from third parties, such *information* would be original and not hearsay.

Admissions. In the same way with *admissions* of the party against his interests, this is regarded as original.

Declarations and Acts. There are certain *declarations* and *acts* which are regarded as original and not hearsay evidence from their connection with the principal fact in issue. Thus, in the trial of Lord George Gordon, the cry of the mob was admitted as original evidence, since it formed part of the *res gestæ*.

[1] Greenleaf, Vol. I, § 100.

While it is admitted that the declarations and acts of the principal parties, as well as the circumstances surrounding them which tend to show the nature of the principal fact, are admissible, yet it is necessary, *first*, that they be closely connected with the principal fact in issue; *second*, that they happened contemporaneously with it. But, as was laid down in an American case,[1] to be *contemporaneous*, they are not required to be *precisely* concurrent in point of time. If the declarations spring out of the transaction—if they elucidate it—if they are voluntary and spontaneous,—and *if they are made at a time so near to it as reasonably to preclude the idea of deliberate design*, they are then to be regarded as contemporaneous. Such declarations are admissible *for*, as well as *against* the parties.

In cases of conspiracy, riot, or other crime, perpetrated by several persons, when once the conspiracy or combination is established, the *act* or *declaration* of one conspirator or accomplice, in the prosecution of the enterprise, is considered the act of all, and is original evidence against all. But, after the common enterprise is at an end, whether by accomplishment or abandonment is not material, no one is permitted, by any subsequent act or declaration of his own, to affect the others. In fine, the declarations of a conspirator or an accomplice are receivable against his fellows only when they are either in themselves acts, or accompany and explain acts for which the others are responsible; but not when they are in the nature of narratives, descriptions, or subsequent confessions.[2]

The declarations or admissions of an agent, in reference to the business of his principal in which he is at the time employed, and within the scope of his authority, are admitted in evidence against the principal, provided they are part of the *res gestæ*.

[1] Mitcham *vs.* The State, 11 Ga., 615.
[2] Greenleaf, Vol. I. § 233.

Exceptions. There are certain exceptions to the rule that hearsay evidence is not admissible:

(1) **Dying Declarations** are, under certain circumstances, admitted in evidence. Eyre, C. B., in giving the reason for this, said, "that the general principle, upon which evidence of this kind is admissible is, that it is of declarations made in extremity, when the party is at the point of death, and when every hope of this world is gone, when every motive to falsehood is silenced, and the mind is induced by the most powerful considerations to speak the truth. A situation so solemn and so awful, is considered by the law as creating an obligation equal to that which is imposed by an oath in court."[1]

The statements of the deceased must be such as would be admissible if he were alive, therefore opinions of the deceased will not be receivable.

Again, the deceased must be a person competent to testify; so, where a person was incompetent from infamy, lunacy, religion, or tender age, the declaration would not be admissible.

The witness, being competent, certain other things are necessary before the dying declaration can be received:

First. It must be proved by the party offering the evidence that the declarations were made under a sense of *impending death.* This may be proved in any way: by his statements, conduct, or other circumstances going to show the state of the declarant's mind.

Second. The declaration of the deceased is admitted only in the case of *homicide,* where the death of the deceased is the subject of the charge, and the circumstances of the death are the subject of the dying declaration.

(2) **Testimony on former Trial.** The testimony on a former trial of a witness, subsequently deceased, is re-

[1] Woodcock's Case, 1 Leach, 502.

ceivable, and may be proved by the testimony of a person who heard it, or by notes made at the time.

The party must be able to swear that his minutes contain the *substance* or the *whole* of the evidence given by the witness, even though he is not able to swear that it contains the exact language used by the witness, or every word spoken by him.

If the witness testifies from memory he must be able to give the substance of the testimony.

CHAPTER XXIV.

THE OBJECT OF EVIDENCE.

The object of evidence is to find out the truth or falsity of the facts at issue.

It has been found by experience that this is best accomplished by the following general rules which are now binding as law:—

(1) *The evidence must be confined to the point at issue.*

(2) *Only the substance of the issue is necessary to be proved.*

(3) *The affirmative of the issue must be proved.*

I. **Evidence confined to Point at Issue.** This rule has been adopted, both in civil and criminal cases, from motives of justice, and especially in criminal cases is there a necessity of its strict enforcement. The reason is that no person can be expected to answer unprepared, and at once, for every action of his life. Thus, under this rule, on a trial of a soldier for mutiny it is not permitted to give evidence of facts, tending to prove another distinct offense, for the purpose of raising the inference that the prisoner had committed the offense in question; still, in an indictment for stealing, for the purpose of showing the identity of the person, it is often important to show that other goods which have been upon an adjoining part of the premises were stolen on the same night and afterwards found in the possession of the prisoner.

It is not competent, even, for the prosecutor to give

evidence of the prisoner's tendency to commit offenses of the kind of which he is charged.[1]

While this general rule seems plain, it is often difficult to apply it. Greenleaf says,—"It is not necessary, however, that the evidence should bear *directly* upon the issue. It is admissible if it *tends* to prove the issue, or constitutes a link in the chain of proof; although alone, it might not justify a verdict in accordance with it. Nor is it necessary that its relevancy should appear at the time when it is offered; it being the usual course to receive, at any proper and convenient stage of the trial, in the discretion of the judge, any evidence which the counsel shows will be rendered material by other evidence, which he undertakes to produce. If it is not subsequently thus connected with the issue, it is to be laid out of the case."[2]

The object of the rule is to exclude evidence of collateral facts which do not bear upon the issue, and which, if allowed, would tend to complicate the case.

Exceptions. To this rule there are certain seeming exceptions, although the law does not regard them as such:

(a) **Guilty Knowledge.** In many cases known to the articles of war, it is necessary to prove a guilty knowledge in the prisoner with regard to the fact at issue. For this purpose evidence may be given of circumstances not connected with, though in some measure relating to, the particular offense, in order to raise a presumption of a guilty knowledge in the prisoner at the time of the offense committed. On this ground evidence of other offenses of the same kind committed by a prisoner, though not charged in the indictment, is admissible against him.

Thus, in the case of an officer charged with false muster under the 14th Article of War, other false reports made

[1] Roscoe, p. 80. [2] Greenleaf, Vol. I., § 51 a.

about the same time may be proved as showing guilty knowledge.

(b) **Intent.** It often happens in the military service that things, in themselves innocent, if done with a certain intent become criminal. Thus, absence without leave becomes desertion if there is an intent to remain away.

In these cases, where the intent has to be proved, evidence of collateral facts may be given if they tend to establish the intent of the prisoner in committing the act in issue. On a charge of desertion, for instance, it might be shown that the prisoner had sold his uniform and bought citizen's clothes shortly before leaving his command, or that he had shortly before drawn money from a bank, or other collateral facts tending to show his intent. So, on a charge of disrespect towards a commanding officer under the 20th Article of War, in sending a threatening letter, other letters, written before or after the one in question, may be read in evidence to show its meaning.

Again, the *declarations* of the prisoner made at a former time are admissible when they tend to prove the intent of the party at the time of commission of offense. Thus, on an indictment for murder, evidence of former grudges and antecedent malices may be given to show the prisoner's malice against the deceased.[1]

(c) **Character.** Another exception to the rule is in the case of character. Courts-martial will always allow prisoners to produce evidence as to character; in fact, the members often advise a soldier to produce such evidence. The most proper person to call for this purpose, generally speaking, will be the prisoner's commanding officer, or, better still, the commander of his company, although any person may give such evidence.

[1] Roscoe, p. 95.

Evidence of character should properly be given after the prisoner has finished his defense by testimony.

Before courts-martial, as in civil courts, evidence of the prisoner's *general* character is allowed. Phillips says,— "The inquiry as to general character ought manifestly to bear some analogy and reference to the charge against him. On a charge of stealing, it would be irrelevant and absurd to inquire into the prisoner's loyalty or humanity; on a charge of high treason it would be equally absurd to inquire into his honesty and punctuality in private dealings. Such evidence relates to the principles of moral conduct, which, however they might operate on other occasions, would not be likely to operate on that which alone is the subject of inquiry; it would not afford the least presumption that the prisoner might not have been tempted to commit the crime for which he is tried, and is, therefore, totally inapplicable to the point in question."[1]

Courts-martial do not so strictly adhere to this rule which requires the evidence to bear analogy to the charge in issue. A prisoner may be permitted to put in proof particular instances wherein his conduct may have been publicly approved by superior officers.[2]

General character, unconnected with the charge, may be received, and would perhaps be of advantage to the prisoner in cases where the punishment is discretionary. It might also influence the reviewing officer to mitigate or remit the sentence.

Value of Evidence as to Character. The exact value of evidence as to character cannot be laid down. It was formerly usual to treat the good character of the party accused as evidence to be taken into consideration only in doubtful cases; and jurors have generally been told that where the facts proved are such as to satisfy their minds

[1] 2 Phillips, 490. [2] VII. Opinions Attorney-General, Jan. 31, 1857.

of the guilt of the prisoner, character, however excellent, is no subject for their consideration. Before courts-martial, however, character should always be taken into consideration. In a clear case of guilt, where punishment is discretionary, it will be of value in determining the amount of punishment; [1] and, in doubtful cases, it would often be of great value in determining whether a person of previous good character was guilty of a particular crime with which he was charged.

Where *intent* is a principal ingredient in the charge, or where circumstantial proof only is adduced, evidence as to character, *bearing on the charge*, may be highly important.[2]

Bad Character. The judge-advocate is not allowed to produce evidence as to bad character, unless the prisoner has brought forward evidence of good character, and, even then, he should only be allowed to rebut the evidence adduced by the prisoner.

Only the Substance of the Issue need be Proved. It is a principle running through the whole criminal law that it is sufficient to prove so much of the indictment as shows that the defendant has committed a substantive crime therein specified. This is specially to be borne in mind by members of courts-martial. In its application a distinction is made between allegations of matter of *substance*, and allegations of matter of *essential description*. The former may be substantially proved; but the latter must be proved with a degree of strictness extending in some cases even to literal precision.[3]

Matter of Substance. This rule, simple enough in itself, is not so easy of application. What constitutes the substance of the issue, and what will justify the court in

[1] Sec. G. C. M. O. 63, A. G. O., 1874, Opinion of J. A. G., May 18, 1875.

[2] Simmons, p. 365, (2 Ed).

[3] Greenleaf, Vol. 1, § 56.

finding guilty, where there is a variance between the charge and the facts proved, is a matter of much importance. This much can be said:—The offense of which the accused is convicted must be of the same class with that which is charged. Cases constantly occur of soldiers charged with *desertion*, being found "not guilty," but "guilty" of *absence without leave*, the substance of the charge being the absence. So also, in cases of officers charged under the 61st Article with *conduct unbecoming an officer and a gentleman*, courts frequently find, where the evidence does not establish the full guilt, "not guilty," but "guilty" of *conduct to the prejudice of good order and military discipline*."

The averments as to the *substance* may be *divisible*. Thus, where a soldier is charged with being absent a certain number of days, he may be found guilty of being absent a less number than stated in the charge; or where a soldier is charged under the 22d Article, with beginning, exciting, or joining in a mutiny with others, while some are acquitted he may be found guilty.

Again, where the *intent* of the prisoner furnishes one of the ingredients in the offense, and several intents are laid in the indictment, each of which, together with the act done, constitutes an offense, it is sufficient to prove one intent only.[1] If a soldier, for example, was charged under the 21st Article with lifting his sword with the intent of striking his superior officer, and with the further intent of exciting a mutiny in the garrison, the averment is divisible; and the court might negative the latter intent, but find guilty of the former.

Matter of Description. In every charge there enters more or less of description; and, under the rule in question, a variance in the description and the proof will

[1] Roscoe, p. 101.

often be fatal. In criminal prosecutions in the civil courts it is believed the defendant is allowed to take advantage of much finer exceptions than is allowed by the custom of courts-martial. The rule in the civil courts is that where a *person* or a *thing*, necessary to be mentioned in an indictment, is described with circumstances of greater particularity than is requisite, yet those circumstances must be proved, otherwise it would not appear that the person or thing is the same as that described in the indictment. Thus, in an indictment for stealing a *black* horse, the animal is necessarily mentioned, but the color need not be stated; yet, if it is stated, it is made descriptive of the particular animal stolen, and a variance in the proof of the color is fatal.[1]

Courts-martial would not fail to correct such a variance in their findings.

In 1840 a prisoner was arraigned for desertion from the navy. At the time of his desertion he was rated as master-at-arms, and was so named in the charge. He pleaded guilty. The court was closed for deliberation, and then, it coming to its knowledge that he had not been rated as master-at-arms since his apprehension, the court thought it had proceeded too far to alter the charge in this way, and adjudged him to be discharged. The attorney-general held that, the fact of his having pleaded to the charge, of his never having in any way made such an exception or defense, and of there being no dispute whatever as to the identity of the prisoner, would have prevented the accused himself from taking advantage of the error at this stage of the case. Of course it offered no ground for the court to refuse to proceed to judgment on the merits.[2]

Averments as to Name. In the trial of a case, the

[1] 1 Starkie, p. 374. [2] III. Opinions Attorney-General, June 24, 1840.

name of the accused, of the parties injured, and of third persons introduced into the charge as descriptive of some person or thing, should be proved as laid in the charge; but here the same particularity does not exist as in the civil courts.

The Judge-Advocate General has held it a fatal variance where the accused is charged under one name and found guilty under another. Where one was arraigned and pleaded guilty as *George* Sheldon, but was found guilty and sentenced as *Charles* Sheldon, it was held fatal; still the court might have corrected this on their finding.[1]

In England the common law upon this subject has been materially modified by statute, and gives, I believe, the practice, with slight variation, of courts-martial in this country. This statute provides that "whenever, on the trial of any indictment for any felony or misdemeanor, there shall appear to be any variance between the statement in such indictment and the evidence offered in proof thereof, in the name of any county, riding, division, city, borough, town corporate, parish, township, or place mentioned or described in any such indictment, or in the name or description of any person or persons, or body politic or corporate, therein stated or alleged to be the owner or owners of any property, real or personal, which shall form the subject of any offense charged therein, or in the name or description of any person or persons, body politic or corporate, therein stated or alleged to be injured or damaged, or intended to be injured or damaged by the commission of such offense, or in the christian name or surname, or both christian name and surname, or other description whatsoever, of any person or persons whomsoever therein named or described, or in the name or description of any matter or thing whatsoever, therein named or described,

[1] Opinions J. A. G., p. 182.

or in the ownership of any property named or described therein, it shall and may be lawful for the court before which the trial shall be had, if it shall consider such variance not material to the merits of the case, and that the defendant cannot be prejudiced thereby in his defense on such merits, to order such indictment to be amended, according to the proof, by some officer of the court or other person, both in that part of the indictment where such variance occurs, and in every other part of the indictment which it may become necessary to amend, on such terms as to postponing the trial to be had before the same or another jury, as such court shall think reasonable." [1]

The only difference seems to be that courts-martial will amend the error on the findings instead of amending during the trial. The words and terms of a charge we have seen cannot be changed after the arraignment of the prisoner.[2]

Averments as to Time. The charges before courts-martial being usually drawn up so as to charge an offense as committed "on or about" a certain time, a variance between the time charged and that proved will be corrected by the court. Where, under a charge of murder, the specification set forth that the crime was committed on the 24th of September, 1863, but the evidence (which fully established the commission of murder in the first degree) showed that it occurred on July 26, 1863, and the accused (who was convicted and sentenced to be hung) took no exception on account of this variance—*held,* that it was not such a fatal one as to affect the validity of the proceedings. But, *advised* in such case, that the court, if not dissolved, be reconvened in order to make a special finding, in terms substituting the proper date for the one indicated in the specification.[3]

[1] 14 and 15 Victoria, c 100.
[2] G. C. M. O. 21, A. G. O., Feb. 17, 1877.
[3] Opinions J. A. G., p. 381.

Averments as to Place. Where crimes are not local in their nature, a mistake in the particular place in which an offense is charged will not be material. Where a soldier is charged with deserting from a particular place the court may find, on evidence adduced, that he deserted from another.

Where the offense is local, however, the name of the place should be correctly stated in the charge and proved as laid; otherwise parties may be found guilty of charges to which, practically, they have not been called on to answer.

Averments as to Mode of Committing an Offense. It is not necessary strictly to prove descriptive averments as to the mode of committing an offense. "It is sufficient," says Greenleaf, "if the proof agree with the allegation in its substance and general character without precise conformity in every particular. In other words, an indictment describing a thing by its generic term is supported by proof of a species which is clearly comprehended within such description. Thus, if the charge be of poisoning by a certain drug, and the proof be of poisoning by another drug; or the charge be of felonious assault with a staff, and the proof be of such assault with a stone; or the charge be of a wound with a sword, and the proof be of a wound with an axe; yet the charge is substantially proved."[1] Though the weapon may not be proved to be the same, yet it must appear that the species of killing was the same. Thus, if the prisoner be indicted for poisoning, it will not be sufficient to prove a death by shooting or strangling.

Averments as to Value. In charges alleging loss, or theft of articles, it is proper to state the value. Such value need not generally be strictly proved.

[1] Vol. I, § 65.

Written Documents. Where a written document is set forth in the charges, the same distinction is now admitted in the proof, between allegations of matter of substance, and matter of description, as has just been explained. In matters not material to the merits of the case, a discrepancy between the document as set forth in the evidence, and the proof of the same, would not be material. Where the document, however, is the foundation of the charge—as for example, disrespect to a commanding officer in sending an abusive letter—the document should be strictly proved.

The Affirmative of the Issue must be Proved. This is a rule of convenience, adopted, not because it is impossible to prove a negative, but because the negative does not admit of the direct and simple proof of which the affirmative is capable.

This rule, like the others we have been discussing, is not always of easy application. Two things must be particularly borne in mind :—

First. Not to confound negative averments, or allegations in the negative, with denials of an affirmative.

Thus, a charge may state that a soldier did *not* appear at a certain roll call. This, although it resembles a negative, is, in reality, a positive averment, and the *onus probandi* would rest with the government.

Second. That the affirmative and negative of the issue mean the affirmative and negative of the issue in *substance*, and not merely its affirmative and negative in form.[1]

Tests. Certain tests have been given for determining where the burden of proof lies; and, as the question may arise at any time during the trial, these tests should be remembered.

(1st) It lies on the party who asserts the affirmative.

[1] Best, Vol. I. p. 510.

Example. An officer or soldier is charged with shooting another. The burden of proof lies on the government to prove the act and attendant circumstances. Should the accused attempt to justify the act by setting up in defense the lawful order of a superior officer, the *onus probandi* would be shifted, and it would rest upon him to show such order.

There are exceptions to this rule, as where the charge sets up negative matter, essential to the issue, which is peculiarly within the knowledge of the other party. Suppose an officer, for example, was charged under the 60th Article with wrongfully selling property belonging to the United States. Here, the officer, if he possessed authority for such sale, could immediately show it without the least inconvenience, while it might be extremely inconvenient to prove the lack of authority. This would be sufficient to shift the burden of proof.

(2d) It lies on the party who would fail if no evidence at all, or no more evidence as the case may be, were given.[1]

(3d) It lies on the party who would fail if the particular allegation was struck out of the charge.[2]

It rests with the court to decide upon whom the burden of proof lies; and it is a well settled rule of law that in a case where the testimony is so evenly balanced as not to admit of a conclusion being drawn from it, the verdict must be against the party upon whom the burden of proving the issue rests.[3]

[1] Best, Vol. I. § 268. [2] Franklyn, p. 120.
[3] Best, Vol. I. § 275, note *a*.

CHAPTER XXV.

THE INSTRUMENTS OF EVIDENCE.

THE instruments of evidence consist of *witnesses* and *documents.*

Witnesses. A witness may be defined to be one who gives evidence under the obligations of an oath.

The testimony given by witnesses is called *parol* evidence, as contradistinguished from that derived from documents, termed documentary.

This division of the subject of evidence will be discussed under the following heads :

(1) Competency of witnesses, (2) Credibility of witnesses. (3) Examination of witnesses.

COMPETENCY OF WITNESSES.

It is the general rule that all persons are competent to give evidence. To this, however, there are certain exceptions, which being proved, will render witnesses incompetent :

Incompetency how ascertained. Proof of such incompetency is necessary, as it is never presumed.

The ordinary mode of ascertaining whether a witness is competent is by examination on the *voire dire* before being sworn. Should he appear incompetent from his answers, he is rejected. If his answers are satisfactory, other witnesses may be called to show his incompetency. It sometimes happens that the incompetency of a witness is not discovered until after he has been sworn and his examination proceeded with a considerable way, or perhaps even brought to a close; under such circumstances the court ought not to consider his evidence in coming to a finding.

Should a ground of incompetency be discovered during the examination of a witness, his examination may be suspended, and he may be put on his *voire dire* to examine him as to his competency.

Exceptions. The exceptions to the general rule that all persons may give evidence may be arranged under the following heads:

1. Want of religious principle. 2. Want of understanding. 3. Interest. 4. Infamy.

Incompetency from Want of Religious Principle. One of the chief requirements of the law for securing truth in parol evidence is that it be given under the *sanction of an oath.* But from the nature of an oath, it would have no sanction if a party did not believe in the existence of a Divine Being, and a state of future rewards and punishments. Persons, therefore, who have not such belief are incompetent to testify.

Nature of Religious Faith required. The particular religion of the party does not affect his competency, so long as he professes a religion that can bind his conscience. An infidel may be allowed to testify if he believes in a God who will punish. Some State courts have gone so far as to require only belief in the existence of a God, without reference to a belief in a state of future rewards and punishments; but the true test seems to be belief of a God, and that he will reward and punish us according to our deserts.[1] It is not material whether the witness believes the punishment will be inflicted in this world or the next.

[1] Greenleaf, Vol. I. § 369, Note 3.

How Proved. Defect of religious principle is never presumed, and the objection to a witness's competency on this ground should be made by the adverse party before he is sworn. Some difference of opinion has existed as to the manner of proving incompetency. The *modern* practice is not to question the witness himself, but to ask third persons to testify whether he has declared his belief in God, and in a state of future rewards and punishment.

Should the witness set up change of belief, this should be shown in the same way by his declarations to third parties.

Witnesses how Sworn. Witnesses should be sworn in the manner which they deem most binding on their conscience. The ordinary mode, as before pointed out, in court-martial proceedings is as follows: The witness, standing, holds up his bare right hand, and the judge-advocate repeats the prescribed oath. It should be administered in the exact language of the law, and by the person authorized to administer it. The court may ask the witness if he considers the form of administering the oath binding on his conscience, and the proper time for making this inquiry is before he is sworn. But if the witness without making any objection, takes the oath in the usual form, he may be afterwards asked whether he thinks the oath binding on his conscience; but it is unnecessary and irrelevant to ask him if he considers any other form of oath more binding, and, therefore, such question cannot be asked.

If witness, without objecting, is sworn in the usual mode, but, being of different faith, the oath was not in a form affecting his conscience, as if, being a Jew, he was sworn on the Gospels, he is still punishable for perjury, if he swears falsely.[1]

[1] Greenleaf, Vol. I. § 371. Wharton's Crim. Trials, § 2205.

Affirmation. The statutes of the United States provide that the requirement of an "oath" shall be deemed complied with by making affirmation in judicial form.[1]

For the violation of the truth in such cases the witness is subject to the punishment of perjury, as if he had been sworn.

Incompetency from Want of Understanding. Under this head will be considered :—

(1st) **Children.** In former times the age of a child was regarded as the criterion of competency; but now competency is determined by the degree of understanding which a child appears to possess. At the age of fourteen the law presumes every person to have common discretion and understanding until the contrary appears; under that age, competency not being presumed, it is proper to make inquiry as to the degree of understanding, and if the child appears to have sufficient natural intelligence, and to have been so instructed as to comprehend the nature and effect of an oath, he is admitted to testify, whatever his age may be. If the child, being a principal witness, appears not yet sufficiently instructed in the nature of an oath, the court will, in its discretion, put off the trial that this may be done.[2]

(2d) **Idiots and Lunatics.** Persons not possessing the full use of their understanding cannot be allowed to testify. An *idiot* is a person who has been *non compos mentis* from his birth, and who has never had any lucid intervals. He cannot be received as a witness. *A lunatic* is a person who has had understanding, but who, by disease, grief, or other accident, has lost the use of his reason. If he has lucid intervals he may be allowed to testify, but he must have been of sound mind at the time the event happened, and also at the time he testifies; and it ought to

[1] § 1, Revised Statutes. [2] Greenleaf, Vol. I. § 367.

appear that no serious fit of insanity has intervened. Intoxicated persons are not allowed to testify until sober.

(3d) **Deaf and Dumb Persons.** Persons deaf and dumb from birth, in contemplation of law, are regarded as idiots. If, however, they are shown by the party adducing them to have sufficient understanding, they may give evidence either by writing, or by signs interpreted to the court.

Incompetency from Interest. The general rule in both criminal and civil suits is that a party interested is not competent.

So far as courts-martial are concerned, the following cases need alone be considered:

(1) **Relationship.** Husband and wife are, in general, incompetent witnesses for or against each other, on the ground of identity of interest, the great danger of perjury, and the extreme hardship of the case. Where the relation of husband and wife has once existed, even after the relation has ceased, the parties are incompetent to testify for or against each other as to matters which occurred during the continuance of the relation.

The rule applies only to *lawful* marriages. Where a woman has cohabited with a man as his wife, but is not so in fact, she is a competent witness for or against him.[1]

Exceptions. There are certain exceptions to this rule, and it should be remembered that where either party is competent *for* they are competent *against*.

(a) **Collateral Proceedings.** In *collateral proceedings*, not immediately affecting their mutual interests, their evidence is receivable notwithstanding it may *tend to criminate*, or may contradict the other, or may subject the other to a legal demand. The reason of this is that they could not be admitted as witnesses, nor could their evidence in the first suit be produced against each other if an

[1] Roscoe, p. 148.

action should be brought; nor could the suit be prejudiced by the testimony in the collateral case.

The principle of this rule requires its application to all cases in which the *interests* of the other party are involved, and, therefore, the wife is not a competent witness against any co-defendant tried with her husband, if the testimony concern the husband, though it be not directly given against him. Nor is she a witness for a co-defendant, if her testimony, as in the case of a conspiracy, would tend directly to her husband's acquittal; nor where, as in the case of an assault, the interests of all the defendants are inseparable; nor in any suit in which the rights of her husband, though not a party, would be concluded by any verdict therein; nor may she, in a suit between others, testify to any matter for which, if true, her husband may be indicted. Yet where the grounds of defense are several and distinct, and in no manner dependent on each other, no reason is perceived why the wife of one defendant should not be admitted as a witness for another.[1]

(b) **Personal Violence.** In cases of personal violence the wife is a competent witness against the husband; otherwise she would be subjected to personal injuries without redress; and on the same principle her dying declarations are admissible on a charge of murder by her husband.

Whether the wife may testify against the husband *with his consent* is a disputed question. The rule seems to be in this country that she cannot.

As to testifying *for* the husband, De Hart cites the case[2] of Lieutenant T., of the artillery, who was arraigned before a general court-martial which assembled at Detroit, upon a charge of "conduct unbecoming an officer and a gentleman," and, among other facts specified, he was

[1] Greenleaf, Vol. I. § 397. [2] P. 399.

charged with violence towards his wife, by striking, etc. In relation to this particular part of the accusation, the prisoner, in his defense, presented his wife as a witness. Being objected to, the court finally decided to admit the witness, and she was accordingly sworn, and gave her evidence, which was a positive denial of the act charged against her husband.

De Hart thought in this case that the court-martial violated the rule of evidence; but, inasmuch as by a recent act of Congress the husband could testify in his own behalf, there seems no good reason now why a wife should not be allowed to testify *for* the husband with his consent.

No other relationship except that of husband and wife excludes from giving testimony. It may affect the credibility of a witness but not the competency.

(2) **Accomplices.** Persons who have been accomplices in the commission of a crime, with which the prisoner stands charged, are competent to give evidence for or against him. This rule arises from the necessity of the case, as it is often impossible to convict an accused without such testimony. If the party can be convicted without the testimony of the accomplice, he should not ordinarily be called.

The court decides whether to allow an accomplice to be called *for the government,* and where he is the *principal* offender he should not be allowed to testify.

Where several persons are charged with the same offense, one may be called *for* the other so long as he is not sentenced for an infamous offense.

If accomplices are tried *jointly,* the custom is not to allow them to testify for each other unless a *nolle prosequi* be entered. The custom in civil courts in joint trials, where there is only slight evidence against an accomplice, is to direct a separate verdict as to him, and, upon his acquittal, to admit him as a witness for the others. This custom in civil courts, though founded on reason and justice, cannot, from the necessity of subsequent approval of the sentence to render the same valid, and the consequent delay incident thereto, be acted on to the full extent by military courts ; but if such a case should arise on a court-martial, the evidence producible proving inadequate or impracticable, there can be but little doubt that the court can proceed to pass judgment on the individual whose testimony is deemed essential, and adjourn for such period as may afford time for confirmation, on the promulgation of which, and the consequent release of the desired witness, the court may reassemble and proceed with the trial. The regular course for a prisoner to adopt, who may desire to avail himself of the evidence of a person involved in the same charge, would be, on receipt of a copy of the charges, to urge the necessity of his separate trial, with the authority ordering the court-martial, and, if not attended to, an application to the court would still be open.[1]

Credibility of Accomplices. Strictly in law a person may be convicted on the testimony of an accomplice without corroborating testimony. In practice, however, owing to the interest which an accomplice may have, it is considered best, in cases of felony, to have confirmation. The amount of confirmation has been a subject of discussion. It is evident it need not be confirmed in every particular. It is considered that it should be confirmed as to some matter *material* to the issue, and also be corroborated as to the particular person. It is a question for the court to decide how much credibility should be given to the testimony of an accomplice, and how far his testimony should be corroborated.

Privileged Communications. Certain persons, though

[1] Simmons, p. 430.

not exactly incompetent, are privileged from testifying in certain cases:

(1) **Attorneys and Counsel.** Where a confidential communication takes place between an attorney or counsel and his client, the communication is privileged. The privilege extends also to the agents and clerks of the attorney, and to an interpreter between the attorney and his client. The privilege is that of the client and not of the attorney, and the courts will prevent the latter, although willing, from making the disclosure. But if the attorney of one of the parties is called by his client, and examined as to a matter of confidential communication, he may be cross-examined as to that matter, though not as to others. The privilege is not limited as to time.

In civil courts a person, though by profession an attorney, if not employed in the particular business which is the subject of inquiry, is not precluded from giving evidence, though he may have been consulted privately. In courts-martial, where officers and soldiers are often employed as counsel, the privilege of not testifying should be extended to them.

There are some cases to which the privilege does not extend:

(a) An attorney is not privileged from disclosing matters communicated to him before his retainer, or after it has ceased.

(b) He may be compelled to disclose facts of which he obtained a knowledge in his individual capacity, and not in his character of professional adviser.

(c) He may be called to prove his client's handwriting, though his knowledge may have been obtained by seeing him write since his retainer.[1]

This privilege does not extend to confidential com-

[1] Roscoe, p. 189.

munications made to any other persons. Confessions to a clergyman, or disclosures to a physician, though made in the strictest confidence, are not privileged.

(2) **State Secrets.** Another class of privileged communications are *secrets of state.*

Under this head come matters communicated confidentially in furtherance of the administration of justice. The rule has been recently settled that, in a public prosecution, no question can be put which tends to reveal who was the secret informer of the government; even though the question be addressed to a witness in order to ascertain whether he was not himself the informer.[1]

In the same class come official communications between *the heads of the department of state, and their subordinate officers.* Thus, communications between a provincial governor and a military officer under his authority; or the report of a military commission of inquiry made to the commander-in-chief; and the correspondence between an agent of the government and a secretary of state, are confidential and privileged matters, which the interests of the state will not permit to be disclosed.[2]

Parties to the Suit. The party who prefers the charges is not incompetent.

The judge-advocate, though representing the interests of the government which is one of the parties, is not incompetent.

A member of the court may testify.

By a recent act of Congress the accused in courts-martial and courts of inquiry is, at his own request, a competent witness, and his failure to make such request is not to create any presumption against him. This rule allowing the accused to testify at his own request is one of the

[1] Attorney-General *vs.* Briant, cited by Greenleaf, § 250, Note 1.
[2] Greenleaf, Vol. I. § 261.

changes which Congress has made in the common law rules of evidence; but is one which several of the States have adopted. The question naturally arises as to whether an accused, once having taken the stand, may be compelled to answer any question which the court deems proper. On this point Judge Cooley says,—"If he does testify he is at liberty to stop at any point he chooses, and it must be left to the jury to give a statement, which he declines to make a full one, such weight, as under the circumstances, they think it entitled to; otherwise the statute must have set aside and overruled the constitutional maxim which protects an accused party against being compelled to testify against himself, and the statutory privilege becomes a snare and a danger." In further explanation of this he said, "What we intend to affirm by it is, that the privilege to testify in his own behalf is one the accused may waive without justly subjecting himself to unfavorable comments; and that if he avails himself of it, and stops short of a full disclosure, no compulsory process can be made use of to compel him to testify. It was not designed to be understood that, in the latter case, his failure to answer any proper question would not be the subject of comment and criticism by counsel; but, onthe contrary, 'it was supposed that this was implied in the remark that it must be left to the jury to give a statement which he declines to make a full one such weight as, under the circumstances, they think it entitled to.' All circumstances which it is proper for the jury to consider, it is proper for counsel to comment upon." The right of comment where the party makes himself his own witness and then refuses to answer proper questions, is as clear as the right to exemption from unfavorable comment when he abstains from asserting his statutory privilege.[1]

[1] Cooley's Constitutional Limitations, § 317, and Note 2.

Judge Campbell, in speaking of the right which the Michigan statute gives to cross-examine a defendant who has made his statement, said :—"While his constitutional right of declining to answer questions cannot be removed, yet a refusal by a party to answer any fair question, not going outside of what he has offered to explain, would have its proper weight with the jury."[1]

An accessory, whether before or after the fact, is not competent to testify for the principal.

A person who receives the reward for arresting a deserter is not rendered incompetent to testify thereby.

Incompetency from Infamy. Persons who have been convicted of infamous offenses are held incompetent to give evidence. But the question immediately arises, what offenses are considered infamous so as to render a witness incompetent. The usual enumeration of offenses having this effect is *treason*, *felony*,[2] and the *crimen falsi*.

Crimen Falsi. Under this head come perjury, subornation of perjury, forgery and some others.

Conviction for desertion will not render incompetent.

How proved. A person can only be disqualified by the judgment of a court of competent jurisdiction; and, the record of that judgment, proved in the ordinary way, or an authenticated copy, must be produced in court. Oral evidence of the guilt of the party, or even the admission of the party himself that he had been convicted of an infamous offense, would not render him incompetent, although it might affect his credibility.

The judgment of a foreign tribunal will not render incompetent, nor that of a State court, unless it would render incompetent in the State where it was given.

How Restored. A person convicted of an infamous offense may have his competency restored.

[1] People vs. Thomas, 9 Mich. 321. [2] For definition, see Chapter XXVI.

(1) By *reversal of judgment.* Proof of this would have to be made in the same way as prescribed for proving the judgment.

(2) By a *pardon.* If the pardon is conditional, the conditions would have to be fulfilled before competency would be restored.

The Revised Statutes prescribe two cases—perjury and subornation of perjury—where competency can be restored only by reversal of judgment.[1]

Serving out the term of imprisonment for a felony, does not restore the party to his competency.[2]

Compellable Witnesses. All persons, not incompetent for any of the before mentioned reasons, are competent and *compellable* witnesses.

It is for the court to decide what witnesses are necessary, and whether or not their testimony is required.

No witness has a right to leave the court until properly discharged. In the case of Captain C., a department commander, called to testify, discharged himself on the ground that, being the reviewing officer, he could not be held at the will of a court ordered by himself. The Judge-Advocate General held that the act of the witness was one without precedent in our military practice, and in a civil case would have constituted a grave contempt of court.[3]

CREDIBILITY OF WITNESSES.

It is the province of the court to decide how much credit it will give to the testimony of any particular witness. It is true they agree to find according to evidence, but, though a number of witnesses may testify to the same fact, and one testify to the contrary, they may give more credit to the one than to all.

[1] Secs. 5392–5393. [2] U. S. *vs.* Brown, 4 Cranch, C. C., 607.
[3] G. C. M. O. 26, A. G. O., May 18, 1878.

How Impeached. After a witness has been examined in chief, his credit may be impeached in various ways:

(1) *By proving that he has made statements out of court contrary to what he has testified at the trial.*

It is, however, only in such matters as are relevant to the issue that the witness can be contradicted; and, before this can be done, it is generally held necessary to ask him as to the time, place, and person involved in the supposed contradiction.

It is not enough to ask him the general question, whether he has ever said so and so, nor whether he has always told the same story.[1]

In rebuttal the opposite party may show that the witness has made the same statement out of court at different times.

If a party asks irrelevant questions for the purpose of impeaching the witness's credibility, he is bound by his answers. Thus, if a witness be asked if he had not been charged with theft on a former occasion, and replies in the negative, other witnesses cannot be brought to prove the truth of this fact, and thus impeach his credibility.

(2) *By general evidence affecting his credit for truth and veracity.*

In this case the examination must be confined to his general reputation, and not be permitted as to particular facts. The regular mode of examining into the general reputation is to inquire of the witness whether he knows the general reputation of the person in question among his neighbors; and what that reputation is; and then, whether from such knowledge the witness would believe that person upon his oath.[2]

In answer to such evidence the other party may cross-

[1] Roscoe, p. 183. [2] Greenleaf, Vol. I. § 461, Note 2.

examine these witnesses as to their means of knowledge, and the grounds of their opinions; or may attack their general character, and, by fresh evidence, support the character of his own witnesses.

(3) *By disproving the facts stated by him, by the testimony of other witnesses.*

Confessions. In this connection will be considered the subject of *confessions,* and the credit to be attached to them.

The confession of a prisoner is, under certain circumstances, admitted as evidence against him:

Voluntary. It must have been freely and voluntarily made, without promises, inducements, or fear; but the inducements, promises, or threats, must have been held out by *one in authority,* otherwise it is receivable. As stated by one judge,—"The inducement must be held out to the accused by some one who has, or who is supposed by the accused to have, some power or authority to assure to him the promised good, or cause or influence the threatened injury."[1] *For example,* a confession made to any of the following persons under inducements, etc., would not be considered voluntary. An officer having the prisoner in custody, or a magistrate, or any one having authority over him, or to a private person in the presence of one in authority.

The official character of the person to whom the confession is made does not affect its admissibility, provided no inducements were employed.

Confessions made to a private individual who had no authority could be properly received in evidence.

The inducements must have reference to some temporal advantage in order to invalidate a confession. Where an accused, charged with a grave crime, is urged

[1] C. J. Shaw, cited in Greenleaf, Vol. I. § 223, Note 6.

by a clergyman "to confess his sins," and so confesses, it would be receivable.

Again, the inducements must have some reference to his escape from the charge. Thus, where a man and his wife were in prison in separate rooms, on a charge of stealing and receiving, and the constable said to the man, "If you will tell where the property is, you shall see your wife," it was held that a confession made afterward was admissible.

It is the province of the court to decide whether a confession is receivable or not. In deciding this point, where the confession is made under an inducement, the court should direct its inquiry as to whether the threat or inducement was such as to be likely to influence the prisoner.

The course of practice is to inquire of the witness whether the prisoner had been told that it would be better for him to confess, or worse for him if he did not confess, or whether language to that effect had been addressed to him.[1]

The confessions of a person are not evidence against an accomplice.

On an indictment against husband and wife her confessions are good against herself, but not against him.

The whole of a confession must be taken, and not parts of it. Thus, where a person acknowledged a debt, but stated that he had paid it, the whole must be considered. The court, however, may believe parts of the confession, and reject others, if they see good grounds for so doing.

Where a fact is discovered in consequence of a non-receivable confession, it may be shown that the fact was discovered through the confession. Thus, where, under a threat, a prisoner confessed to the crime of murder, and

[1] Phillips, (10th Ed.) p. 543.

stated where the weapon with which it was committed could be found, it may be shown that the latter was so found, through the confession, though the latter is not receivable.

Credibility of a Confession. The credit to be given a confession must depend on each particular case. It is not conclusive, although, even if totally uncorroborated, some writers have held that the court may convict upon it. In the United States the prisoner's confession, when the *corpus delicti* is not otherwise proved, has been held insufficient for his conviction.[1]

EXAMINATION OF WITNESSES.

Examination-in-chief. After a witness has been sworn he is examined-in-chief by the party calling him.

It is the custom to require any witnesses before the court to retire before commencing the examination. If a witness remain after an order to retire, it is in the discretion of the court whether he shall be examined. An attorney whose attendance is necessary in court is not expected to retire, though he is to be called as a witness; nor a witness as to character, or experts.

Leading Questions. On the *examination-in-chief* leading questions are not permitted to be asked.

A leading question is one which plainly suggests to the witness the answer desired.

Questions are also objectionable, as leading, which, embodying a material fact, admit of an answer by a simple negative or affirmative.

The interrogatory must not assume facts to have been proved which have not been proved; nor, that particular answers have been given, which have not been given.

Exceptions. In the following cases the rule as to

[1] Greenleaf, Vol. I. § 217.

leading questions on the examination-in-chief does not obtain:—

(1) To questions merely introductory.

(2) Where the witness appears to be hostile to the party producing him, or in the interest of the other party, or unwilling to give evidence.

In either of these cases the judge-advocate or accused should secure permission of the court before asking the question, and this should be noted of record.

(3) Where an omission in his testimony is evidently caused by want of recollection of the witness, which a suggestion may assist.

(4) Where a witness is called to contradict another. Thus, where a witness testifies that certain expressions were used, the judge-advocate may be permitted to ask another witness whether those particular expressions were used, instead of asking the witness to state what was said.[1]

It is the province of the court to decide when leading questions shall be allowed.

On the *cross-examination*, leading questions may be put, but for the single exception that when a witness manifests unmistakable hostility to the party who called him, or an unmistakable bias in favor of the party who is cross-examining him, the court may prohibit leading questions.[2]

Examination-in-chief how Confined. The examination-in-chief should be confined to matters of fact which the witness has perceived, the inferences from these facts being drawn by the court. It is not necessary, however, that he depose to facts with a certainty that excludes all doubt in his mind.

Opinion. In general, a witness must depose to facts,

[1] Greenleaf, Vol. I, §§ 434 and 435.

[2] G. C. M. O. 18, A. G. O., Feb. 26, 1874.

and cannot be asked his *opinion* upon a particular question. To this, exceptions are made in the following cases:

(a) Where a person testifies as an *expert* on questions of science, skill, etc.

On the trial of Col. Q., of the British army, the judge-advocate said, "Every question is admissible of a military man, where it is founded on local knowledge or circumstances which are not within the reach of all the members of the court; but where it is merely a question of military science, to affect the officer undergoing his trial, it is obvious that the court is met for no other purpose but to try that; and that they have before them the facts in evidence, on which they are to ground their conclusions."[1] It is, however, perfectly proper to put questions involving an opinion, to an engineer, as to the progress of an attack, or to an artillery officer, as to the probable effect of his arm, if directed as assumed; these questions, though attaching to military science, are not of that nature to be presumably known to each member of a court-martial.[2]

In the case of Captain C., the Judge-Advocate General held that an officer, might be called to testify as an expert, as to "customs of the service."

Where a witness testifies as an expert, it must first be shown that he is an expert.

An expert cannot give an opinion upon the general merits of the case, but only upon the facts proved; and, if he has heard the evidence, it is held improper to ask him his opinion upon the case on trial, though he may be asked his opinion upon a similar case, hypothetically stated.

(2) A witness may give his opinion or belief as to the identity of a person, or of the handwriting of a particular individual.

[1] Simmons, p. 367 (2d Edition). [2] Simmons, p. 367 (2d Edition) *et seq.*
[3] G. C. M. O. 26, A. G. O., May 18, 1878.

Greenleaf says, "The *opinions* of witnesses are perhaps more frequently called for in military trials than in any others. But it is proper here to add, that where the manner of the act, or of the language with which the prisoner is charged, is essential to the offense, as, whether the act was menacing and insulting, or cowardly or unskillful, or not, or whether the language was abusive, or sarcastic, or playful, the opinion which the witness formed at the time, or the impression it then made upon his mind, being contemporaneous with the fact, and partaking of the *res gestæ*, is not only admissible, but is a fact in the case which he is bound to testify."[1]

Cross-Examination. After the examination-in-chief is finished, the opposite party has the right to cross-examine the witness.

A party, generally speaking, should not cross-examine except as to facts and circumstances connected with the matter stated in the direct examination. If he wishes to examine on other matters he must do so by making the witness his own, and calling him as such in the subsequent progress of the cause. Still it is the accepted opinion, that on the cross-examination the party is not obliged to confine his evidence to the point at issue with the same strictness as on the examination-in-chief; great latitude is often allowed to find out the truth of the matter.

In addition to questions to ascertain his knowledge of the facts, a witness may be asked questions on the cross-examination to ascertain his situation with respect to the parties, and to the subject of litigation, his interest, his motives, his inclination and prejudices, his means of obtaining a correct knowledge of the facts to which he bears testimony, the manner in which he has used those means, his power of discernment, memory, and description. It is

[1] Vol. III. § 478.

not easy for a witness, who is subjected to this test, to impose on a court or jury.[1]

Re-Examination. After the cross-examination is finished, a re-examination is allowed for the purpose of explaining facts which may have come out on the cross-examination. It must be confined to the subject matter of the cross-examination. If new matter is wanted the court may be asked to make the inquiry.

Memorandum. Witnesses are allowed to refresh their memory from a memorandum, made shortly after the occurrence of the fact to which it refers; provided, after inspecting it, they can speak from their own recollection. If, after the inspection, the witness does not remember the facts, nor remember to have recognized the written statement as true, and the writing was not made by him, his evidence is inadmissible.

Where a witness testified that he was present at a conversation, and made a memorandum of it immediately after it took place; that he had now no recollection of all the particulars, but that he had no doubt the facts stated in the memorandum were true; and that he should have sworn to them from recollection within a short time afterwards—the memorandum was admitted in evidence in connection with his testimony, to show the particulars of the conversation.[2]

It is not necessary that the memorandum should have been made by the witness.

Generally speaking the writing should be produced in court to allow the other party to cross-examine.

Criminating Questions. A party cannot refuse to answer a question on the ground that it will criminate him. The Revised Statutes provide that no pleading of a party, nor any discovery or evidence obtained from a party

[1] Greenleaf, Vol. I. § 446. [2] Roscoe, 170, Note 1.

or witness, by means of a judicial proceeding in this or any foreign country, shall be given in evidence, or in any manner used against him or his property or estate, in any court of the United States, in any criminal proceeding, or for the enforcement of any penalty or forfeiture: *Provided*, that this section shall not exempt any party or witness from prosecution and punishment for perjury, committed in discovering or testifying as aforesaid.[1]

Degrading Questions. Much difference of opinion exists as to whether a witness may be compelled to answer a question tending to degrade him.

Greenleaf says: "The conflict of opinion may be somewhat reconciled by a distinction, which has been very properly taken, between cases where the testimony is relevant and material to the issue, and cases where the testimony is not strictly relevant, but is collateral, and is asked under the latitude allowed in the cross-examination. In the former case the witness will be obliged to give evidence, however strongly it may reflect on his character."[2]

In the case of *Marbury vs. Madison*, the Supreme Court held that a witness is not bound to answer any question which may impeach his conduct as a public officer.[3]

If a witness refuses to be sworn, or answer a legal question, he may be punished for contempt. If an officer or soldier he may be ordered into arrest or confinement by the court when charges may be preferred against him.[4] In the case of a *civilian* the Revised Statutes authorize the judge-advocate to issue the like process to compel witnesses to appear and *testify*, which courts of criminal jurisdiction within the State, Territory, or district where such military courts shall be ordered to sit may lawfully issue.[5]

[1] § 860, Revised Statutes. [2] Vol. I. § 454. [3] I. Cranch, 144.

[4] G. C. M. O. 23, A. G. O., Jan. 30, 1873.

[5] In the Articles of War recently submitted to Congress so much of this act as refers to testifying is stricken out.

It is the province of the court to determine, under all circumstances of the case, whether a witness should answer the questions propounded to him as a witness.[1]

A party cannot be allowed to discredit his own witnesses. If, however, a witness testifies differently from what was expected, other witnesses may be called to contradict him and prove the fact.

Number of Witnesses. As to the number of witnesses necessary to prove a fact, the general rule is, that the testimony of one credible witness is sufficient. The *exceptions*, so far as courts-martial are concerned, are in the two cases of *false muster* under the 14th, and perjury under the 60th Articles of War. In the first case two witnesses are required; in the second two witnesses, or one with corroborative evidence.

In the case of perjury a living witness of the *corpus delicti* may be dispensed with, and documentary or written evidence be relied upon to convict of perjury,—*first*, where the falsehood of the matter sworn by the prisoner is directly proved by documentary or written evidence springing from himself, with circumstances showing the corrupt intent; *secondly*, in cases where the matter so sworn is contradicted by a public record, proved to have been well known by the prisoner when he took the oath, the oath only being proved to have been taken; and *thirdly*, in cases where the party is charged with taking an oath, contrary to what he must necessarily have known to be true; the falsehood being shown by his own letters relating to the fact sworn to, or by any other written testimony existing and being found in his possession, and which has been treated by him as containing the evidence of the fact recited in it.[2]

Sufficiency of Evidence. The amount of evidence which will satisfy a court-martial must depend upon each

[1] G. C. M. O. 23, A. G. O., Jan. 30, 1873.

[2] Greenleaf, Vol. I, § 258.

particular case. McArthur cites the case of Lieutenant Thackeray, of the English Navy, who was tried before a naval court-martial on charges preferred by his captain, one of which was, for going into the captain's cabin, when alone at tea, and calling him a *scoundrel* and *liar*. The privacy of the offense excluded all other positive evidence but that of the prosecutor, which was admitted, on the opinion of counsel, and Lieutenant T., was dismissed the service.[1]

To justify conviction there must be "such a moral certainty as convinces the minds of the tribunal as reasonable men, beyond all reasonable doubt."[2]

As a rule *cumulative evidence* (*i. e.* evidence of the same kind to the same fact) is not necessary, unless from the character of the witness, or his testimony, the court is not satisfied.

Judicial Cognizance. In this connection it may be stated that courts of a country take notice of various things without requiring them to be regularly proved: such as public acts, proclamations of war and peace, courts of general jurisdiction, or in fine, of whatever ought to be generally known within the limits of their jurisdiction. Courts-martial, in addition, take judicial cognizance of General Regulations, and General Orders when duly promulgated. Special Orders, as before said, should be regularly proved. In all these cases the court may resort to documents at hand to refresh their memory.

DOCUMENTARY EVIDENCE.

The remaining instruments of evidence are *documents*, and the evidence derived from them is termed *documentary* or *written* evidence.

[1] McArthur, p. 104.

[2] Rule as expressed by Parke, B., cited by Best, Vol. I. § 95.

The term document includes all material substances on which the thoughts of men are represented by writing, or any other species of conventional mark or symbol.[1]

Documents consist, in general, of two kinds : Public and private.

Public Documents are all such records, papers, and acts, as are filed in the public offices of the United States or of the several States; as, for example, public statutes, public proclamations, resolutions of the legislature, the journals of either branch of the legislature, diplomatic correspondence communicated by the President to Congress, and the like.[2]

Proof and Effect. The edition of the *laws aud treaties* of the *United States*, published by Little & Brown, shall be competent evidence of the several public and private acts of Congress, and of the several treaties therein contained, in all the courts of law and equity and of maritime jurisdiction, and in all the tribunals and public offices of the United States, and of the several States, without any further proof or authentication thereof.[3]

Congress under its constitutional authority[4] has provided for the mode of proving, and the effect of public documents of the several States.

Acts of the Legislature. The acts of the legislature of any State or Territory, or of any country subject to the jurisdiction of the United States, shall be authenticated by having the seals of such State, Territory, or country affixed thereto.[5] Courts of the United States take judicial cognizance of the *public* laws of the several States when called on to apply them. Private statutes must be proved in the ordinary way.

Records and Judicial Proceedings. The records

[1] Best, Vol. I. § 215. [2] Bouvier's Law Dictionary, p. 442.
[3] § 908, Revised Statutes. [4] Art. IV. § I. [5] § 905, Revised Statutes.

and judicial proceedings of the courts of any State or Territory, or of any country subject to the jurisdiction of the United States, shall be proved or admitted in any other court within the United States, by the attestation of the clerk, and the seal of the court annexed, if there be a seal, together with a certificate of the judge, chief justice, or presiding magistrate, that the attestation is in due form, and the said records and judicial proceedings, so authenticated, shall have such faith and credit given to them in every court within the United States as they have by law or usage in the courts of the State from which they are taken.[1]

Records not Judicial. All records and exemplifications of books, which may be kept in any public office of any State or Territory, or of any country subject to the jurisdiction of the United States, not appertaining to a court, shall be proved or admitted in any court or office in any other State or Territory, or in any such country, by the attestation of the keeper of the said records or books, and the seal of his office annexed, if there be a seal, together with a certificate of the presiding justice of the court of the county, parish, or district in which such office may be kept, or of the governor, or secretary of state, the chancellor or keeper of the great seal, of the State or Territory, or country, that the said attestation is in due form, and by the proper officers. If the said certificate is given by the presiding justice of a court, it shall be further authenticated by the clerk or prothonotary of the said court, who shall certify, under his hand and the seal of his office, that the said presiding justice is duly commissioned and qualified; or, if given by such governor, secretary, chancellor, or keeper of the great seal, it shall be under the great seal of the State, Territory, or country

[1] § 905, Revised Statutes.

aforesaid in which it is made. And the said records and exemplifications, so authenticated, shall have such faith and credit given to them in every court and office within the United States as they have by law or usage in the courts or offices of the State, Territory, or country, as aforesaid, from which they are taken.[1]

Greenleaf says,—"The Acts of Congress respecting the exemplification of public office books is not understood to exclude any other modes of authentication which the courts may deem it proper to admit."[2]

As records cannot generally be transferred from their place of deposit, courts-martial would ordinarily allow proof by a copy. Where the proof is in this way, an examined copy, duly made and sworn to by any competent witness, is always admissible. It should appear, however, that the record, from which the copy was taken, was found in the proper place of deposit, or in the hands of the officer in whose custody the records of the court are kept.[3]

The proceedings of a court of inquiry may be admitted as evidence by a court-martial, in cases not capital, nor extending to the dismissal of an officer; *Provided,* that the circumstances are such that oral testimony cannot be obtained.[4]

Private Writings produced in evidence must be proved to be genuine.

It is a general rule of evidence that where a fact can be established by written proof, which is regarded as superior to parol proof, the writing ought to be produced.

The *originals* of private writings must be produced, and, until accounted for, oral testimony of their contents or copies will not be received.

How Proved. The proof of deeds, wills, pay rolls,

[1] § 916, Revised Statutes.
[2] Greenleaf, Vol. I. § 489.
[3] Ibid., §§ 485–559.
[4] Article 121.

etc., where there is an attesting witness, should be by him. If he is dead, insane, infamous, or otherwise incompetent, proof of his signature is inadmissible.

Other private writings are proved by the admission of the party, or by proof of handwriting.

Handwriting in a document may be proved in the following ways:

(1) By calling the party who wrote it.

(2) By a party who saw him write it.

(3) By a party who has seen the person write on other occasions, if even once only; but he must swear that he *believes*, not that he *thinks*, it is his writing. The latter will not do.

(4) By a witness who has seen documents purporting to be his writing, and, by subsequent communications with such party, he believes them to be authentic.[1]

In the last two cases the knowledge must not have been acquired with a view to this specific occasion.[2]

(5) By *comparison.* Proof by mere comparison of handwriting is not sufficient, but where *other writings* admitted to be genuine are *already* before the court, the comparison may be made by the members of the court, or by experts.

Upon the testimony of experts to handwriting it seems to be the opinion that little if any reliance should be placed.

There are a class of writings with which courts-martial may frequently have to deal: viz., documents subscribed by affixing near it a mark. Unless there is something to identify it as being the mark of a particular person, the evidence is deemed not admissible.

When a party gives part of a writing in evidence the adverse party has a right to have read all the passages connected with, or which may modify these, but not irrelevant passages.

[1] Franklyn, p. 134. [2] Best, Vol. I, § 236.

CHAPTER XXVI.

CRIMINAL OFFENSES.

COURTS-MARTIAL, by the 62d Article of War, have *at all times* a jurisdiction of "all crimes not capital which officers and soldiers may be guilty of to the prejudice of good order and military discipline;" by the 60th Article, of offenses, such as perjury, forgery, etc., under certain circumstances; and by the 58th Article, *in time of war*, of a large number of offenses cognizable, in time of peace, only by the civil courts.

But few of these offenses have been defined by Congress, and recourse must therefore be had to the common law for their meaning.[1]

Offenses Defined and Classified. An offense which may be the subject of criminal procedure, is an act committed or omitted in violation of public law, either forbidding or commanding it to be done. Offenses, at common law, are divided into three heads; *treasons, felonies* and *misdemeanors*.

Treason. The Constitution provides that "treason against the United States shall consist *only* in levying war against them, or in adhering to their enemies, giving them aid and comfort," and that "no person shall be convicted of treason unless on the testimony of two witnesses to the same overt act, or on confession in open court."

[1] U. S. *vs.* Magill, 1 Wash. C. C. R. 453, U. S. *vs.* Jones, 3 Wash. C. C. R 209.

[2] Article III, § 3, Clause 1, Revised Statutes, § 5331.

Misprision of Treason. Every person owing allegiance to the United States, and having knowledge of the commission of any treason against them, who conceals, and does not, as soon as may be, disclose and make known the same to the President, or to some judge of the United States, or to the governor, or to some judge or justice of a particular State, is guilty of misprision of treason.[1]

Felonies. A felony originally was an offense which occasioned a total forfeiture of either land or goods, or both, at the common law, and to which capital or other punishment might be added according to the degree of guilt.[2] Forfeiture for crime having been generally abolished in the United States, the term felony, in American law, has lost this point of distinction; and its meaning, where not fixed by statute, is somewhat vague and undefined; generally, however, it is used to denote an offense of a higher grade, punishable either capitally, or by a term of imprisonment in the state's prison, and no other, is a felony.[3]

Wharton says: "At common law, in addition to the crimes more strictly coming under the head of treason, the chief, if not the only felonies, were murder, manslaughter, arson, burglary, robbery, rape, sodomy, mayhem and larceny. In this country, with a few exceptions, the common law classification has obtained; the principal felonies being received as they originally existed, and their number being increased as the exigencies of society prompted.[4]

Misdemeanors comprise all offenses lower than felonies which may be the subject of indictment.

Parties to Crimes are divided into principals and accessaries.

Principals. The word *principal* is used in opposition

[1] § 5333, Revised Statutes.
[2] Bouvier's Law Dictionary.
[3] Webster's Dictionary.
[4] § 2.

to *accessary* to show the degree of crime committed by two persons.

A person may be a principal in an offense in the first or second degree.

First Degree. A principal in the first degree is one who is the actor or actual perpetrator of the fact. It is not necessary that he should have committed the act with his own hands, or be actually present when the offense is consummated; for, if one lay poison purposely for another who takes it, and is killed, he who laid the poison, though absent when it was taken, is a principal in the first degree. If he acts through the medium of an innocent or insane medium, he is guilty as a principal in the first degree.

Second Degree. A principal in the second degree is one who is present, aiding and abetting, at the commission of the fact.

To constitute principals in the second degree there must be, in the first place, a participation in the act committed; and, in the second place, presence either actual or constructive, at the time of its commission.

It is not necessary that the party should be actually present, an eye or ear witness of the transaction; he is, in construction of law, present aiding and abetting, if, with the intention of giving assistance, he be near enough to afford it, should occasion arise. Thus, if he be outside the house watching to prevent surprise, or the like, whilst his companions are in the house committing the felony, such constructive presence is sufficient to make him a principal in the second degree.[1]

A party charged as a principal in the second degree may be convicted, though the party charged as principal in the first degree is acquitted. So on an indictment for murder, the court may, in their discretion, try the

[1] Wharton, §§ 112–124.

principal in the second before the principal in the first degree.[1]

Accessaries. An accessary is one who is not the chief actor in the perpetration of the offense, nor present at its performance, but in some way concerned therein, either before or after the fact committed.

Before the Fact. An accessary before the fact is one who, being absent at the time of the crime committed, yet procures, counsels, or commands another to commit it. Absence is necessary.

He who in any wise commands or counsels another to commit an unlawful act is accessary to all that ensues to that unlawful act; but is not accessary to any act distinct from the other.

There can be no accessaries *before* the fact in those offenses which by judgment of law are sudden and unpremeditated, as manslaughter and the like.[2]

When Triable. At common law, accessaries before the fact cannot be punished until the guilt of the principal offender is established.

After the Fact. An accessary after the fact is one who, knowing a felony to have been committed, receives, relieves, comforts or assists the felon. It is, in the *first* place, requisite that he knows of the felony committed; *secondly*, it must be complete at the time of the assistance given; and *thirdly*, he must receive, relieve, comfort or assist the felon. And, generally any assistance whatever, given to a felon to hinder his being apprehended, tried, or suffering punishment, makes the assister an accessary.[3]

There can be no accessaries *before* or *after* the fact in treason, or any offenses under the degree of felony; all persons concerned in these offenses, if guilty at all, are principals.

[1] Wharton, § 130. [2] 4 Blackstone, §§ 36–37. [3] Ibid, § 38.

The 27th Article of War provides that all seconds or promoters of *duels*, and carriers of challenges to fight duels, shall be deemed principals and punished accordingly.

Mere presence at a duel, as a spectator, would not render the party an accessary to the duel.

Punishment. It is the general rule that accessaries shall suffer the same punishment as principals.

Accomplices. This term includes in its meaning every person who has been concerned in the commission of crime, every *particeps criminis,* whether he is considered, in strict legal propriety, as a principal in the first or second degree, or merely as an accessary before or after the fact.

We now come to the meaning of the different offenses, as defined at common law:

Larceny is the wrongful and fradulent taking and carrying away, by one person, of the mere personal goods of another, from any place, with a felonious intent to convert them to his (the taker's) use, and make them his property without the consent of the owner.

To constitute larceny several ingredients are necessary:

(1) There must be a *taking* from the possession, actual or implied, of the owner; hence, if a man finds goods, and appropriates them to his own use, he is not a thief on this account.

The taking must be against the will of the owner, and this may be in some cases where he appears to consent; for example, if a man suspects another of an intent to steal his property, and in order to try him leaves it in his way, and he takes it, he is guilty of larceny.

Where an offender unlawfully acquires possession of goods with an intent to steal them, the owner still retain ing his property in them, such person will be guilty of larceny in taking them.

(2) There must be actual *carrying away*, but the slightest removal, if the goods are completely in the power of the thief, is sufficient.

(3) The property taken must be personal property; a man cannot commit a larceny of real estate, or of what is so considered in law.

Larceny cannot be committed of animals *feræ naturæ*, so long as they are not retained or confined.

(4) The intent of the party must be *felonious*, without any color of right or excuse for the act. If a party takes the goods of another under a claim of right, however unfounded, he has not committed larceny. If again a party takes the property of another with the intent of returning it *ultimately*, it is not larceny.

The possession of property, recently stolen, is *prima facie* evidence of guilt in the possessor of the property; but it may be satisfactorily accounted for.

In some of the States larceny is divided into grand and petit larceny, depending on the value of the property taken; but at the common law it is sufficient to constitute the offense if the thing stolen be of some value.[1]

Robbery is the felonious and forcible taking of the property of another from his person; or in his presence, against his will, by violence or putting him in fear.

(1) Some property must be taken, and the prisoner must have had possession. The value of the property, or the length of possession, is immaterial.

(2) The taking must be from the person, or in his presence. If a person by intimidation is compelled to open his desk, or to throw down his purse, and the money is taken in his presence, this is robbery.[2]

[1] Bouvier's Law Dictionary; Wharton, §§ 1751–1869.

[2] U. S. *vs.* Jones, 3 Wash. C. C. Rep. 209.

(3) The taking must be felonious, and against the will of the party.

If a person takes goods under a *bona fide* claim, without the *animus furandi*, this is not robbery.

(4) The taking must be by violence *or* by putting the party in fear. Either is sufficient. As to the degree of violence, it is held that the sudden taking of a thing unawares from the person, as by snatching a thing from his hand, is not sufficient to constitute robbery, unless some injury be done to the person or there be some previous struggling for the possession of the property.

The fear mentioned may be a fear either to his person, his property, or his reputation.[1]

To secure money, by threatening to charge the party with an unnatural crime, has in several cases been held to be robbery; but this seems to be the only case of fear of reputation sufficient to constitute robbery.

It seems to be immaterial what means are used to induce fear, provided fear was actually created in the mind of the party, and he parted with his property under this fear. This is a question for the court.

This offense differs from larceny from the person in this, that in the latter there is no violence, while in the former the crime is incomplete without an actual or constructive force.

Burglary is the breaking and entering the dwelling-house of another in the night, with intent to commit some felony within the same, whether the felonious intent be executed or not.[2]

To constitute this offense it is necessary:

(1) That there be a breaking and entering. If one enter into a house by a door which he finds open, or through a hole which was made there before, and steals

[1] Roscoe, §§ 898–900.

[2] Wharton, § 1531.

goods, etc., or draws anything out of a house through a door or window which was open before, or enter into a house through a door open in the day time, and lie there till night, and then rob and go away without breaking any part of the house, he is not guilty of burglary.[1]

The slightest breaking however seems sufficient. The lifting a latch, the removing a bolt, the breaking a glass window, the turning a key, whether on the outside of the house, or when within the house, is a breaking as understood in burglary.

The breaking may be actual or constructive. Where one obtains entrance into a dwelling-house by fraud, conspiracy, or threats, in the night time, with a felonious intent, this is constructive breaking, and will constitute burglary.

There must also be an *entry*, but it is not absolutely necessary that the offender's body enter the house. If a man break a window and introduce any instrument for the purpose of committing a felony, this is burglary, but if the instrument is used merely for the purpose of effecting an entry, it would not be.

(2) That the building entered be a dwelling-house. The term dwelling-house seems to comprehend any building in which the occupier and his family usually *reside*, or in other words dwell and lie in.[2] Where no person sleeps in the house it cannot be considered a dwelling-house.

To make it burglary it is not absolutely necessary that any person should be actually within the house at the time of the offense. If the owner leaves it, *animo revertendi*, it is still his dwelling-house.[3] Burglary may be committed in an *out-house*, if it is so near the dwelling-house that it is used with the dwelling-house as appurtenant to it, though not within the same inclosure.[4]

[1] Roscoe, p. 340.
[2] Russell on Crimes, 797.
[3] 2 East, P. C., 496.
[4] Wharton, §1561.

(3) That the breaking be in the night. For this purpose it is deemed night when by the light of the sun a person cannot clearly discern the face or countenance of another.[1] The breaking and entering must both be in the night, but it is not necessary that both be done the same night.

(4) That the *intent* of breaking and entering must be felonious: If a felony however be committed, the act will be *prima facie* evidence of an intent to commit it.[2]

On a charge of burglary the court might find the prisoner guilty of larceny only.[3]

Arson is the willful and malicious burning of the house of another by night or by day.

To constitute this offense it must be proved:

(1) That the offense was committed willfully and maliciously, otherwise, it is only a trespass, and not a felony.[4]

(2) That there was a burning. The least burning is sufficient.

(3) That it was the house of another.

The term house includes all out-houses which are parcel thereof, though not adjoining thereto, nor under the same roof.[5]

By the Revised Statutes of the United States it is declared arson to willfully and maliciously burn any dwelling-house, or mansion house, or any store, barn, or other building, parcel of any dwelling or mansion house, when done within any fort, dock-yard, navy-yard, arsenal, armory or magazine, the site whereof is under the jurisdiction of the United States, or on the site of any light-house, or other needful building belonging to the United States, the site whereof is under their jurisdiction.[6]

[1] 1 Hale, P. C., 550. [2] Ibid, 560.
[3] U. S. *vs.* Dixon, 1. Cr. C. C. Rep. 414. [4] 1 Hale, P. C., 569.
[5] Ibid, 567. [6] § 5385.

It must also be the house of another. It is not arson to burn one's own house, but if a man set fire to his own house, maliciously intending thereby to burn the adjoining house, belonging to another, if the latter house is burned, it is felony; if not, it is a great misdemeanor.[1]

Mayhem is the act of unlawfully and violently depriving another of the use of such of his members as may render him less able, in fighting, either to defend himself or annoy his adversary. Therefore the cutting, or disabling, or weakening a man's hand or finger, or striking out his eye or fore-tooth, or depriving him of those parts, the loss of which abates his courage, are held to be mayhems. But cutting off the ear or nose, or the like, are not held to be mayhems at common law.[2]

By the Revised Statutes, however, every person who, within any of the places upon the land under the exclusive jurisdiction of the United States, or who upon the high seas in any vessel belonging to the United States, or to any citizen thereof, maliciously cuts off the ear, cuts out or disables the tongue, puts out an eye, slits the nose, cuts off the nose or lip, or cuts off or disables any limb or member of any person, with intent to maim or disfigure such person, shall be imprisoned, etc.[3]

Homicide may be defined to be the destruction of life by one human being, either by himself, or by the act, procurement, or culpable omission of another.

Homicides, caused by another, are divided into three general classes, *justifiable*, *excusable* and *felonious*.

Justifiable homicide is of three kinds:

(1) Where the proper officer executes a criminal in strict conformity with his sentence.

(2) Where an officer of justice, in the legal exercise

[1] 1 Hale, P. C. 568. [2] 4 Blackstone, 206. [3] § 5348

of a particular duty, kills a person who resists or prevents him from executing it.

In case of a riot which an officer is ordered to quell, both he and his subordinates, assisting in dispersing the rioters, are justified in killing them at common law, if it cannot be otherwise suppressed.

(3) Where the homicide is committed in prevention of a forcible and atrocious crime; as, for instance, where the deceased was in the act of robbing or murdering another.[1]

Excusable homicide is of two kinds:

(1) Homicide *by misadventure.* Example, where a man doing a *lawful* act, without any intention to hurt, by accident kills another; as for instance, where a soldier firing at a target undesignedly kills a person. But in this case it would have to be shown that proper precautions had been taken in choosing a site for the target.

(2) Homicide in *self-defense,* upon a sudden affray. This is excusable rather than justifiable. It is frequently difficult to distinguish this species of homicide from man-slaughter, in the proper legal sense of the word; but the true criterion seems to be this; where both parties are actually combating at the time when the mortal stroke is given, the slayer is then guilty of man-slaughter; but if the slayer has not begun the fight, or having begun endeavors to decline any further struggle, and afterwards, being closely pressed by his antagonist, kills him to avoid his own destruction, this is homicide excusable by self-defense. For which reason the law requires, that the person who kills another in his own defense should have retreated as far as he conveniently or safely can, to avoid the violence of the assault, before he turns upon his assailant; and that not factitiously, or in order to watch his

[1] Wharton, §§ 936–938.

opportunity, but from a real tenderness of shedding his brother's blood.[1]

Felonious homicide is the killing a human creature without justification or excuse. This includes murder, manslaughter, and suicide.

Murder is where a person of sound memory and discretion unlawfully kills any reasonable creature in being, and in the peace of the commonwealth, with malice prepense or aforethought, either express or implied.[2]

The following things are requisite in murder:

(1) It must be committed by a person of sound memory and discretion. Lunatics and children are held incapable of committing any crime, unless in such cases where they show a consciousness of doing wrong, and of course a discretion or discernment between good and bad.

(2) There must be an unlawful killing.

The unlawfulness arises from the killing without warrant or excuse; and there must also be an actual killing to constitute murder; for a bare assault, with intent to kill, is only a great misdemeanor. The killing may be by any means by which human nature may be overcome.

In order to make the killing murder it is requisite that the party die within a year and a day after the stroke received, or cause of death administered; in the computation of which the whole day upon which the hurt was done shall be reckoned the first.[3]

(3) The person killed must be a reasonable creature in being.

To kill a child in its mother's womb is not murder; and to constitute a birth so as to make the killing of a child murder, the whole body must be detached from that of the

[1] 4 Blackstone, §§ 184–185. [2] Wharton, § 930.
[3] 4 Blackstone, §§ 195–197.

mother; but if it has come wholly forth, but is still connected by the umbilical cord, such killing will be murder.[1]

(4) The person killed must be in the peace of the commonwealth. It is not murder to kill an enemy in time of war; but killing even an alien enemy within the kingdom, unless in the actual exercise of war, would be murder.[2]

(5) The killing must be done with malice aforethought.

Malice is the great test between murder and other kinds of homicide. This malice may be either *express* or *implied*.

Express malice is when one, with a sedate deliberate mind and formed design, doth kill another; which formed design is evidenced by external circumstances discovering that inward intention; as lying in wait, antecedent menaces, former grudges, and concerted schemes to do him some bodily harm.

This takes in the case of deliberate duelling, where both parties meet avowedly with an intent to murder.

Implied. Where no malice is expressed, the law often implies it. Where a man willfully poisons another, in such a deliberate act the law presumes malice, though no particular enmity can be proved. So, if a man kill another suddenly, without any, or without a considerable provocation; if he kill an officer of justice in the legal execution of his duty; if an instrument likely to kill be used; if, intending to do another *felony*, he undesignedly kills another man; in all these cases malice is implied.[3]

Manslaughter is the unlawful and felonious killing of another, without any malice, either express or implied.

The distinction between manslaughter and murder consists in the following: In the former, though the act which occasions the death be unlawful, or likely to be

[1] Bouvier's Law Dictionary. [2] 1 Hale, P. C. 433. [3] Wharton, § 947.

attended with bodily mischief, yet the malice, either express or implied, which is the very essence of murder, is presumed to be wanting in manslaughter.[1]

Manslaughter is of two kinds, *voluntary* and *involuntary*.

Voluntary manslaughter is the unlawful killing of another, without malice, in sudden quarrel or in heat of passion. If upon a sudden quarrel two persons fight, and one of them kills the other, this is manslaughter; and so it is if they, upon such an occasion, go out and fight in a field; for this is one continued act of passion; and the law pays that regard to human frailty, as not to put a hasty and a deliberate act upon the same footing with regard to guilt. So also if a man be greatly provoked, as by pulling his nose, or other great indignity, and immediately kills the aggressor, though this is not excusable *se defendo*, since there is no absolute necessity for doing it to preserve himself; yet neither is it murder, for there is no previous malice; but it is manslaughter.

Involuntary manslaughter is where a man doing an unlawful act, not amounting to felony, by accident kills another.

It differs from homicide excusable *by misadventure* in this, that misadventure always happens in consequence of a *lawful* act; but this species of manslaughter in consequence of an *unlawful* act.

If a person does an act, lawful in itself, but in an unlawful manner, and without due caution and circumspection, this will be either misadventure, manslaughter, or murder, according to the circumstances under which the original act was done; as when a workman flings down a stone or piece of timber into the street, and kills a man; if it were in a country village, where few passengers are,

[1] 1 East P. C. 218.

and he calls out to all people to have a care, it is misadventure only; but if it were in London, or other populous town, where people are continually passing, it is manslaughter, though he gives loud warning; and murder, if he knows of their passing, and gives no warning at all, for then it is malice against all mankind, and, in general, when an involuntary killing happens in consequence of an unlawful act, it will be either murder or manslaughter, according to the nature of the act which occasioned it. If it be in prosecution of a felonious intent, or in its consequences naturally tended to bloodshed, it will be murder; but if no more was intended but a mere civil trespass, it will only amount to manslaughter.[1]

Assault and Battery. An *assault* is an attempt or offer, with force or violence, to do some bodily harm to another, without touching him. If one lifts up his cane or his fist in a threatening manner at another; or strikes at him and misses him, this is an assault.

Abusive words alone cannot constitute an assault.[2]

A *battery* is committed when any injury whatsoever, be it ever so small, is actually done to the person of a man in an angry, revengeful, or rude, or insolent manner, as by spitting in his face, or throwing water on him. A battery includes an assault.

The injury need not be effected directly by the hand of the party.[3]

The 58th Article gives jurisdiction over assault and battery "with an intent to kill or to commit rape." The intent forming the gist of the offense must be specifically proved.

On a charge for assault and battery with intent to kill, it is not necessary to show that the crime would have been murder, had death ensued.[4]

[1] 4 Blackstone, §§ 191–192 [2] Ibid., § 120, and note 3.
[3] Roscoe, 288. [4] U. S. *vs.* Thorp., 5 Cr. C. C. 390.

Rape is the carnal knowledge of a woman by a man, forcibly and unlawfully, against her will.

(1) Some difficulty has arisen in defining what is meant by *carnal knowledge.* In this country proof of some degree of penetration is sufficient.[1]

(2) By the term *man* in this definition is meant a male of the human species, of the age of fourteen and upwards; for an infant under fourteen years is supposed by law incapable of committing this offense.

(3) The knowledge of the woman's person must be *forcibly and against her will;* and if her consent has not been voluntarily and freely given (when she has the power to consent), the offense will be complete, nor will any subsequent acquiescence on her part do away the guilt of the ravisher. A consent obtained from a woman by actual violence, by duress or threats of murder, or by the administration of stupefying drugs, is not such a consent as will shield the offender, nor turn his crime into adultery or fornication. As a child under ten years of age is incapable in law to give her consent, it follows, that the offense may be committed on such a child whether she consents or not.[2]

Embezzlement, at common law, is the fraudulently removing and secreting personal property, with which the party has been intrusted, for the purpose of applying it to his own use.

Congress has, however, enlarged this definition:—

(1) Every disbursing officer of the United States who deposits any public money entrusted to him in any place or in any manner, except as authorized by law, or converts to his own use in any way whatever, or loans with or without interest, or for any purpose not prescribed by law withdraws from the Treasurer or any Assistant Treasurer,

[1] Wharton, § 1139. [2] Bouvier's Law Dictionary,

or any authorized depository, or for any purpose not prescribed by law transfers or applies any portion of the public money entrusted to him, is, in every such act, deemed guilty of embezzlement of the money so deposited, converted, loaned, withdrawn, transferred, or applied.[1]

(2) Every officer or other person, charged by an act of Congress with the safe keeping of the public moneys, who fails to safely keep the same, without loaning, using, converting to his own use, depositing in banks, or exchanging for other funds than as specially allowed by law, shall be guilty of embezzlement of the money so loaned, used, converted, deposited, or exchanged.[2]

(3) Every officer or agent of the United States who, having received public money which he is not authorized to retain as salary, pay or emolument, fails to render his accounts for the same, as provided by law, shall be deemed guilty of embezzlement.[3]

(4) Every person who, having moneys of the United States in his hands or possession, fails to make deposit of the same with the Treasurer, or some Assistant Treasurer, or some public depository of the United States, when required to do so by the Secretary of the Treasury, or the head of any proper department, or by the accounting officer of the treasury, shall be deemed guilty of embezzlement thereof.[4]

(5) Every officer, charged with the payment of any of the appropriations made by any act of Congress, who pays to any clerk, or any employé of the United States, a sum less than that provided by law, and requires such employé to receipt, or give a voucher for an amount greater than that actually paid to and received by him, is guilty of embezzlement.[5]

[1] § 5488, Revised Statutes. [2] Ibid., § 5490.
[3] Ibid., § 5491. [4] Ibid., § 5492. [5] Ibid., § 5483.

Forgery is the false making or altering, *malo animo*, of any written instrument, for the purposes of fraud and deceit.[1]

The offense is consummated by the false making of the instrument with intent to defraud, without any uttering.[2]

A fraudulent insertion, alteration, or erasure, even of a letter, in any material part of an instrument, whereby a new operation is given to it, will amount to a forgery.[3]

Making an instrument in a fictitious name, or the name of a non-existing person, is equally a forgery as making it in the name of an existing person; and although a man may make the instrument in his own name, if he represent it as the instrument of another of the same name, when in fact there is no such person, it will be a forgery in the name of a non-existing person.[4]

The intent must be to defraud another, but it is not requisite that any one should have been injured; it is sufficient that the instrument forged might have proved prejudicial.[5]

Perjury is the crime committed when a *lawful oath* is administered, in some *judicial* proceeding, to a person who swears *willfully*, *absolutely* and *falsely* in a matter *material* to the issue or point in question. It must be shown:

(1) That the oath was a *lawful* one; and the person by whom the oath is administered must have competent authority to receive it.

(2) That it was administered in some *judicial* proceeding. The laws of the United States have enlarged this part of the definition, so that any person who, having taken an oath before a competent tribunal, officer, or person, in any case in which a law of the United States

[1] 2 East, P. C. 852. [2] Wharton, § 1418. [3] 2 East, P. C. 855.
[4] Ibid., 957–963. [5] U. S. *vs.* Moses, 4 Wash. C. C. 726.

authorizes an oath to be administered, that he will testify, declare, depose, or certify truly, or that any written testimony, declaration, deposition, or certificate by him subscribed is true, willfully and contrary to such oath states or subscribes any material matter which he does not believe to be true, is guilty of perjury.[1]

(3) That the party swore *willfully, absolutely* and *falsely*.

In other words the perjury must have been committed *intentionally;* not upon surprise, or the like. The party must *believe* that what he is swearing is fictitious.

If a man swears that he *believes* that to be true which he knows to be false, he swears as absolutely, and is as criminal, in point of law, as if he had made a positive assertion that the fact was, as he swore he believed it to be.

(4) That the matter sworn to was *material* to the issue.

Where the facts sworn to are wholly foreign to the purpose, and altogether immaterial to the matter in question, the oath does not amount to a legal perjury. In general, however, it is sufficient if the matter be circumstantially material to the issue, or affect the ultimate decision. Thus, to swear falsely as to the character of a witness; or swearing falsely that another witness is entitled to credit, if such assertion conduce to the proof of the point in issue, is sufficiently material.

To constitute perjury, at common law, it is not necessary that the false oath should obtain any credit, or occasion any actual injury to the party against whom the evidence is given.[2]

Subornation of Perjury is the offense of procuring

[1] § 5392. Revised Statutes.

[2] 4 Blackstone, § 137 and Notes.

another to take such a false oath as constitutes perjury in the principal.

To render the offense of subornation of perjury complete, either at common law or in the statute, the false oath must be actually taken, and no abortive attempt to solicit will bring the offender within its penalties.

But the criminal solicitation to commit perjury, though unsuccessful, is a misdemeanor at common law, punishable not only by fine and imprisonment, but by corporal and infamous punishment.[1]

[1] 4 Blackstone, § 138 and Note 38.

APPENDIX.

ARTICLES OF WAR.

SECTION 1342.—The armies of the United States shall be governed by the following rules and articles. The word *officer*, as used therein, shall be understood to designate commissioned officers; the word *soldier* shall be understood to include non-commissioned officers, musicians, artificers and privates, and other enlisted men, and the convictions mentioned therein shall be understood to be convictions by court-martial. **Articles of war.**

ARTICLE 1.—Every *officer* now in the Army of the United States shall, within six months from the passing of this Act, and every officer hereafter appointed shall, before he enters upon the duties of his office, subscribe these rules and articles. **Officers shall subscribe these articles.**

ART. 2.—These rules and articles shall be read to every enlisted man *at the time of*, or *within six days* after his enlistment, and he shall thereupon take an oath of affirmation, in the following form: "I, A. B., do solemnly swear (or affirm) that I will bear true faith and allegiance to the United States of America; that I will serve them honestly and faithfully against all their enemies whomsoever; and that I will obey the orders of the President of the United States, and the orders of the officers appointed over me, according to the rules and articles of war." This oath may be taken before any commissioned officer of the army. **Articles to be read to recruits.**

ART. 3.—Every *officer* who *knowingly* enlists or musters into the military service any minor over the age of sixteen years without the written consent of his parents or guardians, or any minor under the age of sixteen **Officers making unlawful enlistments.**

years, or any insane or intoxicated persons, or any deserter from the military or naval service of the United States, or any person who has been convicted of any infamous criminal offense, shall, upon conviction, be dismissed from the service, or suffer such other punishment as a court-martial may direct.

Discharges.

ART. 4.—No *enlisted* man, *duly sworn,* shall be discharged from the service without a discharge in writing, signed by a field-officer of the regiment to which he belongs, or by the commanding officer, when no field-officer is present; and no discharge shall be given to any enlisted man before his term of service has expired, except by order of the President, the Secretary of War, the commanding officer of a department, or by sentence of a general court-martial.

Mustering persons not soldiers.

ART. 5.—Any *officer* who *knowingly* musters as a soldier a person who is not a soldier, *shall be* deemed guilty of knowingly making a false muster, and *punished accordingly.**

Taking money on mustering.

ART. 6.—Any *officer* who takes money, or other thing, *by way of gratification,* on mustering any regiment, troop, battery, or company, or on signing muster rolls, *shall be dismissed* from the service, and *shall thereby* be disabled to hold any office or employment in the service of the United States.

Returns of regiments, etc.

ART. 7.—Every *officer* commanding a regiment, an independent troop, battery or company, or a garrison, *shall,* in the beginning of every month, transmit through the proper channels, to the Department of War, an exact return of the same, specifying the names of the officers then absent from their posts, with the reasons for and the time of their absence. And any officer who, *through neglect or design,* omits to send such returns, shall, on conviction thereof, be punished as a court-martial may direct.

False returns.

ART. 8.—Every *officer* who *knowingly* makes a false

* See Article 14.

return to the Department of War, or to any of his superior officers, *authorized to call for such returns,* of the state of the regiment, troop or company, or garrison under his command; or of the arms, ammunition, clothing or other stores thereunto belonging, *shall,* on conviction thereof before a court-martial, *be cashiered.*

ART. 9.—*All* public stores taken from the enemy shall be secured for the service of the United States; and for neglect thereof the *commanding* officer shall be answerable.

Captured stores secured for public service.

ART. 10.—Every *officer commanding* a troop, battery, or company, is charged with the arms, accoutrements, ammunition, clothing or other military stores belonging to his command, and is accountable *to his colonel* in case of their being lost, spoiled, or damaged otherwise than by unavoidable accident, or on actual service.

Accountability for arms, etc.

ART. 11.—Every *officer* commanding a regiment or an independent troop, battery, or company, *not in the field,* may, when actually quartered with such command, grant furloughs to the enlisted men, in such numbers and for such time as he shall deem consistent with the good of the service. Every officer commanding a regiment, or an independent troop, battery, or company, *in the field,* may grant furloughs not exceeding thirty days at one time, to five per centum of the enlisted men, for good conduct in the line of duty, but *subject to the approval of* the commander of the forces of which said enlisted men form a part. Every company officer of a regiment, commanding any troop, battery, or company, *not in the field,* or commanding in any garrison, fort, post, or barrack, may, *in the absence of his field officer,* grant furloughs to the enlisted men, for a time not exceeding twenty days in six months and not to more than two persons to be absent at the same time.

Furloughs.

ART. 12.—At every muster of a regiment, troop, battery, or company, the commanding officer thereof

Musters.

shall give to the mustering officer certificates, signed by himself, stating how long absent officers have been absent, and the reasons of their absence. And the commanding officer of every troop, battery, or company shall give like certificates, stating how long absent non-commissioned officers and private soldiers have been absent, and the reasons of their absence. Such reasons and time of absence shall be inserted in the muster-rolls opposite the names of the respective absent officer and soldiers, and the certificates, together with the muster-rolls, shall be transmitted by the mustering officers to the Department of War, as speedily as the distance of the place and muster will admit.

False certificates.

ART. 13.—Every *officer* who signs a false certificate, *relating to the absence or pay* of an officer or soldier, *shall be dismissed* from the service.

False muster.

ART. 14.—Any *officer* who *knowingly* makes a false muster of *man or horse*, or who signs, or directs, or allows the signing of any muster-roll, *knowing* the same to contain a false muster, *shall*, upon proof thereof *by two witnesses*, before a court-martial, *be dismissed* from the service, and *shall thereby* be disabled to hold any office or employment in the service of the United States.

Allowing military stores to be damaged.

ART. 15.—Any officer who, *willfully* or *through neglect*, suffers to be lost, spoiled, or damaged, any military stores belonging to the United States, shall make good the loss or damage, *and be dismissed* from the service.

Wasting ammunition.

ART. 16.—Any *enlisted* man who sells or, *willfully or through neglect*, wastes the ammunition delivered out to him, shall be punished as a court-martial may direct.

Losing or spoiling accoutrements, etc.

ART. 17.—Any *soldier*, who sells or, *through neglect* loses or spoils his horse, arms, clothing, or accoutrements, *shall* suffer such stoppages, *not exceeding one-half* of his current pay, as a court-martial may deem sufficient for repairing the loss or damage, *and shall* be punished *by confinement*, or *such other corporal* punishment as the court may direct.

ART. 18.—Any *officer* commanding in any garrison, fort, or barracks of the United States who, *for his private advantage*, lays any duty or imposition upon, or is interested in, the sale of any victuals, liquors, or other necessaries of life, brought into such garrison, fort or barracks, for the use of the soldiers, *shall be dismissed* from the service.

Commanders not to be interested in sale of victuals, etc.

ART. 19.—Any *officer* who uses contemptuous or disrespectful words against the President, the Vice-President, the Congress of the United States, or the chief magistrate or legislature of any of the United States in which he is quartered, shall be dismissed from the service, or otherwise punished, as a court-martial may direct. Any *soldier* who so offends shall be punished as a court-martial may direct.

Disrespectful words against the President, etc.

ART. 20.—Any *officer or soldier* who behaves himself with disrespect toward his *commanding officer* shall be punished as a court-martial may direct.

Disrespect toward commanding officer.

ART. 21.—Any *officer or soldier* who, on any pretense whatsoever, strikes his *superior* officer, or draws or lifts up any weapon, or offers any violence against him, *being in the execution of his office*, or disobeys any *lawful* command of his superior officer, shall suffer death, or such other punishment as a court-martial may direct.

Striking a superior officer, and disobedience of orders.

ART. 22.—Any *officer or soldier* who begins, excites, causes, or joins in any mutiny or sedition, in any troop, battery, company, party, post, detachment, or guard, shall suffer death, or such other punishment as a court-martial may direct.

Mutiny.

ART. 23.—Any *officer or soldier* who, *being present* at any mutiny or sedition, does not use his utmost endeavor to suppress the same, or *having knowledge* of

Failing to resist mutiny.

any intended mutiny or sedition, does not *without delay*, give information thereof to his *commanding officer*, shall suffer death, or such other punishment as a court-martial may direct.

Quarrels and frays.

ART. 24.—All *officers, of what condition soever*, have power to part and quell all quarrels, frays and disorders, whether among persons belonging to his own or to another corps, regiment, troop, battery, or company, and to order officers into arrest, and non-commissioned officers and soldiers into confinement, who take part in the same, until their proper superior officer is acquainted therewith. And whosoever, being so ordered, refuses to obey such *officer* or *non-commissioned officer*, or draws a weapon upon him, shall be punished as a court-martial may direct.

Reproachful or provoking speeches.

ART. 25.—No *officer or soldier* shall use any reproachful or provoking speeches or gestures to another. Any *officer* who so offends *shall* be put in arrest. Any *soldier* who so offends *shall* be confined, and required to ask pardon of the party offended, in the presence of his commanding officer.

Challenge to fight duels.

ART. 26.—No *officer or soldier* shall *send* a challenge to another officer or soldier to fight a duel, or *accept* a challenge so sent. Any *officer* who so offends *shall be dismissed* from the service. Any *soldier* who so offends shall suffer such punishment as a court-martial may direct.

Allowing persons to go out and fight; seconds and promoters.

ART. 27.—Any *officer* or *non-commissioned officer*, commanding a guard, who, *knowingly and willingly*, suffers any person to go forth to fight a duel, *shall* be punished *as a challenger*; and all seconds or promoters of duels, and carriers of challenges to fight duels, *shall* be deemed principals, and *punished accordingly*. It shall be the duty of any officer commanding an army, regiment, troop, battery, company, post or detachment, who *knows* or *has reason to believe* that a challenge has been given or accepted by any officer or enlisted man *under his command, immediately* to arrest the offender and bring him to trial.

ART. 28.—Any *officer or soldier* who upbraids another officer or soldier for refusing a challenge *shall* himself be punished *as a challenger*; and all officers and soldiers are hereby discharged from any disgrace or opinion of disadvantage which might arise from their having refused to accept challenges, as they will only have acted in obedience to the law, and have done their duty as good soldiers, who subject themselves to discipline. **Upbraiding another for refusing challenge.**

ART. 29.—Any *officer* who thinks himself wronged by the *commanding officer of his regiment*, and, *upon due application* to such commander, is refused redress, may complain to the general commanding in the State or Territory where such regiment is stationed. The general *shall* examine into said complaint and take proper measures for redressing the wrong complained of; and he shall, as soon as possible, transmit to the Department of War a true statement of such complaint with the proceedings had thereon. **Wrongs to officers; redress of.**

ART. 30.—Any *soldier* who thinks himself wronged by *any officer* may complain to the *commanding officer of his regiment*, who *shall* summon a *regimental* court-martial for the doing of justice to the complainant. *Either* party *may appeal* from such regimental court-martial to a general court-martial; but if, upon such second hearing, the appeal appears to be groundless and vexatious, the party appealing *shall* be punished at the discretion of said general court-martial. **Wrongs to soldiers; redress of.**

ART. 31.—Any *officer or soldier* who lies out of his quarters, garrison, or camp, *without leave* from his *superior* officer, shall be punished as a court-martial may direct. **Lying out of quarters.**

ART. 32.—Any soldier who absents himself from his troop, battery, company, or detachment, *without leave* from his *commanding* officer, shall be punished as a court-martial may direct. **Soldiers absent without leave.**

Absence from parade without leave.

ART. 33.—Any *officer or soldier* who fails, *except when prevented by sickness or other necessity,* to repair, at the fixed time, to the place of parade, exercise, or other rendezvous appointed by his commanding officer, or goes from the same, without leave from his *commanding* officer, before he is dismissed or relieved, shall be punished as a court-martial may direct.

One mile from camp without leave.

ART. 34.—Any *soldier* who is found one mile from camp, without leave *in writing* from his *commanding* officer, shall be punished as a court-martial may direct.

Failing to retire at retreat.

ART. 35.—Any *soldier* who fails to retire to his quarters or tent at the beating of retreat, shall be punished according to the nature of his offense.

Hiring duty.

ART. 36.—No *soldier,* belonging to any regiment, troop, battery, or company shall hire another to do his duty for him, or be excused from duty, except in cases of sickness, disability, or leave of absence. Every such soldier found guilty of hiring his duty, and the person so hired to do another's duty, shall be punished as a court-martial may direct.

Conniving at hiring duty.

ART. 37.—Every *non-commissioned officer* who connives at such hiring of duty *shall be reduced.* Every *officer* who knows and allows such practices shall be punished as a court-martial may direct.

Drunk on duty.

ART. 38.—Any *officer* who is found drunk on his guard, party, or other duty, *shall be dismissed* from the service. Any *soldier* who so offends shall suffer such punishment as a court-martial may direct. No court-martial shall sentence any soldier to be branded, marked or tattooed.

Sentinel sleeping on post.

ART. 39.—Any sentinel who is found sleeping upon his post, or who leaves it before he is regularly relieved, shall suffer death, or such other punishment as a court-martial may direct.

Quitting guard, etc., without leave.

ART. 40.—Any *officer or soldier* who quits his guard, platoon, or division, without leave from his *superior* officer, *except in a case of urgent necessity,* shall be punished as a court-martial may direct.

ART. 41.—Any *officer* who by *any means whatsoever,* occasions false alarms in camp, garrison, or quarters, shall suffer death, or such other punishment as a court-martial may direct. **False alarms.**

ART. 42.—Any *officer or soldier* who misbehaves himself before the enemy, runs away, or shamefully abandons any fort, post, or guard, *which he is commanded to defend,* or speaks words inducing others to do the like, or casts away his arms or ammunition, or quits his post or colors to plunder or pillage, shall suffer death, or such other punishment as a court-martial may direct. **Misbehavior before the enemy, cowardice, etc.**

ART. 43.—If any commander of any garrison, fortress, or post is compelled, by the officers or soldiers *under his command,* to give up to the enemy or to abandon it, the officers or soldiers so offending shall suffer death, or such other punishment as a court-martial may direct. **Compelling a surrender.**

ART. 44.—*Any* person *belonging to the armies of the United States* who makes known the watchword to any person not entitled to receive it, according to the rules and discipline of war, or presumes to give a parol or watchword different from that which he received, shall suffer death, or such other punishment as a court-martial may direct. **Disclosing watchword.**

ART. 45.—*Whosoever* relieves the enemy with money, victuals, or ammunition, or *knowingly* harbors or protects an enemy, shall suffer death, or such other punishment as a court-martial may direct. **Relieving the enemy.**

ART. 46.—*Whosoever* holds correspondence with, or gives intelligence to, the enemy, either directly or indirectly, shall suffer death, or such other punishment as a court-martial may direct. **Corresponding with the enemy.**

ART. 47.—Any *officer or soldier* who, *having received pay,* or having been *duly enlisted* in the service **Desertion.**

of the United States, deserts the same, shall, *in time of war,* suffer death, or such other punishment as a court-martial may direct; and in *time of peace, any* punishment, excepting death, which a court-martial may direct.

Deserter shall serve full term.

ART. 48.—Every *soldier* who deserts the service of the United States shall be liable to serve for such period as shall, with the time he may have served previous to his desertion, amount to the full term of his enlistment; and such soldier *shall be tried* by a court-martial *and punished,* although the term of his enlistment may have elapsed previous to his being apprehended and tried.

Desertion by resignation.

ART. 49.—Any *officer* who, having tendered his resignation, quits his post, or proper duties, *without leave,* and *with intent to remain permanently absent therefrom,* prior to due notice of the acceptance of the same, shall be deemed and punished as a deserter.

Enlisting in other regiment without discharge.

ART. 50.—No *non-commissioned officer* or *soldier* shall enlist himself in any other regiment, troop, or company without a regular discharge from the regiment, troop or company in which he last served, on a penalty of being reputed a deserter, and suffering accordingly. And in case any *officer* shall *knowingly* receive and entertain such non-commissioned officer or soldier, or shall not, after his being discovered to be a deserter, *immediately confine* him, and *give notice* thereof to the corps in which he last served, the said officer *shall,* by a court-martial, *be cashiered.*

Advising to desert.

ART. 51.—Any *officer or soldier* who advises or persuades any other officer or soldier to desert the service of the United States, shall, *in time of war,* suffer death, or such other punishment as a court-martial may direct; and *in time of peace, any* punishment, excepting death, which a court-martial may direct.

Misconduct at divine service.

ART. 52.—It is earnestly recommended to all *officers and soldiers* diligently to attend divine service. Any *officer* who behaves indecently or irreverently at any place of divine worship shall be brought before a general court-martial, there to be publicly and severely reprimanded *by the president* thereof. Any *soldier* who so offends shall, for his first offense, forfeit one-sixth of a dollar; for each further offense he shall forfeit a like sum, and shall be confined twenty-four hours. The money so forfeited shall be deducted from his next pay, and shall be applied, by the captain or senior officer of his troop, battery, or company, to the use of the sick soldiers of the same.

Profane oaths.

ART. 53.—Any *officer* who uses any profane oath or execration shall, for each offense, forfeit and pay one dollar. Any *soldier* who so offends shall incur the penalties provided in the preceding article; and all moneys forfeited for such offenses shall be applied as therein provided.

Officers to keep good order in their commands.

ART. 54.—Every *officer commanding* in quarters, garrison, or on the march, shall keep good order, and, to the utmost of his power, redress all abuses or disorders which may be committed by any officer or soldier under his command; and if, upon complaint made to him of *officers or soldiers* beating or otherwise illtreating any person, disturbing fairs or markets, or committing any kind of riot, to the disquieting of the citizens of the United States, he *refuses* or *omits* to see justice done to the offender, and *reparation* made to the party injured, *so far as part of the offender's pay shall go toward such reparation*, he shall be dismissed from the service, or otherwise punished, as a court-martial may direct.

Waste or spoil, and destruction of property without orders.

ART. 55.—All *officers and soldiers* are to behave themselves orderly in quarters and on the march; and whoever commits any waste or spoil, either in walks or trees, parks, warren, fish-ponds, houses, gardens, grain-fields, inclosures, or meadows, or maliciously destroys any property whatsoever *belonging to the inhabitants of the United States* (*unless* by order of a general officer commanding a separate army in the field) shall, *besides* such penalties as he may be liable to by law, be punished as a court-martial may direct.

Violence to persons bringing provisions.

ART. 56.—Any *officer or soldier* who does violence to any person bringing provisions, or other necessaries, to the camp, garrison, or quarters of the forces of the United States *in foreign parts,* shall suffer death, or such other punishment as a court-martial may direct.

Forcing a safeguard.

ART. 57.—*Whosoever, belonging to the armies of the United States in foreign parts,* or at any place within the United States or their Territories, *during rebellion* against the supreme authority of the United States, forces a safeguard, *shall suffer death.*

Certain crimes during rebellion.

ART. 58.—*In time of war, insurrection, or rebellion,* larceny, robbery, burglary, arson, mayhem, manslaughter, murder, assault and battery, with an intent to kill, wounding, by shooting or stabbing, with an intent to commit murder, rape, or assault and battery with an intent to commit rape, shall be punishable by the sentence of a general court-martial, *when committed by persons in the military service of the United States,* and the punishment in any such case *shall not be less* than the punishment provided for the like offense by the laws of the State, Territory, or district in which such offense may have been committed.

Offenders to be delivered up to civil magistrate.

ART. 59.—When *any officer or soldier* is accused of a capital crime, or of any offense against the person or property of any citizen of any of the United States, *which is punishable by the laws of the land,* the commanding officer, and the officers of the regiment, troop, battery, company, or detachment, to which the person so accused belongs, are required, *except in time of war,* upon *application duly made by or in behalf of the party injured,* to use their utmost endeavors to deliver him over to the civil magistrate, and to aid the officers of justice in apprehending and securing him, in order to bring him to trial. If, upon such application, any officer refuses or willfully neglects, *except in time of war,* to deliver over such accused person to the civil magistrates, or to aid the officers of justice in apprehending him, he *shall be dismissed* from the service.

ART. 60.—Any person in the military service of the United States who makes or causes to be made any claim against the United States, or any officer thereof, *knowing such claim to be false or fraudulent;* or

Certain crimes of fraud against the United States.

Who presents or causes to be presented to any person in the civil or military service thereof, for approval or payment, any claim against the United States, or any officer thereof, *knowing such claim to be false or fraudulent* ; or

Making false claim. Presenting false claim.

Who enters into any agreement or conspiracy to defraud the United States by obtaining, or aiding others to obtain, the allowance or payment of any false or fraudulent claim, or

Agreement to obtain payment of false claim.

Who, for the purpose of obtaining, or aiding others to obtain, the approval, allowance, or payment of any claim against the United States, or against any officer thereof, makes or uses, or procures or advises the making or use of, any writing, or other paper, *knowing the same to contain any false or fraudulent statement ;* or

False paper.

Who, for the purpose of obtaining, or aiding others to obtain, the approval, allowance, or payment of any claim against the United States or any officer thereof, makes, or procures or advises the making of, any oath to any fact or to any writing or other paper, *knowing such oath to be false ;* or

Perjury.

Who, for the purpose of obtaining, or aiding others to obtain, the approval, allowance, or payment of any claim against the United States, or any officer thereof, forges or counterfeits, or procures or advises the forging or counterfeiting of, any signature upon any writing or other paper, or uses, or procures or advises the use of, any such signature, *knowing the same to be forged or counterfeited* ; or

Forgery

Who, having charge, possession, custody or control of any money or other property of the United States, furnished or intended for the military service thereof, *knowingly* delivers, or causes to be delivered, to any person having authority to receive the same, any amount

Delivering less property than receipt calls for.

thereof less than that for which he receives a certificate or receipt; or

Giving receipts without knowing truth of.

Who, being authorized to make or deliver any paper certifying the receipt of any property of the United States, furnished or intended for the military service thereof, makes, or delivers to any person, such writing, *without having full knowledge* of the truth of the statements therein contained, and *with intent* to defraud the United States; or

Stealing, wrongfully selling, etc.

Who steals, embezzles, *knowingly and willfully* misappropriates, applies to his own use or benefit, or *wrongfully or knowingly* sells or disposes of any ordnance, arms, equipments, or ammunition, clothing, subsistence stores, money, or other property of the United States, *furnished or intended for the military service thereof;* or

Buying public military property.

Who *knowingly* purchases, or receives in pledge for any obligation or indebtedness, from any soldier, officer, or other person who is a part of or employed in said forces or service, any ordnance, arms, equipments, ammunition, clothing, subsistence stores, or other property of the United States, such soldier, officer, or other person not having lawful right to sell or pledge the same,

Shall, on conviction thereof, be punished by fine or imprisonment, or by such other punishment as a court-martial may adjudge. And if any person, being guilty of any of the offenses aforesaid, while in the military service of the United States, receives his discharge, or is dismissed from the service, he shall continue to be *liable* to be arrested and held for trial and sentence by a court-martial, *in the same manner and to the same extent* as if he had not received such discharge nor been dismissed.

Conduct unbecoming an officer and gentleman.

ART. 61.—Any *officer* who is convicted of conduct unbecoming an officer and a gentleman, *shall be dismissed* from the service.

Crimes and disorders to prejudice of military discipline.

ART. 62.—*All* crimes *not capital,* and all disorders and neglects, which officers and soldiers may be guilty of, *to the prejudice of good order and military disci-*

pline, though not mentioned in the foregoing articles of war, are to be taken cognizance of by a general, or a regimental, garrison, or field-officer's court-martial, according to the nature and degree of the offense, and punished at the discretion of such court.

Retainers of camp.

ART. 63.—All *retainers to the camp*, and all persons *serving with the armies of the United States in the field*, though not enlisted soldiers, are to be subject to orders, according to the rules and discipline of war.

All troops subject to articles of war.

ART. 64.—The *officers and soldiers* of *any* troops, whether militia or others, *mustered and in pay* of the United States, shall, *at all times* and *in all places*, be governed by the articles of war, and shall be subject to be tried by courts-martial.

Arrest of officers accused of crimes.

ART. 65.—*Officers* charged with crime shall be arrested and confined in their barracks, quarters, or tents, and deprived of their swords by the commanding officer. And any officer *who leaves his confinement* before he is set at liberty by his commanding officer *shall be dismissed* from the service.

Soldiers accused of crime.

ART. 66.—*Soldiers* charged with crimes shall be confined until tried by court-martial, or released by proper authority.

Receiving prisoners.

ART. 67.—No provost-marshal, or officer commanding a guard, shall refuse to receive or keep any prisoner committed to his charge by an officer belonging to the forces of the United States; *provided* the *officer committing* shall, *at the same time*, deliver an account *in writing, signed by himself*, of the crime charged against the prisoner.

Report of prisoners.

ART. 68.—Every *officer* to whose charge a prisoner is committed, shall, *within twenty-four hours* after such commitment, or as soon as he is relieved from his guard, report *in writing*, to the commanding officer, the name of such prisoner, the crime charged against him, and the name of the officer committing him ; and if he fails to make such report, he shall be punished as a court-martial may direct.

Releasing prisoner without authority ; escapes.

ART. 69.—Any *officer* who presumes, *without proper authority*, to release any prisoner committed to his charge, or suffers any prisoner so committed to escape, shall be punished as a court-martial may direct.

Duration of confinement.

ART. 70.—No *officer or soldier* put in arrest shall be continued in confinement more than *eight* days, or until such time as a court-martial can be assembled.

Copy of charges and time of trial.

ART. 71.—When an *officer* is put in arrest *for the purpose of trial*, except *at remote military posts or stations*, the officer by whose order he is arrested shall see that a copy of the charges on which he is to be tried be served upon him within *eight* days after his arrest, and that he is brought to trial within *ten* days thereafter, *unless the necessities of the service prevent such trial ;* and *then* he shall be brought to trial within *thirty* days after the expiration of said ten days. If a copy of the charges be not served, or the arrested officer be not brought to trial, as herein required, the arrest *shall cease.* But officers *released* from arrest, under the provisions of this article, may be tried, whenever the exigencies of the service shall permit, within twelve months after such release from arrest.

Who may appoint general courts-martial.

ART. 72.—Any *general* officer commanding the army of the United States, a separate army, or a separate department, shall be competent to appoint a general court-martial, *either in time of peace or in time of war.* But when any such commander is the *accuser or prosecutor* of any *officer under his command*, the court *shall be* appointed by the President, and its proceedings and sentence *shall* be sent directly to the Secretary of War, by whom they *shall* be laid before the President, for his approval or orders in the case.

Commanders of divisions and separate brigades may appoint in time of war.

ART. 73.—*In time of war* the commander of a division, or of a separate brigade of troops, shall be competent to appoint a general court-martial. But when such commander is the *accuser or prosecutor* of *any person under his command,* the court *shall be* appointed by the next higher commander.

ART. 74.—Officers who may appoint a court-martial, shall be competent to appoint a judge-advocate for the same. Judge-advocate.

ART. 75.—*General* courts-martial *may* consist of any number of officers from five to thirteen, inclusive; but they shall not consist of less than thirteen when that number can be convened without manifest injury to the service. Members of general courts-martial.

ART. 76.—When the requisite number of officers to form a general court-martial is not present in any post or detachment, the commanding officer shall, in cases which require the cognizance of such a court, report to the commanding officer of the department, who shall, thereupon, order a court to be assembled at the nearest post or department at which there may be such a requisite number of officers, and shall order the party accused, with necessary witnesses, to be transported to the place where the said court shall be assembled. When. requisite number not at a post.

ART. 77.—Officers of the *regular* army shall not be competent to sit on courts-martial to try the officers or soldiers of other forces, except as provided in Article 78. Regular officers; on what courts may sit.

ART. 78.—Officers of the Marine Corps, *detached for service with the Army by order of the President,* may be associated with officers of the *Regular* Army on courts-martial for the trial of offenders *belonging to the Regular Army,* or to forces *of the Marine Corps so detached;* and in such cases the orders of the senior officer of either corps, who may be present and *duly authorized,* shall be obeyed. Marine and Regular Army officers associated on courts.

ART. 79.—*Officers* shall be tried *only* by general courts-martial; and no officer shall, *when it can be avoided,* be tried by officers inferior to him in rank. Officers triable by general courts-martial.

Field-officers courts.

ART. 80.—*In time of war* a field-officer may be detailed in every *regiment,* to try soldiers thereof for offenses not capital; and no soldier, *serving with his regiment,* shall be tried by a regimental (a) garrison court-martial when a field-officer of his regiment may be detailed.

Regimental courts.

ART. 81.—Every officer *commanding a regiment or corps* shall, subject to the provisions of article eighty, be competent to appoint, for his own regiment or corps, courts-martial, consisting of *three* officers, to try offenses not capital.

Garrison courts.

ART. 82.—Every officer commanding a garrison, fort, or other place, *where the troops consist of different corps,* shall, subject to the provisions of article eighty, be competent to appoint, for such garrison or other place, courts-martial, consisting of *three* officers, to try offenses not capital.

Jurisdiction of field-officers', regimental, and garrison courts.

ART. 83.—Regimental and garrison courts-martial, and field officers detailed to try offenders, shall not have power to try *capital cases* or *commissioned officers,* or to inflict a fine exceeding one month's pay, or to imprison or put to hard labor any non-commissioned officer or soldier for a longer time than one month.

Oath of members of courts-martial.

ART. 84.—The judge-advocate shall administer to each member of the court, before they proceed upon any trial, the following oath, which shall also be taken by all members of regimental and garrison courts-martial: "You A B, do swear that you will well and truly try and determine, according to evidence, the matter now before you, between the United States of America and the prisoner to be tried, and that you will duly administer justice, without partiality, favor, or affection, according to the provisions of the rules and articles for the government of the armies of the United States, and if any doubt should arise, not explained by said articles, then according to your conscience, the best of your understanding, and the custom of war in

(a) The word *or* omitted from the roll.

like cases; and you do further swear that you will not divulge the sentence of the court until it shall be published by the proper authority; neither will you disclose or discover the vote or opinion of any particular member of the court-martial, unless required to give evidence thereof as a witness, by a court of justice, in a due course of law. So help you God."

Oath of judge-advocate.

ART. 85.—When the oath has been administered to the members of a court-martial, the president of the court shall administer to the judge-advocate, or person officiating as such, an oath in the following form: "You, A B, do swear that you will not disclose or discover the vote or opinion of any particular member of the court-martial, unless required to give evidence thereof, as a witness, by a court of justice, in due course of law; nor divulge the sentence of the court to any but the proper authority, until it shall be duly disclosed by the same. So help you God."

Contempts of court.

ART. 86.—A court-martial may punish, *at discretion any* person who uses any menacing words, signs, or gestures, *in its presence,* or who disturbs its proceedings by any riot or disorder.

Behavior of members.

ART. 87.—All members of a court-martial are to behave with decency and calmness.

Challenges by prisoner.

ART. 88.—*Members* of a court-martial may be challenged by a prisoner, but only for cause stated to the court. The court shall determine the relevancy and validity thereof, and *shall not* receive a challenge to more than one member at a time.

Prisoner standing mute.

ART. 89.—When a prisoner, arraigned before a general court-martial, *from obstinacy and deliberate design,* stands mute, or answers foreign to the purpose, the court may proceed to trial and judgment, as if the prisoner had pleaded not guilty.

Judge-advocate, prosecutor and counsel for prisoner.

ART. 90.—The judge-advocate, or some person deputed by him, or by the general or officer commanding the army, detachment, or garrison, shall prosecute in the name of the United States, but *when the prisoner has made his plea*, he shall *so far* consider himself counsel for the prisoner as to object to any leading question to any of the witnesses, and to any question to the prisoner, the answer to which might tend to criminate himself.

Depositions. ART. 91.—The depositions of witnesses *residing beyond* the limits of the State, Territory, or district, in which any military court may be ordered to sit, if taken on *reasonable notice* to the opposite party and *duly authenticated*, may be read in evidence before such court in cases *not capital*.

Oath of witness. ART. 92.—All persons who give evidence before a court-martial *shall* be examined on oath, or affirmation, in the following form: "You swear (or affirm) that the evidence you shall give, in the case now in hearing, shall be the truth, the whole truth, and nothing but the truth. So help you God."

Continuances. ART. 93.—A court-martial *shall*, for reasonable cause, grant a continuance to either party, for such time, and as often, as may appear to be just: *provided*, That if the prisoner be in close confinement, the trial shall not be delayed for a period longer than sixty days.

Hours of sitting. ART. 94.—Proceedings of trials shall be carried on *only* between the hours of eight in the morning and three in the afternoon, *excepting* in cases which, in the opinion of the officer appointing the court, require immediate example.

Order of voting. ART. 95.—Members of a court-martial, in giving their votes, shall begin with the youngest in commission.

Sentence of death. ART. 96.—No person shall be sentenced *to suffer death*, except by the concurrence of *two-thirds* of the members of a general court-martial, and *in the cases herein expressly mentioned.*

Penitentiaries. ART. 97.—No person in the military service shall, under the sentence of a court-martial, be punished *by* *confinement in a penitentiary,* unless the offense of which he may be convicted would, by some statute of the United States, or by some statute of the State, Territory, or district in which such offense may be committed, or by the common law, as the same exists in such State, Territory, or district, subject such convict to such punishment.

Flogging, etc.

ART. 98.—No person in the military service shall be punished by flogging, or by branding, marking, or tattooing on the body.

Discharge and dismissal of officers.

ART. 99.—No *officer* shall be discharged or dismissed from the service, except by order of the President, or by sentence of a general court-martial; and *in time of peace* no *officer* shall be dismissed, except in pursuance of the sentence of a court-martial, *or in mitigation thereof.*

Publication of officers cashiered for cowardice or fraud.

ART. 100.—When an officer is dismissed from the service for cowardice or fraud, the sentence *shall* further direct that the crime, punishment, name, and place of abode of the delinquent shall be published in the newspapers in and about the camp, and in the State from which the offender came, or where he usually resides; and *after such publication* it shall be scandalous for an officer to associate with him.

Suspension of officers' pay.

ART. 101.—When a court-martial suspends an officer from command, it *may* also suspend his pay and emoluments for the same time, according to the nature of his offense.

No person tried twice for same offense, etc.

ART. 102.—No person shall be tried a second time for the same offense.

Limitation of time of prosecution.

ART. 103.—No person shall be liable to be tried and punished by a general court-martial for any offense which appears to have been committed more than two years before the issuing of the order for such trial, unless, by reason of having absented himself, or of some other manifest impediment, he shall not have been amenable to justice within that period.

Approval of sentence by officer ordering court.

ART. 104.—No sentence of a court-martial shall be carried into execution until the *whole* proceedings shall have been approved by the officer ordering the court, or by the officer commanding for the time being.

Confirmation of death sentence.

ART. 105.—No sentence of a court-martial, *inflicting the punishment of death*, shall be carried into execution until it shall have been confirmed by the President; *except* in the cases of persons convicted, *in time of war*, as spies, mutineers, deserters, or murderers, and in the cases of guerilla marauders, convicted, in time of war, of robbery, burglary, arson, rape, assault with intent to commit rape, or of violation of the laws and customs of war; and in such excepted cases the sentence of death may be carried into execution upon confirmation by the commanding general in the field, or the commander of the department, as the case may be.

Confirmation of dismissals in time of peace.

ART. 106.—*In time of peace* no sentence of a court-martial, *directing the dismissal of an officer*, shall be carried into execution until it shall have been confirmed by the President.

Dismissal by division or brigade courts.

ART. 107.—No sentence of a court-martial, *appointed* by the commander of a division or of a separate brigade of troops, *directing the dismissal of an officer*, shall be carried into execution until it shall have been confirmed by the general commanding the army in the field to which the division of brigade belongs.

General officers; sentences respecting.

ART. 108.—No sentence of a court-martial, either in time of peace or in time of war, *respecting a general officer*, shall be carried into execution, until it shall have been confirmed by the President.

Confirmation by officer ordering court.

ART. 109.—All sentences of a court-martial *may be confirmed and carried into execution* by the officer ordering the court, or by the officer commanding for the time being, where confirmation by the President, or by the commanding general in the field, or commander of the department, is not required by these articles.

ART. 110.—No sentence of a field-officer, detailed to try soldiers of his regiment, shall be carried into execution, until the whole proceedings shall have been *approved* by the brigade commander, or, in case there be no brigade commander, by the commanding officer of the post. **Confirmation of field officers' sentences.**

ART. 111.—Any officer who has authority to carry into execution the *sentence of death,* or *of dismissal* of an officer, *may suspend* the same until the pleasure of the President shall be known; and, in such case, he shall *immediately* transmit to the President a copy of the order of suspension, together with a copy of the proceedings of the court. **Suspension of sentences of death or dismissal.**

ART. 112.—Every officer who is authorized to order a general court-martial, shall have power to *pardon or mitigate any punishment* adjudged by it, *except* the punishment of death or of dismissal of an officer. Every officer commanding a regiment or garrison in which a regimental or garrison court-martial may be held, shall have power to *pardon or mitigate any punishment* which such court may adjudge. **Pardon and mitigation of sentences.**

ART. 113.—Every judge-advocate, or person acting as such, at any general court-martial, shall, with as much expedition as the opportunity of time and distance of place may admit, forward the original proceedings and sentence of such court *to the Judge-Advocate General of the Army,* in whose office they shall be carefully preserved. **Proceedings forwarded to Judge-Advocate General.**

ART. 114.—Every party tried by a general court-martial *shall upon demand* thereof, *made by himself* or *by any person in his behalf,* be entitled to a copy of the proceedings and sentence of such court. **Party entitled to a copy.**

ART. 115.—A court of inquiry, to examine into the nature of any transaction of, or accusation or imputation against, any officer or soldier, *may* be ordered by the *President* or by any *commanding officer*; but, as courts of inquiry may be perverted to dishonorable **Courts of inquiry; how ordered.**

purposes, and may be employed, in the hands of weak and envious commandants, as engines for the destruction of military merit, they *shall never* be ordered by any *commanding officer, except* upon a demand by the officer or soldier whose conduct is to be inquired of.

Members of court of inquiry. ART. 116.—A court of inquiry shall consist of one or more officers, *not exceeding three,* and a recorder, to reduce the proceedings and evidence to writing.

Oaths of members and recorder of court of inquiry. ART. 117.—The recorder of a court of inquiry shall administer to the members the following oath : "You shall well and truly examine and inquire, according to the evidence, into the matter now before you, without partiality, favor, affection, prejudice, or hope of reward : so help you God." After which the president of the court shall administer to the recorder the following oath : "You, A. B., do swear that you will, according to your best abilities, accurately and impartially record the proceedings of the court and the evidence to be given in the case in hearing : so help you God."

Witnesses before courts of inquiry. ART. 118.—A court of inquiry, and the recorder thereof, shall have the same power *to summon* and *examine* witnesses as is given to courts-martial and the judge-advocates thereof. Such witnesses shall take the same oath which is taken by witnesses before courts-martials, (a) and the party accused shall be permitted to examine and cross-examine them, so as fully to investigate the circumstances in question.

Opinion; when given by. ART. 119.—A court of inquiry *shall not* give an *opinion on the merits* of the case inquired of, unless specially ordered to do so.

Authentication of proceedings of court of inquiry. ART. 120.—The proceedings of a court of inquiry *must be* authenticated by the signatures of the recorder and the president thereof, and delivered to the *commanding* officer.

(a) *Sic* in the Roll.

ART. 121.—The proceedings of a court of inquiry may be admitted as evidence by a court-martial, *in cases not capital*, nor extending to the *dismissal of an officer*: *Provided*, That the circumstances are such that *oral testimony* can not be obtained.

Proceedings of court of inquiry used as evidence.

ART. 122.—If, upon marches, guards, or in quarters, different corps of the army happen to join or do duty together, the officer highest in rank of the line of the army, marine corps, or militia, by commission, there on duty or in quarters, shall command the whole, and give orders for what is needful to the service, *unless* otherwise specially directed by the President, according to the nature of the case.

Command, when different corps happen to join.

ART. 123.—In all matters relating to the rank, duties, and rights of officers, the same rules and regulations shall apply to officers of the Regular Army and to volunteers commissioned in, or mustered into said service, under the laws of the United States, for a limited period.

Regular and volunteer officers on same footing as to rank, etc.

ART. 124.—Officers of the militia of the several States, when *called* into the service of the United States, shall, on all detachments, courts-martial, and other duty wherein they may be employed in conjunction with the regular or volunteer forces of the United States, take rank next after all officers of the like grade in said regular or volunteer forces, notwithstanding the commissions of such militia officers may be older than the commissions of the said officers of the regular or volunteer forces of the United States.

Rank of milita officers on duty with officers of regular or volunteer forces.

ART. 125.—In case of the death of any *officer*, the *major* of his regiment, or the officer doing the major's duty, or the second officer in command at any post or garrison, as the case may be, shall immediately secure all his effects then in camp or quarters, and shall make, and transmit to the office of the Department of War, an inventory thereof.

Deceased officers' effects.

Deceased soldiers' effects.

ART. 126.—In case of the death of any *soldier*, the *commanding officer* of his troop, battery, or company shall immediately secure all his effects then in camp or quarters, and shall, in the presence of two other officers, make an inventory thereof, which he shall transmit to the office of the Department of War.

Effects of deceased officers and soldiers to be accounted for.

ART. 127.—Officers charged with the care of the effects of deceased officers or soldiers shall account for and deliver the same, or the proceeds thereof, to the legal representatives of such deceased officers or soldiers. And no officer so charged shall be permitted to quit the regiment or post until he has deposited in the hands of the commanding officer all the effects of such deceased officers or soldiers not so accounted for and delivered.

Articles of war to be published once in six months to every regiment, etc.

ART. 128.—The foregoing articles *shall* be read and published once in every six months, to every garrison, regiment, troop, or company in the service of the United States, and shall be duly observed and obeyed by all officers and soldiers in said service.

Spies.

SEC. 1343.—*All* persons who, *in time of war*, or *of rebellion* against the supreme authority of the United States, shall be found lurking or acting as spies in or about any of the fortifications, posts, quarters, or encampments of any of the armies of the United States, or elsewhere, shall be triable by a general court-martial, or by a military commission, and *shall*, on conviction thereof, *suffer death*.

APPENDIX.

FORM I.

Order appointing a General Court-Martial.

HEADQUARTERS, DEPARTMENT OF ——,
—— —, 187-.

SPECIAL ORDERS,
No. —

A General Court-Martial is hereby appointed to meet at West Point, N. Y., on Monday the — day of ——, 187-, at 11 o'clock, A. M., or as soon thereafter as practicable,[1] for the trial of such persons as may properly be brought before it.

Detail for the Court.

1. Major —— —— Corps of Engineers,
2. Major —— —— —— Artillery,
3. Captain —— —— —— Cavalry,
4. Captain —— —— Ordnance Department,
5. First Lieutenant —— —— —— Infantry,
6. First Lieutenant —— —— —— Infantry,
7. First Lieutenant —— —— —— Cavalry,

First Lieutenant —— —— —— Artillery, Judge-Advocate.

No other officers than those named can be assembled without manifest injury to the service.[2]

The court is authorized to sit without regard to hours.[3]

By command of Major-General ——,

[Name] —— ——,
Asst. Adjt. General.

[1] The orders from some of the Departments here read, "for the trial of such persons as may be brought before it by authority from these Headquarters."

[2] This clause is not added when the court consists of thirteen members.

[3] This clause would only be added when the court is authorized to sit beyond the prescribed hours.

FORM II.

Order appointing a Garrison Court-Martial.

HEADQUARTERS, FORT ——,
January —, 187–.

ORDERS, }
No. — }

A Garrison Court-Martial will convene at this post on the — day of ——, at 11 o'clock, A. M., or as soon thereafter as practicable, for the trial of such prisoners as may properly be brought before it.

Detail for the Court.

1. Captain —— —— —— Artillery,
2. First Lieutenant —— —— —— Artillery,
3. Second Lieutenant —— —— —— Artillery.

By command of Colonel ——.

[Name] —— ——,
[Rank] —— ——,
Post Adjutant.

FORM III.

Order appointing a Court of Inquiry.

HEADQUARTERS, DEPARTMENT OF ——,
—— —, 187–.

SPECIAL ORDERS, }
No. — }

On the application of Captain —— ——, —— Artillery,[1] a Court of Inquiry is hereby appointed to meet at —— ——, on Monday, the — day of ——, 187–, at 11 o'clock, A. M., or as soon thereafter as practicable, to examine into the nature of certain accusations against Captain ——, contained in a communication from —— —— to —— —— of date ——, 187–.

Detail for the Court.

1. Colonel —— —— —— Artillery,
2. Major —— —— —— Cavalry,
3. Captain —— —— —— Infantry,

First Lieutenant —— —— —— Cavalry, Recorder.

[1] Where a court is ordered by the President the order reads, "By direction of the President a Court of Inquiry is hereby appointed, etc." If it is on application of an officer, this appears in the order.

The Court will report the facts and give their opinion on the merits of the case.[1]

By command of Major-General ———,

[Name] ——— ———,

Asst. Adjt. General.

FORM IV.

Record of Proceedings of a Court-Martial.

Page 1.[2]
Case 1.

Proceedings of a General Court-Martial, convened at West Point, N. Y., by virtue of the following order:[3]

HEADQUARTERS, DEPARTMENT OF ———,

——— —, 187-

SPECIAL ORDERS, }
No. — }

A General Court-Martial is hereby appointed to meet at West Point, N. Y., on Monday, the — day of ——, 187-, at 11 o'clock, A. M., or as soon thereafter as practicable, for the trial of such persons as may properly be brought before it.

Detail for the Court.

1. Major ——— ——— Corps of Engineers,
2. Major ——— ——— —— Artillery,
3. Captain ——— ——— —— Cavalry,
4. Captain ——— ——— Ordnance Department,
5. First Lieutenant ——— ——— —— Infantry,
6. First Lieutenant ——— ——— —— Infantry,
7. First Lieutenant ——— ——— —— Cavalry,

First Lieutenant ——— ——— —— Artillery, Judge-Advocate.

No other officers than those named can be assembled without manifest injury to the service.

[1] When not required to give an opinion the latter part of this clause would be omitted.

[2] Each page should be numbered.

[3] The record should be written down one page of legal cap paper, then commencing at the top of the next when turned, and so on.

The court is authorized to sit without regard to hours.

By command of Major-General ——,

[Name] —— ——,

Asst. Adjt. General.

WEST POINT, N. Y.,

—— —, 187–.

The court met pursuant to the foregoing order at 11 o'clock, A. M.

Present.

1. Major —— —— Corps of Engineers,
2. Major —— —— —— Artillery,
3. Captain —— —— —— Cavalry,
4. Captain —— —— Ordnance Department,
5. First Lieutenant —— —— —— Infantry,

First Lieutenant —— —— —— Artillery, Judge-Advocate.

Absent.

1. First Lieutenant —— —— —— Infantry,
2. First Lieutenant —— —— —— Cavalry.

[*The cause of absence, if known, should be here inserted, and the judge-advocate should ascertain the cause if possible. If letters, or medical certificates are furnished, they should be appended, properly marked and referred to.*]

The court then proceeded to the trial of First Lieutenant —— ——, — Regiment of Infantry, who then came before the court, and having heard the order convening it read, was asked, if he objected to any member present named in the order; to which he replied in the negative.

Or, The accused submitted the following objection to Captain ——.

[*Here insert the cause of challenge.*]

The challenged member then stated that:

[*Here insert statement of challenged member.*]

[*Should the accused desire that the challenged member be placed on his* voire dire, *the record would continue as follows:*]

The accused then requested that the challenged member be sworn on his *voire dire.*

Captain ——— was then duly sworn by the Judge-Advocate, and testified as follows:

Question by accused * * * *

Answer * * * * *

* * * * * *

[1] The court was then cleared, the challenged member retiring, and after due deliberation the court was re-opened, the accused and challenged member being present, and the decision of the court was announced by the Judge-Advocate, that the challenge is sustained, and that Captain ——— is excused from serving as a member of the court (or) [that the challenge is not sustained.]

The members of the court were then severally duly sworn by the Judge-Advocate, and the Judge-Advocate was duly sworn by the President of the court; all of which oaths were administered in the presence of the accused.[2]

The accused then requested to introduce —— —— as his counsel, which request was granted.[3]

[*Should the court refuse to receive a particular person as counsel, the cause should appear upon the record.*]

[*Should a delay or postponement of trial be desired this is the proper time to make it; the application and decision of the court being here entered upon the record. Should no delay be required the record would continue.*]

The accused was then duly arraigned on the following charges and specifications.

Charge I. * * * * *

Specification I. * * * * *

Specification II. * * * * *

Charge II. * * * * *

Specification I. * * * * *

To which the accused pleaded as follows:

To the first Specification first Charge, "Guilty" (or) "Not "Guilty."

To the second Specification first Charge, "Guilty" (or) "Not "Guilty."

[1] Where the challenged member is not sworn on the *voire dire* this clause would follow his statement.

[2] In a Garrison or Regimental Court-Martial the Record would here read, "The court, including the Recorder, was then duly sworn according to law in the presence of the prisoner."

[3] Application for the introduction of counsel may be made at any time of the trial, though this is, generally speaking, the proper time.

To the first Charge, "Guilty" (or) "Not Guilty."

To the first Specification second Charge, "Guilty" (or) "Not "Guilty."

To the second Charge, "Guilty" (or) "Not Guilty."

[*Any other plea, in bar of trial, or in bar of judgment, which the accused may make, any arguments upon the same by the accused or judge-advocate, the decision of the court, etc., would be entered in lieu of the plea to the general issue.*]

Captain ——— ———, ——— Cavalry, a witness for the prosecution, was then duly sworn by the Judge-Advocate, and testified as follows:

Question by Judge-Advocate * * * *
Answer * * * * *
Question by Judge-Advocate * * * *
Answer * * * * *

Cross-Examination.

Question by accused * * * *
Answer * * * * *
Question by accused * * * *
Answer * * * * *

Re-Examination.

Question by Judge-Advocate * * * *
Answer * * * * *
Question by Court * * * * *
Answer * * * * *

[*If the accused declines to cross-examine the witness it should appear upon the record.*]

[*When all the witnesses for the prosecution have been called the record will note as follows:*]

The Judge-Advocate announced that the prosecution here rested.

[*Supposing an adjournment at this time, the record would read:*]

The Court then, at — o'clock, P. M., adjourned to meet tomorrow at — o'clock, A. M.

[Name] ——— ———,
[Rank] ——— ———,
Judge-Advocate.

WEST POINT, N. Y.,
——— —, 187–.

The court met pursuant to adjournment at — o'clock, A. M.

Present.

* * * * * *

Absent.

* * * * * *

The accused and his counsel also present.

The proceedings of the — instant, were then read and approved.

Lieutenant ——— ———, —— Artillery, a witness for the defense, was then duly sworn by the Judge-Advocate, and testified as follows:

Question by accused * * * *
Answer * * * * *

Cross-Examination.

Question by Judge-Advocate * * * *
Answer * * * * *

Re-Examination.

Question by accused * * * *
Answer * * * * *
* * * * * * *
Question by Court * * * * *
Answer * * * * *

The accused having no further testimony to offer, made the following statement in his defense; (*or*), submitted a written statement which was read to the court and is hereto appended, marked "A;" (*or*), requested until to-morrow to prepare his statement; (*or*) declined to make any statement in his defense.

The court was then cleared for deliberation, and having maturely considered the evidence adduced (or where no evidence is offered on either side, "having maturely considered the case,") finds the accused ——— ———, —— Regiment of Infantry,

Of the first Specification, first Charge: "Guilty" (or) "Not Guilty."

Of the second Specification, first Charge: "Guilty" (or) "Not Guilty."

Of the first Charge: "Guilty" (or) "Not Guilty."

Of the first Specification, second Charge: "Guilty" (or) "Not Guilty."

Of the second Charge: "Guilty" (or) "Not Guilty."

And the Court does therefore sentence him ——— ———, —— Regiment of Infantry [*here insert the sentence*] (or) the Court does therefore acquit him ——— ———, —— Regiment of Infantry.

——— ———,
Major of Engineers,
President.

——— ———,
First Lieutenant, —— Artillery,
Judge-Advocate.

There being no further business before it, the court at — o'clock, P. M., adjourned *sine die.*[1]

——— ———,
Major of Engineers,
President.

——— ———,
First Lieutenant, —— Artillery,
Judge-Advocate.

FORM V.

Record of Revision.

Revision.

WEST POINT, N. Y.,
——— —, 187–.

The court re-convened pursuant to the following order at — o'clock, A. M.

Present.

* * * * * *

Absent.

* * * * * *

The following communication from the reviewing officer, setting forth the causes for re-convening the court, was then read by the Judge-Advocate.

[*Here insert the communication.*]

[*Whatever action the court may take would be here inserted, something as follows:*]

[1] To be placed on the final case.

The court then proceeded to reconsider the sentence [or finding, or etc.], and, after mature deliberation, revokes the former sentence, [or, etc.] and, in lieu therefor does sentence him, ——— ———, —— Regiment of Infantry, etc.

——— ———,
Major of Engineers,
President.

——— ———,
First Lieutenant, —— Artillery,
Judge-Advocate.

There being no further business before it, the court at — o'clock, A. M., adjourned *sine die.*

——— ———,
Major of Engineers,
President

——— ———,
First Lieutenant, —— Artillery,
Judge-Advocate.

Form VI.

Indorsement of Court-Martial Proceedings.[1]

West Point, N. Y.
January —, 187–.

Proceedings of a General Court-Martial, convened by Special Orders No. —, dated Headquarters Department of ———, January —, 187–.

Major ——— ———,
Corps of Engineers,
President.

1st. Lieut. ——— ———,
—— Artillery,
Judge-Advocate.

Case Tried.

1st. Lieut. ——— ———,
—— Infantry.

[1] The record is folded twice and indorsed on the first fold. It should occupy about three-fourths of the fold.

FORM VII.

Order confirming or disapproving the Proceedings of a General Court-Martial.

HEADQUARTERS DEPARTMENT OF ——,
—— ——, 187–.

GENERAL COURT-MARTIAL, ORDER No. —.

I. . . . Before a General Court-Martial which convened at ——, ——, January —, 187–, pursuant to Special Orders No. —, Headquarters Department of ——, January —, 187–, and of which Major —— ——, Corps of Engineers, is President, was arraigned and tried :

First Lieutenant —— ——, —— Infantry.

Charge : * * * * * *

Specification : * * * * *

[*Insert all the Charges and Specifications.*][1]

To which charges and specifications the accused, First Lieutenant —— ——, —— Infantry, pleaded as follows :

[*Here insert the pleas of the accused.*]

FINDING.

The Court having maturely considered the evidence adduced, finds the accused, First Lieutenant —— ——, —— Infantry, as follows :

[*Here insert the findings.*]

SENTENCE.

And the court does therefore sentence him, First Lieutenant —— ——, —— Infantry.

[*Here insert the sentence.*]

II. The proceedings, findings, and sentence of the General Court-Martial in the foregoing case of First Lieutenant —— ——, —— Infantry, are approved, and the sentence will be duly executed.

III. The General Court-Martial of which Major —— —— is President, is dissolved.[1]

By command of Major-General ——.

[Name] —— ——,
Asst. Adjt. General.

[1]This clause is not necessary, and is now omitted frequently in Orders from the Headquarters of the Army.

FORM VIII.

Indorsement of Envelope forwarding Court-Martial Proceedings.

PROCEEDINGS OF A GENERAL COURT-MARTIAL.

Judge-Advocate General,[1]
Washington,
D. C.

FORM IX.

Record of a Field Officer's Court.

Proceedings of a Field Officer's Court-Martial, convened at ——— ———, by virtue of the following order:

[*Here insert a copy of the order.*]

——— ———,
——— —, 187–.

The Court met pursuant to the foregoing order, at — o'clock, A. M., and proceeded to the trial of Private ——— ———, ——— Infantry, who was duly arraigned on the following charge and specification:

Charge: * * * * * *
Specification: * * * * *

To which Charge and Specification the accused pleaded "not guilty."

[1] When the Court is convened by a Department Commander the letter is addressed to the Assistant Adjutant General; when by a Post Commander, to the Post Adjutant.

After mature deliberation on the evidence adduced, the court finds the prisoner as follows:

[*Here insert findings.*]

And the court does therefor sentence him.

[*Here insert, sentence.*]

[Name] ——— ———,

[Rank] ——— ———.

FORM X.

Charges and Specifications.

Charge and Specification preferred against Private C—— D——, Company "A," —— U. S. Infantry.

CHARGE: Drunkenness on duty in violation of the 38th Article of War.

SPECIFICATION: In this, that Private C—— D——, Company "A," —— U. S. Infantry, having regularly marched on guard on the morning of —— —, 187–, was found so drunk between the hours of five and six P. M., as to be unable properly to perform his duties as a sentinel.

This at Fort ——— ———, on the — day of ———, 187–.[1]

[Name of officer preferring charge] ——— ———,

Captain —— Artillery.

Witnesses:

Captain ——— ———, —— Infantry,

Sergeant ——— ———, Co. — —— Infantry.

[1] When there is more than one Charge or Specification they follow each other in succession on the same sheet of paper.

Form XI.

Indorsement referring Charges for Trial.

1st Indorsement.

Headquarters Dept. of ——,

—— ——, —— —, 187–.

Respectfully referred for trial to First Lieutenant —— ——, —— Artillery, Judge-Advocate of the General Court-Martial, convened by Special Order No. —, Headquarters Department of ——.

By command of Major-General ——,

[Name] —— ——,

Asst. Adjt. General.

Form XII.

Subpœna for Civilian Witnesses.

General Court-Martial Room,

—— ——,

—— ——, 187–.

The President of the United States of America:

To —— ——, *greeting:*

Pursuant to Section 1202, Revised Statutes of the United States, you are hereby required to be and appear, in your own proper person, on the — day of ——, 187–, at — o'clock in the — noon, before a general court-martial of the United States, convened at said —— by virtue of Special Orders No. — of ——, from the Headquarters of the Department of ——, to testify and give evidence, all that you may know, concerning the pending case, then and there to be tried, of the United States *versus* —— ——, accused of —— under the laws of the United States, and have you then and there this precept.*

Witness, [*Here insert name of presiding officer*], president of said court, this — day of ——, 187–.[2]

[Name] —— ——,

[Rank] —— ——.

Judge-Advocate.

[*The following would be here added to secure the production of papers:*]

*You will bring with you to be used in evidence in said case the following documents.

[*Here set forth the documents required.*]

Affidavit of service of subpœna.

STATE OF ——
COUNTY OF ——. } *ss.*

—— —— being sworn, says: The witness hereafter named was subpœnaed by deponent, as hereafter stated; that deponent at the time and place below set forth served the annexed subpœna upon the witness named therein, by exhibiting the annexed original subpœna to such witness, and delivering to him a duplicate original thereof.

On ——, at ——, N. Y., on the — day of ——, 187–.

[*Signature of party serving subpœna.*]

Subscribed and sworn to
before me this — day of
——, 187–. }

[*Signature of officer administering oath.*]

[1] These subpœnas should be issued in duplicate by the Judge-Advocate or Recorder.

[2] This form is the proper one for any military court, altered, of course, to set forth the objects of the court.

Form XIII.

Summons for a Military Witness.

General Court-Martial Rooms,
West Point, N. Y.,
—— ——, 187–.

To —— ——,
—— Infantry.

Sir: You are hereby summoned to appear as a witness on the — day of ——, 187–, at — o'clock, a. m., before a General Court-Martial, convened at ——, by Special Orders from ——, for the trial of —— ——, —— Artillery.

[Name] —— ——,
[Rank] —— ——,
Judge-Advocate.

Form XIV.

Court-Martial Service—Citizen Witness.

The United States,
To ————, *Dr.*

187–.		Dolls.	Cts.
	For actual cost of his transportation, or travel-fare, while journeying to and from a Military Court, convened at ——, under the orders and per summons and statement hereto annexed:		
	From —— to ——, between the — day of —— and the — day of ——, in traveling to said court..............................		
	From —— to ——, between the — day of —— and the — day of ——, in returning from said court........................		
	For per diem while traveling to and returning from said court between the places and dates above specified, —— days at $— per day		
	For per diem while attending on said court as a citizen witness from the — day of —— to the — day of ——, inclusive, at $— per day, as per certificate herewith.........................		

____________ COUNTY, *ss:*

On this ____ day of ________, one thousand eight hundred and seventy-_____ personally appeared before me, a ____________ in and for the County aforesaid, __________, and made oath in due form of law that the above account is correct and just; that the statement annexed exhibits the actual expenses of his transportation for and during the journeys above specified; that he was actually and necessarily occupied the number of days and between the dates stated in traveling to and returning from the court in obedience to the summons annexed; and that he traveled in the customary reasonable manner.

____

RECEIVED at __________________, the ____ of ________ 187–. of _________________, Paymaster, United States Army, the sum of ________________________ dollars and _________________ cents, in full of the above account.

(DUPLICATE.)

____

Certificate on back of Voucher.

I CERTIFY that ________________________ a citizen, has been in attendance as a material witness from the __________ day of ___________________, 187 , to the _______________ day of ___________________, 187 , inclusive, before a General Court-Martial duly and legally appointed by Special Orders No. ______, Headquarters _________________________________, and holden at this place, and that he was duly summoned thereto from _______

DATE, ______________

PLACE, ____________________ ____________________

Judge-Advocate.

NOTE I.—The above certificate is to be given in duplicate by the Judge-Advocate, who will also administer the oath in case of "citizen witnesses." Should the witness be a "Government employé," those words will be inserted in the above certificate in place of the word "citizen."

NOTE II.—In completing this voucher Judge-Advocates will be governed by the provisions of G. O. 97, A. G. O., September 8, 1876.

Form XV.

Process of Attachment.

THE PRESIDENT OF THE UNITED STATES OF AMERICA:

To ——— ———,

Stationed at ———.

Greeting:

WHEREAS, a General Court-Martial of the United States was duly convened at ———, on the — day of ——, 187–, pursuant to Special Orders No. —, of ——, 187–, from Headquarters ———, a copy of which said order is hereto annexed, marked "A;" and *whereas*, on the — day of —, 187–, at ——, the said General Court-Martial having been first duly sworn, ——— of the United States Army, was duly arraigned and his trial proceeded with on a certain charge, instituted at the prosecution of the United States, for the offense of —— under the laws of the United States, a copy of which is hereto annexed, marked "B." And *whereas*, one ——— of —— in the —— was, on the — day of ——, 187–, personally served with a subpœna (a duplicate of which is hereto annexed, marked "C"), directing him to appear and testify in said cause at the time and place therein commanded; and, *whereas*, the said —— did, on the — day of ——, 187–, fail and neglect to appear before said court or testify in said cause, as required by said subpœna, and still fails and neglects to appear and testify in said cause, he being a necessary and material witness therein, and no just excuse has been offered for such neglect:

NOW, THEREFORE, under and by virtue of Section 1202 of the Revised Statutes of the United States, you are hereby commanded that you take the said ——— ——— wherever he may be found within the United States, and him safely keep, and bring you his body without delay before the said General Court-Martial convened at said ———, and of which ——— ———, United States Army, is President, at the court-room thereof on the —— day of ——, 187–, at — o'clock in the forenoon, at the opening of said court, to then and there testify in the said cause of the United States *versus* ——— ———, now depending, and then and there to be continued and tried.

And have you then and there this writ.

By order of the Court.

In witness whereof, I, as Judge-Advocate of said Court, duly appointed and sworn, have hereto set my hand and seal, at ———, this —— day of ——, 187–.

[Name] ——— ———, [SEAL]
[Rank] ——— ———.
Judge-Advocate.

FORM XVI.

Application for a Writ of Habeas Corpus ad Testificandum.[1]

TO THE HONORABLE ——— ———,
Judge of the United States for the ——— ———:

The petition of ——— ——— [*Name of Judge-Advocate*] respectfully shows that a General Court-Martial of the United States was duly convened at ——— on the — day of ——, 187–, pursuant to Special Orders No. — of ——, 187–, from Headquarters ———, a copy of which said order is hereto attached, marked "A," and that on the — day of ——, 187–, at ——— the said General Court-Martial having been first duly sworn, ——— ——— of the United States Army, was duly arraigned and his trial proceeded with on a certain charge, instituted at the prosecution of the United States, for the offense of —— under the laws of the United States, a copy of which is hereto annexed, marked "B;" and your petitioner further says that ——— ——— [*Name of witness*] is, as he believes, a material and necessary witness for the prosecution [*or defense*] in said trial, that the trial cannot safely proceed without his testimony, and that it is not practicable to take his deposition under the 91st Article of War. And your petitioner further says that, as he is informed and believes, said ——— ——— is now confined in the ———, charged with [*or undergoing sentence for*] ———, in the custody of the sheriff of ———, [*or as the case may be,*] and unable to attend as a witness in said trial.

Wherefore your petitioner, as Judge-Advocate of said General Court-Martial, and at request of said Court, prays that a writ of *habeas corpus ad testificandum* may be issued by this honorable Court, commanding the production of said ——— ——— before said General Court-Martial at ——— on the — day of ——, 187–,

[1] Gardner's Practical Forms.

to then and there testify, according to law, all that he may know concerning the pending cause then and there to be continued and tried of the *United States versus* ———.

[*Name of Judge-Advocate*] ——— ———,
[*Rank*] ——— ———.

STATE OF ———, }
COUNTY OF ———. } *ss:*

On the — day of ———, 187–, personally appeared before me, the above named ——— ——— [*Name of Judge-Advocate*], and made oath to the truth of the foregoing petition.

——— [*Signature of officer administering oath*].

FORM XVII.

Interrogatories and Annexed Deposition.[1]

GENERAL COURT-MARTIAL.

THE UNITED STATES *vs.* ——— ——— [*Name of prisoner.*]	To ——— ——— [*Name of person and address who takes deposition. If not known then to be filled up on return.*

Interrogatories to be administered, under the 91st Article of War, to ——— ———, [*Name of witness*], of ——— ——— [*residence*], in the above entitled case now pending, and to be tried before the United States General Court-Martial convened at ——— ———, pursuant to Special Orders No. — from Headquarters Department of the ———, of ———, 187–, and whereof ——— ——— is President, and ——— ——— is Judge-Advocate.

Interrogatories by the Judge-Advocate [*or prisoner.*]

First Interrogatory: Please state your full name, occupation, and present residence ?

Second Interrogatory: Do you know ——— ———, the prisoner [*or accused, as the case may be,*] if so, state how long you have known him, and how you know him to be the defendant in this trial ?

Third Interrogatory: * * * *

Fourth Interrogatory: etc., etc.

* * * * * *

* * * * * *

[1] Gardner's Practical Forms.

Last Interrogatory: Do you know anything further relating to this cause now in hearing, if so, state it?

Cross-Interrogatories by prisoner [or Judge-Advocate.]

First cross-interrogatory: * * * *
Second cross-interrogatory: etc., etc., etc.

* * * * * *

* * * * * *

Re-direct Interrogatories by Judge-Advocate [or prisoner.]
First re-direct interrogatory:

* * * * * *

* * * * * *

Re-cross Interrogatories by prisoner [or Judge-Advocate.]
First re-cross interrogatory:

* * * * * *

* * * * * *

First Interrogatory by Court: [where Court desires to propound questions.]

* * * * * *

* * * * * *

By order of the Court.

[Name] ——— ———,
[Rank] ——— ———,
Judge-Advocate.

ANNEXED DEPOSITION.

THE UNITED STATES
vs.
——— ——— [*Prisoner's name.*]
} *Deposition of witness under* 91*st Article of War.*

STATE OF ———,
COUNTY OF ———.
} *ss:*

——— ———, the witness above named, being carefully examined and cautioned, and duly sworn [*or affirmed*] according to law, to tell the truth, the whole truth, and nothing but the truth, relating to the above entitled case, doth depose [*or affirm*] and say for full answers in evidence, respectively, to all and each of the foregoing interrogatories and cross-interrogatories as follows:

To the first interrogatory by Judge-Advocate [*or prisoner.*]

* * * * * *

To the second interrogatory by Judge-Advocate [*or prisoner.*]

* * * * * *

To the first cross-interrogatory by prisoner [*or Judge-Advocate.*]

* * * * * *

&c. &c. &c. &c. &c.

and further deponent [*or affiant*] saith not.

Subscribed and sworn [*or affirmed*] to before me this — day of ——, 187–. } [*Signed by witness*] —— ——.

[*Signature of officer administering oath.*] —— ——,

Form XVIII.

Return to a writ of Habeas Corpus issued by a State Judge, requiring production of the body of an enlisted man.[1]

New York Supreme Court, City and County of New York. }

In *re* application on Habeas Corpus for the production of Private —— ——, Battery "M," 3d Artillery.

To the Honorable ——, *Judge of* ——.

Sir:

I have the honor to make return to the within writ of *habeas corpus* issued in the case of —— ——, a private soldier in the service of the United States; that the said —— —— is a regularly enlisted soldier, and held to service in the Army of the United States by virtue of said enlistment; that the said —— —— was regularly enlisted in the service of the United States according to the rules and regulations of the recruiting service for enlisting recruits, by his signing the proper statement or declaration, and by taking the oath required for recruits to take; and that the recruit was regularly examined by the surgeon appointed for that purpose.

[1] This corresponds largely to the actual form used by General Butterfield while in charge of the recruiting service, at a time when such writs were constantly issued from State courts.

That under the decisions of the United States Supreme Court it is not my duty to produce the body of the said ——— ——— in court.

That such declination and denial of the jurisdiction of your honor is a matter of official duty, and not from any disrespect of your honorable Court.

Your attention is respectfully invited to the enclosed triplicate enlistment paper of the said ——— ———, marked "A," and to the decisions of the United States Supreme Court upon this subject in the cases of Ableman *vs.* Booth, (21 Howard, 506,) and U. S. *vs.* Tarble (13 Wallace, 397).

Dated Jan. —, 187–, Fort ———, New York Harbor.

I have the honor to be,
Very respectfully,
Your obedient servant.

[*Name of officer making return*] ————,

Captain ———, U. S. Artillery.

[*Should the writ issue from a United States Court, the form of return would read:*]

I have the honor to make return to the within writ of habeas corpus in the case of ——— ———, by producing the said ——— ——— before this honorable Court in obedience thereto; and by certifying that the said ——— ——— is a regularly enlisted soldier, etc.

PRINCIPAL ENGLISH AND AMERICAN PUBLICATIONS ON MILITARY LAW.*

ENGLISH.

WARD. *Animadversions of Warre.* 1639.
BRUCE. *Military Law.* (Edinburgh) 1717.
SULLIVAN. *Martial Law.* 1784.
GROSE. *Military Antiquities.* 1786.
ADYE. *Courts-Martial.* (First edition written during Revolutionary War.)
TYTLER. *Military Law.* 1799.
DELAFONS. *Naval Courts-Martial.* 1850.
MCARTHUR. *Courts-Martial.* 1813.
SAMUEL. *Law Military.* 1816.
JAMES. *Regimental Companion.* 1805.
Collection of Charges, Opinions and Sentences of General Courts-Martial. 1820.
DUPIN. *View of the History and Actual State of the Military Forces of Great Britain.* (Translated with notes by an Officer. London. 1822.)
KENNEDY. *Courts-Martial.* 1824.
HOUGH. *Practice of Courts-Martial.* 1825.
Military Law Authorities. 1839.
Precedents in Military Law. 1855.
MCNAGHTEN. *Annotations on the Mutiny Act.* 1828.
SIMMONS. *Courts-Martial.* 1836.
NAPIER. *Remarks on Military Law and Flogging.* 1837.
HUGHES. *Duties of Judge-Advocates.* 1845.
MARSHALL. *Military Miscellany.* 1846.
PRENDERGAST. *Law relating to Officers of the Army.* 1849.

* The dates here given are believed to be those of the first edition of the respective works. Many of them have passed through several editions.

MAWSON. *Records of the Indian Command of General Sir Charles James Napier* (Calcutta). 1851.

THOMSON. *Military Forces and Institutions of Great Britain.* 1855.

D'AGUILAR. *Courts-Martial and Courts of Inquiry.* 1858.

PIPON AND COLLIER. *Manual of Military Law.* 1860.

SKINNER. *Rules for the Guidance of Courts-Martial* (Bombay, 1863.)

CLODE. *Military Forces of the Crown.* 1869.

Military and Martial Law. 1872.

TULLOCH. *Elementary Lectures on Military Law.* 1872.

FRANKLYN. *Military Law and Laws of Evidence.* 1874.

AMERICAN.

MACOMB. *Martial Law.* 1809.

Courts-Martial. 1841.

MALTBY. *Courts-Martial.* 1813.

DEHART. *Courts-Martial.* 1846.

O'BRIEN. *American Military Law and Courts-Martial.* 1846.

BENET. *Military Law and Courts-Martial.* 1862.

Digest of Opinions of the Judge-Advocate General of the Army (3d. Ed. 1868).

HARWOOD. *Naval Courts-Martial.* 1867.

KAUTZ. *Customs of the Service for Officers of the Army.* 1866.

Customs of the Service for Non-Commissioned Officers and Soldiers. 1864.

SCOTT. *Analytical Digest of the Military Laws of the United States.* 1873.

LIEBER. *Observations on the Origin of the Trial by Council of War.* 1876.

Meaning of the term "Martial Law" in Petition of Right and Preamble to Mutiny Act. 1877.

GARDNER. *Practical Forms for use in Courts-Martial.* 1876.

Law of Evidence in Courts-Martial. 1877.

REAGAN. *Judge-Advocate's and Recorder's Guide.* 1877.

INDEX.

A.

B.

C.

F.

G.

H.

I.

J.

L.

M.

N.

O.

P.

R.

S.

U.

V.

W.